Live That Dream

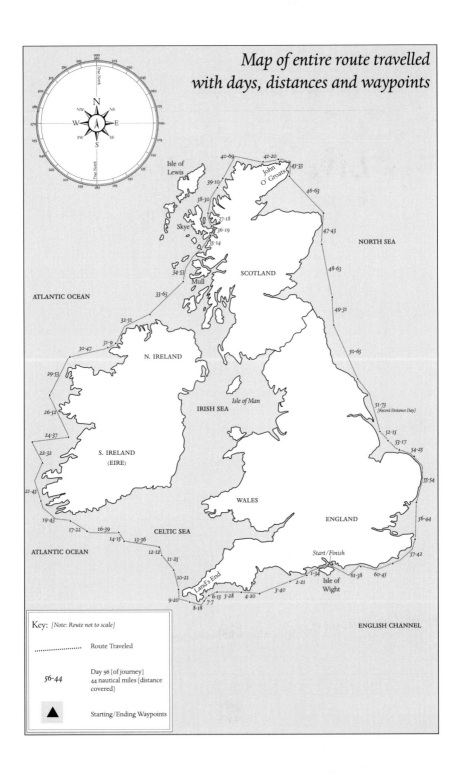

Map of entire route travelled with days, distances and waypoints

ATLANTIC OCEAN

NORTH SEA

Isle of Lewis

John O' Groats

SCOTLAND

Skye

Mull

N. IRELAND

Isle of Man

IRISH SEA

S. IRELAND
(EIRE)

WALES

ENGLAND

CELTIC SEA

Land's End

Start/Finish

Isle of Wight

ATLANTIC OCEAN

ENGLISH CHANNEL

40-69
41-20
45-33
39-10
46-63
38-30
47-43
37-18
36-19
35-14
48-63
34-53
33-63
49-31
32-51
31-9
50-65
30-47
29-53
51-73
[Record Distance Day]
26-52
52-15
53-17
24-37
54-25
22-32
55-54
21-45
56-44
19-43
17-22 16-39
14-15   13-36
12-12
57-42
11-25
10-21
1-34
2-21
3-40
61-38 60-45
9-20
6-15 5-28 4-20
8-18   7-7

Key: *[Note: Route not to scale]*

.... Route Traveled

56-44 Day 56 [of journey]
44 nautical miles [distance covered]

▲ Starting/Ending Waypoints

Live That Dream

Richard Cooper

The Pentland Press
Edinburgh – Cambridge – Durham – USA

© R. Cooper, 2000

First published in 2000 by
The Pentland Press Ltd
1 Hutton Close
South Church
Bishop Auckland
Durham

ISBN 1-85821-824-1

Typeset in Monotype Dante

by Carnegie Publishing, Carnegie House, Chatsworth Road, Lancaster
Printed and bound by Antony Rowe Ltd, Chippenham

To Rosie, Jack, George and Amy whose young hearts are so full of dreams to be lived, and who were as proud of me for a day as I will be of them always

Contents

Illustrations

Foreword

*B*eing an island race means that before we can go anywhere, we have to start by crossing the sea. Today that journey might be by super-ferry or aircraft, but in days gone past it meant the risk of a voyage in a small wind-powered boat. As a people our journeys started with such unpredictable exposure to the will of the elements, and perhaps this has shaped a disproportionate number of us to embrace adventure as a way of life. Certainly the British have been a very adventurous race, which explains our leading place in exploration, sailing, and mountain climbing.

With the world mapped from satellites, and made smaller by instant communications, people often ask what is there left to be done, but for the adventurous there is always something that can catch the imagination. A new route ascending a perilous rock face is just as satisfying as a faster mile; but both have one thing in common: the single-minded determination to achieve the objective.

Richard Cooper's chosen objective was to become the first person to windsurf around the British Isles. Our island is often on the receiving end of a succession of Atlantic depressions, and any plan made on the basis of an existing weather forecast is almost certain to have been completely changed a week later. As I know from bitter experience, when you set out to circumnavigate the British Isles, you take what comes, good or bad, and make the most of it. Richard set about achieving his dream with the same careful planning and preparation that must precede all successful ventures, but the planning is only a part. To succeed requires stubborn determination, tunnel vision as far as achieving the objective is concerned, and the adaptability to change the plan when circumstances dictate. It was never going to be an easy venture, but if it had been easy why bother doing it? It is by taking on real challenges that we add zest to our lives.

Richard was and still is a fairly normal guy, married with four children, and having worked hard to climb the corporate ladder and generate a comfortable standard of living. As far as I know, he does not hold any strange radical beliefs, or have any unusual needs or hobbies. His background is maybe more varied and travelled than most, but his story is certainly no bestselling biography. He tells me that he believes in living life to the full, in honesty and integrity, and in the human need for progress and achievement, and to love and be loved.

Through the following pages he tells his colourful and very human story, how he gave up his comfortable and predictable lifestyle to implement one of the toughest sailing challenges ever. Many of us think of taking a time-out to live a long-held dream. Some take the plunge, some just continue dreaming. For them the implementation may be too risky, or personal circumstances do not allow. Maybe the time-out is more valuable than living the dream itself. Maybe sometimes we are afraid that the living of the dream will disappoint, and thus stay happy just dreaming. Richard decided that he had no intention of getting to sixty, and looking back with regret at not having the guts to try and make his dream happen.

If you see yourself as another 'normal guy' but somehow incomplete, and reluctant to implement your own dream, then read on, and let Richard Cooper take you through his own emotional journey from project conception and reaction of friends and family and potential sponsors, through the wonderful but nerve-wracking start, the deep depressions when failure seemed much more likely than success, to the climatic and tearful completion, and the combined emotional afterglow and hangover when it was all over.

It is a physical journey round an ever-changing coastline, through awe-inspiring landscapes and seascapes, passing spectacular and daunting headlands, seeing wonderful marine wildlife, and the awful debris of humanity; and also visiting an amazing variety of coastal stopovers, including idylic anchorages, trendy marinas, busy smelly fishing harbours, and depressed decaying ports.

It is also a very human journey, charting Richard's own doubts, frustrations, and glories, and the developing and sometimes deteriorating relationships of those on his support team, who were sharing his but also living their own dreams.

For the reader, it can also be your own journey. If you are dreaming of a challenge, read on, and maybe you will also turn a dream into reality, and not be left pondering what might have been. Richard wanted zest and no regrets, and this is his story.

Sir Robin Knox Johnston
July 2000

(Sir Robin Knox-Johnson was the first person to sail solo and non-stop around the world, and has since held numerous other sailing records. Sir Robin already has his place in the history of maritime voyages; and his perceptive foreword illustrates the understanding and respect he has for Richard Cooper's achievements, and the clear advice he has for other would-be adventurers.)

Acknowledgements

First and foremost I would like to thank my wife Amanda for putting up with my crazy ambition, and looking after our four highly demanding children during my absence. Thereafter the list is endless. I will remain eternally in debt (i.e. good for a drink) to those who inspired the dream in the first place, those who helped me get to the start line, and of course those who helped me make it round. My sponsors, and in particular Classic FM were superb, as were all the other myraid suppliers of discounted or free-of-charge products and services. A special thanks to Duncan Walpole, my photographer, who captured all the images contained in the book. The whole thing was a rich and varied life tutorial for me, and I would like to thank the plethora of colourful characters who showed us such wonderful hospitality en route. I also owe an apology and a thank-you to all the unsuspecting persons who feature in and add depth and reality to this story. And then perhaps closest to my heart, I thank all those friends, family, colleagues, and interested general public, who followed my endeavours with such enthusiasm, and who kept me going when all seemed lost.

Dramatis Personnae

Those who helped me get to the start line:

Simon Bornhoft:	Well-known windsurf guru, and technique coach during the training period.
Euan McGrath:	Sports science lecturer, and fitness coach.
Pete Cunningham:	Fitness coach to our Olympic sailors, and advisor to RC.
Sue Crayfer:	Physio to our Olympic sailors, and advisor to RC.
Sue Cotgrove:	Pre-event physio.
Jon White:	Head of RYA windsurfing.

Those who helped me make it round:

Terry Nielsen:	Owner and skipper of the mother ship Maiden.
Kevin Fuller:	Mate and reserve skipper on Maiden.
Duncan Walpole:	Team photography, press liaison & Maiden crew.
Sarah Aynesworth:	Documentary filming, TV/Radio/VNR liaisson & Maiden crew.
John Beecroft:	Documentary filming & Maiden crew.
Denise Hendrie:	Maiden crew and physio (weeks 1–3).
Sophie Thomas:	Galley manager/medical officer/Maiden crew (weeks 1–5).
Peter Head:	Maiden crew (weeks 7–9).
Lindsay Porter:	Galley manager/Maiden crew (weeks 7–9).
Damian Ward:	Maiden crew (weeks 5–8).
Steve Potter:	RIB Coxwain and safety officer (weeks 1–7).
Gary (Gaz) McKay:	RIB Driver (weeks 1–4).
Stuart (Spider) Webster:	RIB Driver (weeks 4–8).
Andy Crocker:	Caddy/navigator (weeks 1–6) & RIB driver/safety officer (weeks 8–9).
Philippe Falle:	RIB Coxwain and navigator (weeks 7–9).
Tim Birkes:	Van driver/Maiden crew (weeks 1–6) and caddy/navigator (weeks 7–9).

Prologue

To be what we are, and to become what we are capable of is the only
end in life.

Robert Louis Stevenson

What a day! One hour earlier I had become only the second human being to
windsurf round the infamous and treacherous Fastnet rock off the south-west
tip of Ireland, and had felt absolutely elated and so totally alive. Now the seas
off Dursey Island had suddenly become huge and frightening with 25 ft foot
swells breaking onto the safety boat. The wind had increased from a gentle
force 3 to a near gale, and I was stranded with a huge sail impossible to use
in these worsening conditions. We were also less than half a mile from, and
being blown towards a violent-looking cliff face. We simply had to get my
weakened body into the safety boat, before we became a second Fastnet
disaster. The safety boat was being tossed around like a lazy piece of flotsam,
and several times as I tried to swim close enough to be hauled aboard, its hull
came crashing down perilously close to my unprotected skull. Through a
combination of good luck, bad language and brute strength, I was somehow
dragged aboard, and the crisis averted. Some minutes later as I lay speechless
and emotionally empty in the safety boat, I caught myself wondering why
the hell I was putting myself through this torture, and pined almost to the
point of tears to be back at home eating supper with my family after a long
comfortable day at the office. Two hours later I was back on top of the world
again. The intoxicating cocktail of triumph and trauma had worked its magic
spell again.

I woke cold, clammy and shaken. That was quite a dream ... or was it?
Was I looking forward or looking back? There is always that period of
horrible insecurity, when the conscious gradually takes over from the
subconscious, but which part is responsible for what is so painfully blurred.
The sloshing slapping sounds of the sea, and the smells of eleven other
acrid salty bodies bunked into the bowels of a yacht, gave it away before
my eyes opened to confirm that I had woken aboard our mother ship, in
Dingle marina. It was true. I had rounded the Fastnet in awesome conditions
the previous day, and we had eventually turned north. The story of how
I had come to be in such a situation was well documented on my cerebral
hard-disk; but what lay ahead of the remaining three-quarters of my planned
journey, was still a heady mixture of subconscious fantasy and nightmare,

and conscious analysis and fear. The analytical side of me correctly concluded that our probability of success was less than 20 per cent, and that I was a complete idiot for starting on this crazy venture; but the dreamer could only think of that moment of triumph when the familiar landmarks of the beach I had left three long weeks ago appeared out of the horizon. The heart yet again was ruling the head.

Chapter I

A Dream, a Plan and a Decision

Until one is committed, there is hesitancy,
The chance to draw back, always
Ineffectiveness.

Concerning all acts of initiative,
There is one element of truth,
The ignorance of which kills countless ideas and splendid plans
That moment one commits oneself,
Then providence moves all.

Whatever you can do or dream you can, Begin it.
Boldness has genius, power and magic in it.

Begin it now.

Goethe

*I*t was always in there somewhere, the idea to take a time-out from normality, and push myself to the limit having a go at something extraordinary. Maybe it relates back to childhood days organising a 'Mini-Olympics' for the village kids in our back field with gold, silver and bronze medals made out of clay and baler twine. With a very average collection of sporting achievements, maybe I still needed to have a go at my own gold medal for grown-ups! My working life had been reasonably successful, but somehow this was not enough. I needed to leave my mark, to step out and be someone different. I didn't want to get to retirement and regret not having had a go at achieving something exceptional. I also liked the silly romantic idea of talking through my epic adventure with loving grandchildren. At least it might give them something to brag about in the playground for a day or two.

Psychologists would perhaps look for my own childhood experiences to explain this need to step out of normality. My father was and still is a more natural ball player than I will ever be. He supported my sporting adolescence, as most fathers do, but I was acutely aware that despite hours and hours of practice, I simply didn't have the natural ability to become anything other than average. Even if I was impacted by my perception of his hidden disappointment, he still (by deed and instruction) gave me a fierce determination to succeed and a never-give-up mindset.

A big part of my adolescence (at least in my memory) was spent walking and day-dreaming through the Lancashire fields and woods near the family's farm. As I read recently in that well-known literary journal *Windsurf* magazine: 'Its simply a fresh air thing, you either want it or you don't, and when you've got it, you don't need anything else.' Perhaps a somewhat extreme statement, but I definitely caught that 'fresh air thing' at an early age, and have had it bad ever since. Man-made *beauty* has never given me anything like the feeling of glowing wonderment I get when discovering or being reunited with a special landscape or seascape. What makes somewhere or something special? Who knows? Maybe some answers will emerge within the body of this book ... Anyway I knew that I would be in seventh heaven on a daily diet of the ever-changing sea and coastline around Britain and Ireland.

I first had a go at windsurfing on a day trip to the Red Sea, whilst working in Cairo in my early twenties. I wasn't immediately hooked, but I always loved messing about in and on the water; and this seemed a rather clean, simple, physically demanding, and dare I say visible means of water-borne travel. Were the girls on the beach watching, and impressed as I flipped another muscular tack? Of course not, but even if they had accidentally looked seaward at just the right moment, most males look the same from 400 yards away, which was clearly to my advantage! During the mid-1980s back in the UK, I became seriously addicted. With windsurfing, like surfing, the addiction is fuelled by a futile desire for the 'perfect day'. We listen diligently to the weekend wind forecast, lose masses of marital brownie points, and drive expectantly to the coast on a promise of clear skies and a solid force 4–5; only to encounter a smothering sea mist and zero breeze. The 'perfect conditions' always come on days when obligated to attend a family gathering. However, always after a period of frustrating wasted journeys to the beach which terminally weaken the awful addiction, there comes a 'near-perfect day' to break the cure. I can remember seven or eight of those near-perfect days during the 1980s, as clear as if yesterday. It is not like a cup final. There is no winning, just a tremendous inner glow. The wind is just right. You feel at one with the perfectly tuned board and sail. The fluffy cumulous clouds are skidding across a cool blue sky, and the waves can be felt and read through the soles of your feet on the board. You are sailing way beyond your normal level with smooth-flowing gybes, and effortless speed, and you don't realise how exhausted you have become during this extended period of pleasure, until you pack up and start the long drive home.

Anyway, I guess the bottom line is that of all the sports I'd tried to become competent at, windsurfing seemed to be the one where I was in the top rather than the bottom half of the average brigade. If I was to take on an epic journey then why not as a windsurfer? Having said that, the furthest I'd ever windsurfed before was about 18 miles in the round Mersea race during 1987. It took me about four hours, and I could hardly walk for days afterwards. During the next ten years I managed to get married, sire four delightful but highly demanding children, and hold down a sensible but also highly demanding job based in landlocked Marlborough, Wilts. I had no choice. I was a beaten man. I could not have sustained regular enough trips to the coast without destroying my marriage and/or my career. My windsurfing during these 'sensible' years was limited to five or six outings per year, mostly whilst on holiday in Cornwall or Greece. So I had a ten-year sabbatical from windsurfing, ultimately replaced by an eight-month sabbatical from normal life.

Some fourteen years ago I had read a book by Tim Batsone, the first man to windsurf around Britain, and had never totally dismissed the idea that I could do something similar. In the late 1990s, the idea grew into something that highjacked my thoughts more and more regularly. I would casually talk to friends and work colleagues of my impossible dream, but always ending with a dismissive postscript that the work and family practicalities were insurmountable. I also started to read more and more sailing, climbing and adventure books, such as those of Pete Goss, the round-the-world yachtsman, and David Hempleman-Adams, the polar explorer and mountaineer. They all seemed like ordinary blokes who had made extraordinary dreams come true. I also talked a lot to a business friend who had just taken an eleven-month sabbatical to sail round the world on one of the BT Global Challenge yachts. As a normal working man with a wife, four kids and a big mortgage, I found it difficult to see myself giving it all up to chase an adventuring lifestyle, which would enrich me, but probably impoverish my family. I needed a compartmentalised fix, something I could do in a six- to eight-month window, which would not leave my kids fatherless for too long, and not render me unemployable afterwards. Tim Batstone had taken ten weeks to windsurf around Britain; I naively concluded that with modern equipment and a better support system, it should be possible to register a first and go around Ireland as well in six to eight weeks. It needed to be a first to justify the effort and sacrifice, and to attract sponsors and media attention. I also ideally needed at least six months off work to get myself in shape physically and to organise the whole event.

Apparently there are sound physiological and hormonal reasons why individuals need and become almost addicted to hard physical exercise. I certainly feel frustrated if denied a regular 'fix', but also often employ big quantities of will power to drag myself out for a run or to the gym, when my mind tells me there are many much more pleasant ways to spend an evening. Once out and working hard, there is some sort of release, and a feeling of mental and physical well-being; but the bigger motivation is as a means to an end, where the end is normally getting fitter and therefore ready for an event such as a half marathon or triathlon. The other driver is simply progress. In the age of 'objectives-driven man' I exhibit typical fitness anorak behaviour writing down my objectives, and recording all times and performances. When evaluating all the different elements of the challenge I was considering, I would look forward to having the time and goal to implement a really serious fitness campaign. It would almost be like being a professional athlete. I started from a very good base level for my age and I knew that with six months hard work I could get into the best shape of my life. It was also a way to see how hard I could push myself, and thus how fit I could actually get without the normal time constraints.

So I had something to prove or achieve (depending upon which school of thought we follow), a love of journeys through wild and beautiful environments, a psyche that gained considerable pleasure from pushing my body to its limit, and an unhealthy love of windsurfing. I had the motive, and the means to commit this crazy crime against sensibility. All that was missing was the opportunity (meaning time off work) and a more informed assessment of feasibility (meaning input from some experts). I also needed a charitable cause. I had never done much for charity, and felt that this was my opportunity to find a cause I believed in, and to use the venture to spread the word and raise cash.

Some three to four years before the Round Britain and Ireland Windsurf idea became a serious obsession, I had decided that after some twenty years on the working treadmill (meaning 1999/2000), I would step off and do all those life-enhancing things there had never been enough time for. The list of life-enhancing activities at first was very vague, but in 1996 I approached my boss and asked for a six-month sabbatical in five years' time. He was an open-minded, modern-thinking manager who probably regretted not having done something similar himself, so he said yes, with some caveats about timing and providing it could be done without negatively impacting the business I was managing. Unfortunately during the intervening years I was promoted and won a much less understanding boss. The encroaching sabbatical was mentioned at every end-of-year review, and my new boss tried to say yes and no at the same time. This was one of the skills he practised regularly, but it was always a consistently useless tactic. Like the proverbial dog with a bone, I had no intention of giving up, and nagged him mercilessly during 1998, to the extent that he now started to think I was more committed to the sabbatical than to the success of the business I was managing. I was still committed to my job, but I could no longer tolerate his indecision. Either he gave an absolute no, meaning I had to decide whether to give up on the sabbatical or resign; or an absolute yes with clear dates, my proposal being to start the sabbatical in autumn 1999. It didn't help that my casual conversations in the pub about 'time out' and what I was going to do with it, started to leak back into the work environment. I had trapped myself, but my boss was still holding the key. Finally in January 1999 I delivered some bad profit news, and his frustrations with me boiled over and precipitated an unholy row, and the usual threats and counter threats. Colleagues who had seen this coming persuaded both of us to back down from our silly positioning, and the compromise to give us both some space and distance was a sooner rather than later sabbatical. My request to start in autumn 1999 had been with a view to a spring 2000 attempt on the record. He offered an eight-month 'unpaid leave' starting June 1999, and returning February 2000. This meant no option other than to go for a late summer 1999 start, which was far from ideal but after about thirty minutes of deliberations I accepted. In the end, two weeks after this resolution, the whole group was acquired, and my boss put out to grass. Also, the new structure and culture did not look like easily accommodating my re-entry post sabbatical. Anyway ... what the hell ... I would deal with that issue in February 2000.

The unavoidable conclusion was to set sail late August from a south coast venue. I could not leave any sooner, as this would shift the planning and preparation time frame from very challenging to impossible; and we could not go any later, for risk of being trapped by worsening winter weather. The late summer/autumn wind statistics I had been given by the Met Office were far from ideal. Favourable sea breezes tend to be much more prevalent in the spring and early summer when the land is warming up but the sea still quite cool. Also the risk of a windless, immovable high-pressure system was much higher in August than May, and if for whatever reason our progress was much slower than expected we would be running into colder more wintry weather and shortening day length. To cap it all the records show that the year's most severe storms statistically occur around the autumn equinox, when I could well be off the north-west coasts of Ireland or Scotland, the most exposed and dangerous coastlines of the British Isles. But I had a target to work towards, which was still progress from where I had been in December 1998.

Before getting anywhere near the final sabbatical approval in January 1999, I had channelled my frustrated energies into talking to a plethora of experts and potentially useful contacts. My business training had drilled into me the need to collect and process information from all possible useful sources before considering options and formulating a plan. I had never windsurfed more than 20 miles before. I had never raised sponsorship or optimised media exposure before. Neither had I run a significant charity fundraising campaign, nor put together the team and infrastructure for a fairly major maritime expedition. For my own internal evaluation, I needed to better understand the factors which would determine success or failure, and I needed a feeling for probability of success, and risk of serious injury or death. Also I didn't like being asked questions to which I had no answer. To get respect and commitment from those asked to support me, I needed to at least give the impression of being professionally prepared. So moving into 'investigative journalist' mode I made a list of targets, and started to seriously bother people with my daft questions.

The first call was to Bill Dawes the editor of *Boards* magazine, one of the UK's major windsurfing publications. He was predictably sceptical, but did give me contact details for Simon Bornhoft. Simon is one of the UK's top windsurfers, and a well-known equipment and technique guru. He also holds various long-distance and endurance windsurfing records, and had himself put together a round Britain windsurf attempt. His attempt had to be aborted at the eleventh hour when a major sponsor pulled out, but he had gone through the same planning process that I was just starting. After several long telephone conversations, when he poured huge doses of reality onto some of my more naive notions, I eventually pinned him down to a meeting in a London hotel bar on 16 October 1998. This was my first encounter with someone who made their living out of windsurfing. He matched my mental image fairly well: compact, muscular, tanned and dressed in that trendy-untidy way that wouldn't work for a 41 year old. He had a quietly enthusiastic manner and a blatant passion for everything to do with the sport. It was an exciting, illuminating, but sobering discussion covering the sails and boards I would need, and how difficult it would be to get the logistics, crew, sponsorship and media exposure organised. Simon's conclusion was that I would need at least twelve months, £100k, and a lot of professional help. I think that at the time, Simon was being a nice polite professional. He had not seen me windsurf (thank God!), had been bombarded with my naïve questions, and deep down probably put my probability of success at zero. Anyway, we got on well, and he agreed to advise me on a structured consultancy basis. I was thus starting to spend money long before I had won any sponsorship.

One of the biggest differences of opinion I had with Simon was over how to organise the supporting logistics. He felt that using a yacht as mother ship or moving base camp, would be a recipe for disaster. Firstly, it would be too slow to keep up with me on the good days, meaning I and the safety boat could end up 70 miles ahead, with nowhere to stay for the night. Maximum speed of the yacht would be about 12–14 knots whereas mine could be 25 knots. Secondly, it could severely limit our nightly stopover options, as the draft on the type of ocean racing yacht I had envisaged could be 3–4m, meaning we could not get into many harbours and marinas. Lastly it would be very uncomfortable for a tired and aching windsurfer sleeping in an 18″ wide hammock. Simon's recommendation was to come ashore every night, using a mobile home as our base camp. But I was hooked on the ethos of a maritime journey, living 'on the water', and also felt that one of our best chances of getting into the media was through spectacular photos, of windsurfer and yacht crashing through the swells together. We were both right and both wrong, as the unfolding story will illustrate.

Unfortunately Simon then disappeared for most of the next three months, on various exotic overseas assignments, so his input was limited to a couple of long e-mails. We were working together on a schedule to spend most of 1999 getting organised, and to then set sail spring 2000. In early February 1999, I gave him the classic good news-bad news scenario. My sabbatical had finally been approved, but it had to be from June 1999 until February 2000, meaning I had no choice but to set sail late summer 1999, giving six rather than twelve months to get everything in place. Simon at first thought we should abort the whole thing. In his opinion probability of success had dropped to unrealistic levels. No time, and bad timing, was his summary. I suspect he was under the influence of alcohol at the time, but he eventually relented and agreed to give me his full support despite my ludicrous time schedule. The next step was for him to see me sail in late February, whereupon he could advise more specifically of what kit would suit my ability, and how to focus my windsurfing improvement programme.

In those last few months of 1998, and early 1999, I talked to many people seeking advice, but the meeting with Sir Chay Blythe was perhaps the most useful and colourful. Chay had sailed around the world single handed, and now ran the very successful BT Global Challenge race, where anyone (approved by Chay) could sign on, pay £25k, and spend eleven months racing a 67-ft yacht the wrong way (against prevailing winds and tides) around the world. Chay asked, 'Why should the media be interested in some nutter with a following entourage of yacht and safety boat taking eight weeks to windsurf around the British Isles?' In his subtle, indirect way he stressed that it was too slow, meaning they would lose interest, and not dangerous enough, meaning the public would not engage. He further added that if I couldn't convince sponsors of virtually guaranteed media coverage, then they would not commit any cash, and that many sponsors shied away from sponsoring individuals. Sponsoring a team or an event was far less risky. Having said all this, he seemed impressed with my enthusiasm, gave me some very useful sponsorship and media contacts, and left me with the message that persistence is everything ...

I next tracked down Tim Batstone, whose book had inspired me fourteen years before, and who was still the only person to have successfully windsurfed around Britain. Tim was certainly surprised to get the call and gave me the impression that he had long since given up windsurfing. He agreed with my preference to go for an ocean-going yacht as mother ship, but thought that the spring/summer was the only possible time to take on this mammoth journey.

An important issue for me was whether I could rely on support from the windsurfing industry and the governing body of the sport, namely the windsurfing section of the Royal Yachting Association (RYA). The first press release I sent out was butchered into two disparaging sentences by *Windsurf* magazine ending with the conclusion that 'he will be lucky if he makes it back by Christmas'. Jon White and Barrie Edgington at the RYA, however, took me seriously, and were enthusiastic supporters of the whole project. Jon White suggested I contact Euan McGrath, as my fitness advisor, and Sue Crayfer to give me a musculoskeletal screen, and physio advice. Euan is a sports science lecturer at the Southampton Institute, who also coaches our junior Olympic windsurfing squad, and Sue is physio to our Olympic windsurfing and sailing squads. These two individuals subsequently had a huge role to play in getting my ageing and fault-ridden body into the best possible condition for my gruelling physical challenge. Before going to see Euan and Sue, I had plenty of energy and determination but I simply didn't have a clue how to train.

I also talked to David Hemery, our 400m Gold Medal winner in the Mexico Olympics; Sue Stockdale, who was the first British woman to walk to the magnetic north pole; Jock Wishart who had skippered the record-breaking Cable and Wireless round-the-world powerboat venture; and Susan Preston-Davies, whose company handled the PR for Tim Batstone, and had been heavily involved with the BT Global Challenge. They all gave me different leads and ideas, but one consistent message, namely that if I wanted it badly enough, then I would make it.

My feasibility research, directed at a highly varied collection of 'experts', had yielded a reasonably consistent picture. All aspects of the venture, namely, getting fit enough, improving my windsurfing enough, raising enough sponsorship, getting enough media interest, and organising good enough supporting logistics, were going to be very very challenging! However, almost all reacted positively to my determination, persistence and professional approach. To see others get excited by what I was planning was a huge boost to me, and probably the factor which tipped me over into a final decision to go for it. Despite others thinking I had a professional approach, with the benefit of hindsight, I was still incredibly naïve, and ironically if I'd known then what I know now, I almost certainly would have given up, but where would the world be without blind optimists? I was naïevely confident I could get to the start line well prepared and well supported. Thereafter I concluded that our probability of success would be down to the weather, and staying free of debilitating injury. With normal weather conditions, and no big injuries, I put a successful outcome at 50:50. Too much or too little wind, or winds consistently from the wrong direction, could easily push our success probability down to less than 10 per cent. Providing I had an experienced and reliable support infrastructure, and we followed a policy of always sheltering during storms, the general consensus was that the risk of death or serious injury was no greater than that of commuting round the M25 every day. The counter to that was that the seas around our shores are dangerously unpredictable, and prone to punish those who take liberties. It would all be about managing the risk, and being fit enough, and well resourced enough to get out of trouble.

My first ports of call whilst looking for a suitable charity were the big children's, wildlife and cancer charities. Their response was typified by the guy I spoke to at the BBC's Children in Need, who said, 'Yes, great, go ahead and do it and send us the cheque afterwards.' This was not my vision. I then realised that I needed to work *with* the charity on the fundraising, understand where the money raised would go, and preferably align myself with a smaller charity where our contribution would be enough to really make a difference. After some quick Internet research and a recommendation from a sponsorship contact, I called the Marine Conservation society. They were a small, focused operation dedicated to improving our beaches, seas, and environments for our marine wildlife. They were also prepared to work with us, and gave us an additional task of surveying sea-surface litter and logging marine wildlife sightings. I also liked the people, and we immediately started work on a joint logo for my sails.

Secretly I believed that through my wide and quite senior-level business network, I could raise the necessary sponsorship, and that despite Chay Blythe's warnings it would be relatively easy to get the media coverage. I had tended to worry the most about whether my windsurfing would be up to it. I also felt it would not be too difficult to put an enthusiastic and competent group of volunteers together as the core of the support team. Surely there were individuals out there who would jump at the chance to be a part of this history-making venture?

So at the end of January 1999 I now had motive, means, opportunity, charitable cause and a decent understanding of the feasibility. It was decision time. If I was to put together a support team, commit to charter both safety boat and mother ship, send out press releases and pitch for sponsorship, then I had to give a firm start date, and ethically could not change my mind, when others had arranged their business and personal schedules around my venture. I talked at length to my wife and parents. They were all apprehensive, and would certainly not have shed any tears if I had called the whole thing off. My wife was concerned that the windsurf project would dominate my eight months off work, leaving no time for all the family experiences we had planned; and she was not over the moon at being potentially left on her own for eight weeks with our four young children. I did feel terribly selfish, and tried to rationalise that if successful, the venture could open up new job opportunities for me, where I could make decent money without being a sixty-hours-a-week slave to the corporate machine. My tenuous argument was that the venture could thus indirectly improve our overall quality of life. My wife pretended to believe this pathetic pitch, but was sensible enough not to make me look even sillier by asking what sort of job I was expecting to appear out of the ether, just because I'd windsurfed around the British Isles. My parents were simply worried that I would not come back at all. Neither my mother nor father had any interest in, or experience of, the sea and sailing. To them, it was simply big, powerful, unpredictable and very dangerous. My mum pleaded with me to avoid ever getting out of sight of land, which would have made the crossing to Ireland somewhat tricky. Despite all the worries, counter arguments, and knowing how selfish I was being, I was emotionally too far down the track to turn back, and I knew it had to be NOW or it would be NEVER. A date of 22 August was fixed for the start, I wrote the first press release, and started to call people and deliver the 'its definitely on' message.

Chapter II

Of Wind and Windsurfing

*W*indsurfing is the most impractical means of long-distance transport imaginable. The windsurfer is always stood up, and 99 per cent of the time has two arms and two legs fully occupied. There is nowhere on a windsurfer to store food, drink, navigational equipment and spare kit. Eating and drinking are difficult to say the least, and neither is there anywhere to rest (let alone sleep). The waterborne equivalent of 'mending a puncture' is a tad difficult on a rough sea and with a board that hardly floats. Whereas the yacht sailor can reef down the mainsail when the wind increases, a windsurfer has to change to a smaller sail, and often a smaller board.

As if this were not enough, a windsurfer (like all other sail-driven craft) can only zig-zag or tack 'upwind' (when the desired direction of travel also happens to be the direction from which the wind is blowing) ; and unlike other sail-driven craft, the windsurfer is often very difficult to sail 'down-wind' (or in the same direction as the wind is blowing). Most windsurfers spend most of their time sailing 'across the wind', meaning their board is travelling at around 90 degrees to the direction of the wind. Sailing across the wind or 'beam reaching' is the fastest, most comfortable 'point of sail', but anyone needing to cover any distance on a windsurfer (such as anyone daft enough to consider circumnavigating Britain and Ireland!) will inevitably spend most of their time sailing upwind or downwind (see illustration on following page).

At its simplest windsurfing requires a board, a rig and an operator, with the rig comprising a sail, a mast and a boom. At its most complicated, windsurfing can compete with any other sport for endless techno-speak jargon. For the purposes of this book (and because I am not really young enough to know what the latest techno-jargon really means), the bits and pieces are as per the illustration on page 13.

Fortunately there are only two sides to a rig, meaning the person windsurfing is either sailing on a starboard tack (right hand nearest the mast) or port tack (left hand nearest the mast); and in further keeping with its simple nature, there are only two ways for the operator to move from one side of the sail to another, and thus change direction. If sailing upwind, the operator stalls the board by letting it point head to wind, and then swings the sail over the back of the board whilst walking round the front of the mast to the other side. This manoeuvre where the nose of the board

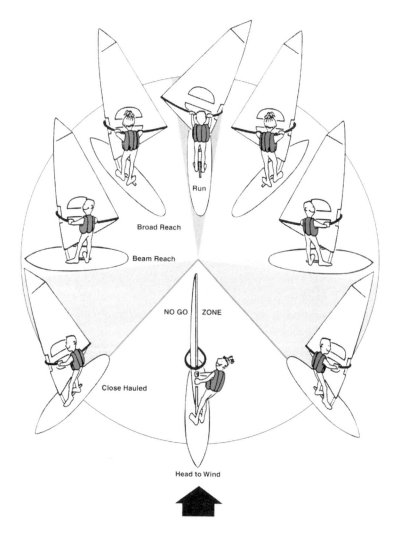

Fig 1. The Points of Sailing
(Illustration courtesy of RYA Windsurfing)

passes through the eye of the wind is called 'tacking'. When sailing downwind, the sail is flipped over the front of the board, and as the back of the board passes through the eye of the wind, the operator moves from one side of the board to another to complete a 'gybe'. Lastly but consistently there are two ways to get going on a windsurfer. In light winds the operator simply heaves the sail out of the water with a piece of rope called the 'uphaul' and grabs the boom to initiate the forward motion. Not surprisingly this technique is known as 'uphauling'. For intermediates and in

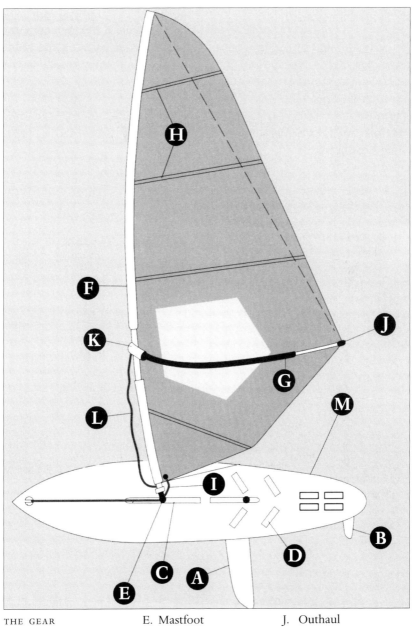

THE GEAR

A. Daggerboard	E. Mastfoot	J. Outhaul
B. Fin	F. Mast	K. Boom Clamp
C. Mastrack	G. Boom	L. Uphaul
D. Footstraps	H. Battens	M. Rails
	I. Downhaul	

Fig 2 – Illustration courtesy of RYA Windsurfing

stronger winds, the best way to get going is by 'waterstarting', where the operator lifts the leading edge of the sail clear of the water, puts one foot on the board, and by holding onto the boom lets the wind in the sail lift his or her body onto the board. In principle and whilst watching, this method is not dissimilar to a waterskier being pulled out of the water by the tow rope.

Windsurfers talk incessantly about the wind strength which in true British maritime tradition is measured in knots, but often categorised according to the Beaufort scale.

Force	General Description	Open Sea State	Limit of velocity in Knots
0	Calm	Sea like a mirror	1
1	Light air	Ripples with the appearance of scales are formed but without foam.	1-3
2	Light breeze	Small wavelets, still short but more pronounced. Crests have a glassy appearance and do not break.	4- 6
3	Gentle breeze	Large wavelets, crests begin to break; foam of glassy appearance, perhaps scattered white horses.	7-10
4	Moderate breeze	Small waves becoming longer; fairly frequent white horses.	11-16
5	Fresh breeze	Moderate waves taking a more pronounced long form; many white horses are formed (chance of some spray).	17- 21
6	Strong breeze	Large waves begin to form and white foam crests become more extensive (probably some spray).	22-27
7	Near gale	Sea heaps up and white foam from the breaking waves begins to be blown in streaks along the direction of the wind.	28-33
8	Gale	Moderately high waves of greater length, edges of crests begin to break into spindrift. The foam is blown in well-marked streaks along the direction of the wind.	34-40
9	Strong gale	High waves; dense streaks of foam along the direction of the wind. Crests of waves begin to topple and roll over, spray may effect visibility.	41- 47

Fig 3. The Beaufort Wind Scale
(Courtesy of RYA Windsurfing)

Sailors, mariners and even pilots also tend to measure the speed of their craft in knots. Why knots? Why not simple miles per hour? Why is a speed of 10 knots equivalent to 11.5 mph? I didn't have an answer to this question myself, until I undertook this little project. A windsurfer travelling at a speed of 1 knot will cover one nautical mile in one hour. So why the hell do we need nautical miles as well as land miles? The answer lies in the man-made system of longitude and latitude which enables accurate positioning of individual points on the Earth's surface. Britain lies roughly between 50 and 60 degrees of latitude north of the equator. Each degree of latitude is divided into 60 minutes, and coincidentally each minute is one nautical mile. Thus for pilots and mariners who fix a grid reference for their craft in latitude and longitude, it is much easier to use nautical miles as a measure of distance and thus knots as a measure of speed. Any reference to miles in this book are thus nautical miles.

I did not carry my own navigational equipment on the windsurfer. This service was effectively provided by the experts and their specialist equipment on the safety boat. Our navigational mainstay was the GPS (Global Positioning System) which uses the feedback from a network of satellites to give an accurate position. At the end of each day's sailing the GPS reading at our 'waypoint' would be recorded and witnessed, with an example entry being: Finish position 51 degrees, 25.459 minutes North & 9 degrees, 27.507 minutes West (to the layman we were 4.5 nautical miles north-east of the Fastnet Rock. The next day's sailing would logically begin at the previous day's finish position or way point. The GPS also gave us our speed over the ground (SOG) and heading. The second-most used piece of equipment was the plotter, which gave us a picture on the screen of the safety boat superimposed onto a zoomable map of the area. More detailed nautical charts, a compass, an anemometer and radar were used to supplement these two essential systems.

Wind strength is impossible to predict accurately, particularly when weather fronts are passing through, and wind strength and direction can vary enormously. When the wind direction shifts in a clockwise direction it is said to be veering, whereas a wind direction shifting anti-clockwise is said to be backing. The wind not only powers the windsurfer, but also has a big impact on the watery terrain over which it has to pass.

The sea state is heavily influenced by the local wind strength and direction, but also by distant depressions. The more regular, often well spaced, and shallow incline 'swells' are normally caused by more distant weather systems; whereas shorter, steeper more confused seas are normally the result of local wind effects. The difficulty is that most of the time around our shores we have both, meaning the sea is more often than not lumpy and confused. Normally a swell only becomes a wave when it breaks. Swells normally only break when running into shallower water, but wind and tidal effects can also cause the tops of swells to break in deeper water.

The next complication for any long distance windsurfer is the horrendously complicated tides around our shores. My understanding was that the tide flows out (ebbing) for six hours and roughly twenty minutes, and then comes in (flooding) for a further six and a bit hours. This turned out not always to be the case, with an eight- and five-hour cycle encountered off northern Scotland. Don't ask me to explain this phenomenon, or the even stranger case off Cape Wrath where despite the tide, the water always flows east to west. Tidal flows vary in speed from less than 1 knot to more than 10 knots. The water flow associated with big spring tides is obviously that much faster than with weaker neap tides, but in this case spring has nothing to do with the season between winter and summer. The tidal range follows a two-week lunar cycle, with the highest 'spring' tides occurring at the time of a full and new moon. However to partly justify the terminology, it is true that the most extreme tides of the year occur in spring and autumn. As any offshore sailor will know, the problem is not the tides per se, but the consequences of a large volume of water having to pass through or round or over a natural obstruction. In such situations tidal flows accelerate to create a 'tidal race'.

The windsurfing equipment needed for a round Britain and Ireland venture had to be able to accommodate the highly variable windspeed, and a predominance of upwind and downwind sailing. It also had to be fast and comfortable to use; two qualities that are not normally listed together on the same specification.

For the planned venture I had three different boards graded in size to accommodate different wind strengths, and sea states. The lighter the wind the bigger the board and vice versa. The biggest, floatiest board was 3.80m long, with a volume of some 270 litres. For the technically minded it was the F2 3.80 Raceboard, with very deep boxy sides, sharp rails, and a huge retractable daggerboard. It was the biggest board I have ever sailed, but its designers had 'done a blinder'. It was much easier to sail upwind or downwind than any raceboard I had been on before, and just did not feel its size. Big in this case was beautiful and very effective, and our pre-event plan was that this board would mostly be used in F1/3 conditions. To the non-windsurfer comparing this board to the others in my set, it would look long, wide and thick. I couldn't help likening it to my recently acquired Big Bertha golf club, which was also bigger than anything I had ever used before, but much more effective. There was no argument. The 3.80 race-board had to be christened Big Bertha. As a personality Big Bertha was domineering and possessive. She had good connections, and on many occasions when shunned in favour of her smaller brethren would wield her influence to cause the wind to drop, such that I had no choice but to reinstate her under my feet.

The next smallest in the family was a 3.05m long F2 Thommen, with a volume of around 160 litres. In the technical jargon this was a first-generation, wide-style, early-planing board, designed for racing in F3/4 conditions. It also had sharp rails, and when used with a huge 50-cm fin was faster and higher pointing into wind, than any similar-sized earlier designs. This was the board I had spent most of my training time on, and thus the board I was most comfortable on. It was a buxom and curvaceous creation, but built for speed and performance. It was also a survivor, and had come back from the dead several times, after major surgery. With the film *Titanic* and its curvy, indestructible heroine still fresh in everyone's minds, this board was evidently the Kate Winslett of windsurfing, and became known as Katie. Katie was a laid-back but incredibly robust and adaptable character.

My 2.77m long F2 Ride, with around 105 litres volume, was ideally for use in winds of F4 and above. It has a sleek, elegant appearance, and would be a classic rather than exotic beauty. To me it was a soft-riding, almost naïve creature, but mysteriously jinxed, and happier being pampered than ridden. This very feminine individual was pretty to look at but very rarely used, as I tended to take the easier to manage, more robust, bigger options. This board had to be Lady Di. With my weight of around 85 kg and at least another 15 kg of rig, wetsuit and survival/communications kit on my back, this board was close to being a sinker. A sinker is a board that does not have enough buoyancy to keep its rider above the surface of the water in light wind conditions. As a general rule, when the weight upon the board exceeds its volume, it sinks.

We also took on the trip ten Tushingham sails varying in size from 4 square metres to 10.7 square metres, eight carbon-fibre masts with the biggest 5.20m long, eight carbon-fibre booms, and a truckload of widgets, ropes, pulleys and repair kits. The biggest 10.7m sail was designed for use in winds of maximum 8 knots (F3), whereas a 4.0m sail would not really work unless exposed to a good F6. I also managed to acquire four Neil Pryde wetsuits (varying in thickness and thus warmth), three pairs of neoprene boots, a collection of neoprene helmets and undervests, and a specially made life vest, with pockets both back and front for safety equipment, and food/fluids.

Main: The huge 10.7m sail on Bertha for light wind days

Inset: Carrying curvacious Katie ashore during training

Chapter III

No Turning Back

It is not because things are difficult that we do not dare
It is because we do not dare that they are difficult.

Seneca

We had been three days stormbound in Scrabster on the north-east tip of Scotland waiting for the weather to ease enough to allow us to safely negotiate the treacherous Pentland Firth. Much of the time during the three days had been spent looking at one of the world's strongest and most famous tidal races from the cliff tops, planning our route and tactics. The large volume of water running to the west at 12 knots against a 35-knot gale from the west, was throwing up some horrendous 10–15 ft standing waves. A group of ocean-going cargo freighters were sitting it out south of Duncansby Head, waiting for the seas to ease, so there was certainly no way through for a 12-ft windsurfer. I had been for a chat to the Scrabster coastguard who told me that the wind was forecast to ease by tomorrow, and that one tide should be enough to flatten the seas back to something manageable. He also told me that if we set sail from our waypoint east of Dunnet Head at dawn, we would have maximum three hours, to sail the 12 miles west, and out past the worst of the race off Duncansby head before the tide turned against us. This was it; our window of opportunity before conditions turned for the worst again. I didn't sleep much, and neither did the crew talk much during our pre-dawn ride out to the waypoint in light westerly winds with an inky black sky above us and undulating inky black sea below. Steve, the safety boat coxswain and safety officer, made one final call to the coastguard and asked for confirmation that we had three hours of favourable tide. It was a different coastguard on duty, and his reading of tide tables told us that we had no more than fifty minutes of favourable tide. If his information was correct, then we didn't have a hope in hell of getting through.

Steve was furious calling me all sorts of names starting with 'impatient' and ending with something more basic. I lost my rag and swore back suggesting that with all his years of experience at sea, he should have taken time to read the ✶✶✶✶✶✶ tide tables himself, rather than relying on the ✶✶✶✶✶✶ coastguard. When faced with one piece of positive information and one piece of negative information on the weather or tides, Steve would always believe the pessimistic scenario, and I the optimistic scenario. He was doing his job as safety officer, but I was running out of time to complete this gruelling journey. I somehow persuaded Steve that we had nothing to lose by rigging up rapidly, and even if today's coastguard were correct, with the light winds and gentle seas we would at least get a few miles nearer our target before the tide turned. Steve's view was that forty minutes of sailing to cover 3–4 miles did not justify getting up at 4.30 a.m., and that we should head back into Scrabster to sit out the next six or seven hours of unfavourable tide. My problem with this approach was that if yesterday's coastguard was right we would end up waiting nine rather than seven hours, and risk running out of light at the other end of the day. We simply could not afford to miss this window. The wind could easily pick up later, or swing to the east, giving us wind over tide conditions. Even worse the storms could return forcing us to sit out another three days. I set off sailing in absolute silence, and drifted past Dunnet Head on the weakening east-flowing tide at about 4 knots SOG (speed over ground). No-one dared speak to Steve or myself for fear of reigniting the row. I however gleefully broke the stony silence by pointing out to Steve after seventy minutes that the bubbling water flow around a lobster pot buoy we were passing suggested the east-going tide was still running at around 3 knots. Yesterday's coastguard was right, bless his cotton socks!

Two hours later I just managed to get past the imposing Duncansby Head before the tide turned, and they pulled me into the safety boat and recorded our GPS position, before I was swept backwards. A great great feeling to have at last got through this monster, and some quiet satisfaction that my impatience and optimism had in this case paid off. Two weeks earlier, I had set myself a time limit that we had to get round the north coast of Scotland by Friday, 8 October. Beyond this arbitrary cut-off we were slipping too far into winter, and I knew that if I didn't complete the journey by the end of October, I would lose most of my voluntary crew and the RIB support. We got through the Pentland Firth three days before the deadline. Now there was definitely no turning back. We simply had to finish. Despite the angry start to the day, Steve was as thrilled as me to have got round the top, and perhaps fittingly it was also his last night before being replaced by Philippe. We had a warm and relieved session in the pub that night, and openly discussed what made us tick in such completely different ways.

*P*rior to the event, I had worried most about the sea and the weather and whether my body would cope. During the event, I spent at least as much time stewing over people issues. Perhaps I should have designed the whole project as a sociological experiment, or as an outdoor equivalent to psychometric testing. We ended up with twelve very different personalities from a wide spectrum of backgrounds, brought together on 21 August 1999, to live for eight weeks in one 14′ by 10′ yacht cabin, with no heating and no shower. The passage above is one of many illustrations of the conflicts that arose when we were faced with difficult decisions in a physically demanding and stressful environment. There were also many glorious moments of togetherness and mutual success, and to counter-balance the silent and not so silent conflicts, some deep friendships formed that may well last for life. I did not pick the mostly voluntary team in any systematic way. I met people and if I thought they would fit, they were hired. Some who were offered the job turned it down. Some said yes and then subsequently changed their minds. Some came with the hardware I was to charter, namely the safety boat crew, and the skipper and first mate of the mother ship. All had relevant skills, but perhaps as would have been the case with a totally random selection, four were absolute rocks, who I would immediately hire for any similar future venture, six were good strong functionally effective members of the team, and two didn't really fit at all.

In February 1999 I sat down with a blank sheet of paper, and listed the skills and functional roles that I would ideally need, in addition to the core crew of the safety boat and mother ship:

Medical/first aid officer
Photographer
Film cameraman
Physio
Equipment manager/caddy
Navigator
Safety officer
Cook and provisions manager
Media liaison/PR manager
Charity fundraising manager
Van driver
Budget manager

It was obvious that one person could handle more than one role, but also obvious that the first thing I had to do was secure a mother ship and safety boat, and therefore know the people and thus skills that came with the hardware.

Despite the advice from Simon Bornhoft and others to avoid using a yacht as mother ship, I charged headlong into the charter market. I bought myself a copy of *Yachts and Yachting*, and spent many hours ringing round anybody who might have a 50–65ft, 12-berth, reasonably quick, ocean-going yacht for hire at a sensible price. My hypothesis was that if my schedule avoided any of the major races, and the summer corporate entertaining season, then someone somewhere would have a boat (and possibly crew) lying idle, costing money. The owner might also identify with my crazy adventure, and believe my story that we would get masses of publicity;

and that a picture of me in foreground and yacht behind, blasting past the Needles on the front page of the *Daily Telegraph*, would be great PR for his charter business. One of my first calls was to Group 4, who had bought an ex-BT Global Challenge boat from Chay Blythe. They at first seemed quite interested in providing this eminently suitable yacht at cost or less, providing Group 4 effectively became the title sponsor. The yacht was already decked out with Group 4 logos, and the simplicity of this solution appealed to me, even if I was worried about losing control of the project. Anyway, they were patently unable to make a decision one way or the other, and when I had got no response from my persistent phone calls I took this as a 'no', and focused my attentions elsewhere. Coming from a business background, where people had to be reliable, I found the yacht charter business very frustrating. Many I spoke to had time to discuss things over the phone, and gave the impression of being interested and enthusiastic, but getting any sort of proposal or decision out of them was next to impossible. Many of the smaller operators seemed to be individuals from other walks of life who had succumbed to their addiction to the sea and sailing by selling out of whatever they were in before, and buying a big yacht to enjoy and to make money from. The problem was that they often seemed to find it difficult to decide whether they were in 'enjoy' or 'make money' mode. The larger operators like Sunsail acted like a large operator and didn't take me seriously.

My first conversation with Terry Nielsen, the owner of the yacht Maiden was typically enthusiastic, as per the norm with other owner/operators. Maiden had been made famous by Tracy Edwards and her highly successful Whitbread round-the-world race, skippering an all-female crew. Terry did however agree to meet at the Boat Show, and the idea of using a yacht that had been almost a household name was a big plus for me. With a yacht such as Maiden, it should be easier to guarantee media coverage and thus attract sponsors.

Terry was an immediately likeable individual, with lots of ideas and visions. True to type he had sold out of his legal practice in Edinburgh to live his lifelong passion of ocean racing. We got on well at the Boat Show, and agreed a two-tiered charter price, the plan being to pool energies on winning sponsorship, and he would receive a normal market charter rate if we were successful, but would do it at cost if we were not. Terry and I shared a blind optimism, which some would see as a personality defect. He did not necessarily fit the image of a grumpy, white-haired, wizened, old seadog, but his brusque 'this is the way we will do it' manner, and tendency to throw the occasional temper tantrum certainly upset several of the crew once we were on our way. I had only a verbal agreement with Terry. Nothing was committed to paper which made me nervous, but the mutual trust was there, and he didn't have any other jobs for Maiden at that time of year. Terry had committed himself to me, and that for me meant no turning back. He was also always keen to help put me onto others who were either potential crew volunteers, or could support the project in some other way. In fact three of the final crew came via Terry's network.

Terry's first mate, and in fact replacement as skipper for the last five weeks of the trip, was a swarthy northerner named Kevin who had given up his business operating fish and chip shops to live aboard Maiden for much of the year, as Terry's maintenance man cum-reserve skipper. Kevin immediately struck me as a straightforward bloke who needed his pints, fags, girlfriend and sailing, but not much else. His relationship with Terry seemed to be one of mutual dependence, and dislike. Terry effectively exploited Kevin's addiction to the sailing life, and lifestyle, by paying him very little, and using him as a verbal punchbag when Kevin had made a mistake; but Terry had a broader frustration to vent. Whereas a business breakthrough was often round the corner for Terry, escape from his Terry-dependency was always around the corner for Kevin. When Terry was skippering Maiden Kevin seemed grumpy and disgruntled. When Terry had to leave the project after four weeks to attend to other business interests, Kevin took over and crew harmony seemed to improve. Terry as the owner/skipper was always coming from a more difficult direction, whereas Kevin's more flexible 'one of the lads' approach just seemed to be right for our situation. In Terry's defence it was not a normal skippering context, with absolute decision-making authority, and a necessary *he who must be obeyed* culture. We were effectively four independent but interdependent teams. Overall we were a team headed by Richard Cooper, with an overriding objective to become the first to windsurf around Britain and Ireland. We had a media team of three (one photographer, and two documentary makers) whose objective was to optimise the quality of the footage and images they were after, and to maximise media exposure and general publicity. We then had a RIB/safety boat team, who were concerned with keeping me out of danger, keeping the RIB (the industry abbreviation for Rigid Inflatable Boat) running, and maintaining my equipment. The RIB team was effectively a service to me, and the Maiden team a service to the other three teams. They provided our accommodation, food and moving base camp.

I had imagined Maiden as a sleek, spectacular, state-of-the-art creation. The pictures on Terry's website, of Maiden at full power gliding through rough seas, only served to strengthen this image. Never mind the windsurfing, it would be a wonderful enough experience making this 2,000-mile journey on a yacht with such an aura and history. My first visit to Moody's

Above: Battleship grey Maiden with Terry at the helm.

Below: Steve and Spider on our RIB (Rigid Inflatable Boat).

boatyard where Maiden was moored was a huge eye-opener. Maiden was painted what to me looked like battleship grey (in fact the colours of Royal Jordanian Airlines, Tracy Edwards' original sponsor), had nothing on deck except ropes, winches and more ropes and winches, and down below was musty, spartan and tatty. She was effectively a fifteen-year old racing yacht, with absolutely no concessions to comfort, and badly in need of serious refurbishment. She was living off her name, like some respected but over-the-hill film star. After the initial shock, I started to fall for her dank, grey, metallic form, and sleeping on board for the first time in early May, I lay awake for hours dreaming of the stories this boat could tell. The first time we sailed together was also a relationship-building experience. We were out in the Solent cruising up and down, and having great difficulty getting in position for our photographer to get his perfect shot. It was like a mismatched couple trying to dance together but apart, with the incompatibility blindingly obvious to all except the dancers. When seen under full sail from water level 50 yds away, Maiden was huge and majestic, and I metaphorically salivated at the prospect of sailing together round some of our famous headlands, with crowds on the cliffs watching this odd but beautiful Little and Large show.

The reality was of course very different. For logistical reasons we very rarely sailed together, but when we did it invariably made the day that much more memorable. Maiden was effectively our seaborne hotel and nerve centre. We ate, slept, planned, fell out, celebrated, and became familiar with each other's body odours on Maiden! She had twelve narrow hammocks strung in four blocks of three, off the sloping walls of the main cabin. Depending upon the chosen alignment, it was possible to sleep with one's head no more than 3 ft away from five pairs of smelly salty feet, or alternatively five snorting, snoring, wheezing faces. The galley (kitchen to the non-sailors) was only 5' 10" high, meaning that those over 6 ft would return from a session on washing-up duty with neck irreversibly angled 45 degrees to right or left. The head (toilet) was basic, not at all private, and only 6 ft across the corridor from the galley. There was no door, only a plastic curtain with unreliable velcro. Once one's job was done, it was necessary to violently yank the vacuum pump back and forth until the said jobs had hopefully been evacuated. On a diet unusually biased towards high-energy carbohydrates and dried fruit, my jobs were far from normal, and at times stubbornly refused to evacuate with the normal amount of yanking. This caused great hilarity among the crew, particularly when I totally blocked the heads, and had to disassemble the pump and remove the offending blockage before being allowed out on my board. Maiden had no heating, a hot water system that worked some of the time, and a makeshift hand-held 'too hot/too cold' shower that could be used whilst sitting naked on the toilet seat. A strange experience, which only I tried, and then only once. Despite Maiden's failings, when we arrived in port for the night, heads always turned, and we often had a constant stream of visitors on guided tours.

Maiden had no need to follow the same course as me. She effectively hopped from port to port or anchorage to anchorage, whereas the safety boat and myself would plan the shortest straightest course along the coastline, and at the end of each day's windsurfing we would take a GPS position (satellite-derived map reference), often miles offshore, pack up and motor into wherever Maiden was to be for the night. Maiden could motor directly into the wind or tide, whereas I would have to zig-zag patiently upwind and sometimes on light wind days wait for the favourable tide. Sometimes I was much quicker than her, sometimes much slower. Sometimes we got well ahead of her scheduled stopover, and had to motor back, and sometimes the opposite.

Stopovers fell into six categories. The best option was always to get into a marina, where we could moor up alongside a pontoon, get a hot shower, and have easy access to pubs and shops. Not all marinas could accommodate Maiden's 3.3m draft, and in the more remote regions, marinas full of expensive leisure craft are not exactly common. Out of our sixty-one days at sea we spent twenty-one nights in the relative comfort of a marina. The next best option was a town-quay or dock-wall tie-up, where we had ready access to land, but not the laid-on facilities. We had some great town-quay and dock-wall stopovers adding up to sixteen nights. The least aesthetic, hospitable option was when we had no other choice but to tie up outside a series of oily, rusty, and not very sweet-smelling fishing boats, in ports such as Killibegs and Newlyn. We also had some absolutely stunning anchorages, in the lee of islands like Lindisfarne and Aranmore, and some less stunning nights tied up to a mooring buoy in places like Harwich. For three nights whilst crossing the Celtic sea, we simply drifted on the weak tide, and employed an overnight watch to make sure we were not run down by an errant freighter.

The appeal of this existence was its unpredictability, and the journey through an incredibly varied coastal landscape was fascinating and full of surprises. Not knowing what is round the next headland will always be one of the charms of any coastal journey. In many of the more exposed landscapes, the sight of a stubby, wind-battered tree clinging to the side of a shadowy gully was a surprise in itself. Many times on the journey we were out of sight of land, due either to the curvature of the earth or poor visibility. Seeing land and its shape and character emerge out of the misty horizon was always captivating. Similarly we had no idea what our anchorage or berth for the night would look like until we got there.

In parallel with my efforts to find a suitable mother ship, I also needed to find and hire a suitable safety boat. This time there were no differences of opinion. By far the most practical solution, as used by all others who have done or tried something similar, was to find a suitable RIB. RIBs have soft, inflatable, wrap-around tubes, and a rigid (normally fibreglass) hull. They are fast, light, very safe, and easy to climb into from the water. They normally come with either an inboard diesel or outboard petrol engine, and can be anything from 4 to 12m long. The RIB would have to be big enough to carry all my boards and sails that we would potentially need on a given day, be able to carry four or five bodies comfortably, be capable of speeds up to and beyond 30 knots, and preferably have a small cabin to store food and dry clothes, and for emergency hypothermia situations. It would also need to be an offshore 'ocean-going' RIB with all necessary communication and navigation equipment, and have a reliable and economical inboard diesel engine. *Yachts and Yachting* was an easy buy from WH Smiths. Once I'd discovered the existence of *International RIB* magazine, and become a lifelong subscriber, it was an easy second step to begin ringing round the industry experts and RIB service/charter companies.

The RIB business with by far the most experience of supporting windsurfing events was an imaginatively named outfit called International RIB Services or IRS, based out of Lymington in Dorset, run by two ex-marines, Steve Potter and Russ Kerslake. I met Russ and Steve in a Dorset pub in mid-February 1999, and after several pints and a lot of RIB chat, their conclusion seemed to be that I was a guy they could work with. I had stressed to them that the success of this venture was for the most part down to the quality of the RIB support. This was a somewhat exaggerated precis of my true feelings, but Russ and Steve gave me the impression that the rest of the world had yet to truly appreciate the potential of RIBs, and thus I did not see it necessary to talk about other critical success factors such as my fitness, and my windsurfing ability. I also took to them. They had strong opinions but seemed enthusiastic, honest, and were also very into the details. They had just returned from providing the RIB support for a transatlantic windsurf race, which had apparently been an organisational nightmare, and had been a massive learning experience in how not to run long-distance windsurfing events. The RIB owned by IRS were too small for this job, but they were in partnership with a professional yachting photographer named Philippe Falle, who had built an 8.5m inboard diesel RIB, complete with all necessary gadgets and a small cabin; a perfect solution. The contract negotiations with Russ and Steve were certainly different. They alternated between phases of extreme and almost naïve flexibility, to moods of reactive, aggressive stubbornness. They had both been twenty years in the Marines, and the Special Boat Service, the Navy's equivalent of the SAS. I got the feeling they had only partly adapted to life on the outside, and in times of stress and frustration with the softness and unreliability of life on civvy street, reverted back to type.

Steve and Russ actually looked a bit like their beloved RIB, which tend to be wider than a conventional craft and more curvy. Steve was squat, round and muscular, with little or no neck. Russ was taller but barrel-chested and similarly round and powerful. Steve was the safety boat coxswain and safety officer for all but the last three weeks of the trip. We had some major disagreements, but also shared some moments of great elation, and of all the support team, I often felt that Steve was perhaps one of the most committed to our overall success. He was just as down as me when things went wrong, and had to endure some very tough days, both out on the RIB in heavy seas trying to keep an exhausted and useless windsurfer going, and back on Maiden stormbound and watching our probability of success slip inexorably downwards. He obviously did not feel comfortable in a consensus-driven, decision-making environment, where the needs of four different teams, had to be accommodated, and I was always trying to get wider buy-in. For Steve it was simple. It was either his call, in which case discussion was unnecessary, and it was time for everyone to get out and get on with it, or it was someone else's call, in which case he would grumpily do as he was told. Steve was very cautious in his role as safety officer, and head navigator. In my opinion and that of others on the team, this over-cautious approach cost us time and distance; but to his credit, I and the rest of the RIB team made it round without serious injury or having to face any life-threatening situations. He also matured as the journey progressed, and became more flexible on some of the contentious navigational and logistical issues.

For the first four weeks, Steve's co-driver, and second coxswain was another ex-marine called Gary, or more accurately Gaz. As an individual Gaz gave the impression of being a happy-go-lucky party animal. He had bleached blonde hair, the ubiquitous ear ring, and a predictably raunchy-looking girlfriend. In a team environment Gaz was adept at diffusing the tension with a clever quip, and did offer input when Steve might be sulking in the background waiting for someone to take a bloody decision. Gaz was good for morale as the team joker and wide boy, but I often felt that he was only there to do his job, have a laugh and collect his IRS wages. If he was doing what Steve had 'ordered' he was fine, but if Steve had reluctantly accepted an alternative decision, he could be quite petty and obstructive.

I thanked Gaz when he left, but inside was looking forward to getting a more serious and committed replacement. His successor, who of course was another ex-marine, was a totally different species. Spider was recently married, and so obviously devoted to his new wife. He was quiet, willing and much easier to co-exist with on the often tense environment of the RIB. Spider (or as his wife called him, Stuart) was long limbed, dark and wiry (hence the name). He spoke slowly and deliberately, and had a serious responsible air, but also a good sense of humour; and often helped me get Steve out of his perennial grumps, which normally persisted until lunchtime.

After six weeks, Steve had to go back to Lymington, and was replaced as RIB coxswain by Philippe, the RIB owner, and absolute chalk to Steve's cheese. Philippe was a university-educated, fast-living, London-based, professional photographer. He had crewed on a round-the-world racing yacht and to my mind was the best judge of acceptable weather risk we had on the team. This yachting background made the RIB-Maiden relationship easier. He was also less of a morning faffer, and thus we invariably got out sailing sooner. Philippe's only drawback was his tendency to coerce others into finding serious pub lock-in situations, which often resulted in an absolutely legless troupe of would-be circumnavigators crashing back onto Maiden at 3.00 a.m. waking a tired and emotional windsurfer. Philippe's stamina, after a heavy session and three hours sleep, and his resistance to the biting east coast cold, was remarkable. On the way out to our morning start point he would cheerfully don his two layers of lightweight clothing, assume his position as RIB driver, and spend one to two hours crashing his boat through 10-ft swells, and minus something windchill, out to our starting waypoint.

By the end of February 1999, with Maiden, the RIB and their respective owner/operators forming the four-man core of my infrastructure, I decided that my next priority was to find specialists who would ensure we had a professional media liaison package. I needed pre-publicity, and to be able to tell potential sponsors that we had the ability to get top-quality photographs and releases into the national press, and to gather film footage for both news releases and documentary/feature use.

My first port of call was a quiet beer with an old skiing mate, Duncan Walpole. Duncan is a professional winter sports photographer, and is married to the owner of a successful ski-holiday company. I knew Duncan was big on adventures and sailing, and guessed that August to October should be his quiet time. It took Duncan twenty-four hours to consult with senior management and return with a yes decision. The idea was that Duncan would help sail Maiden, and thereby get valuable experience for his yachtmaster qualification, take the appropriate photos, and run all press liaison. He also became our IT specialist, part-time electrician, emergency van driver and afternoon siesta specialist. Duncan became variously labelled by the rest of the team as Duncan Disorderly, Dangerous Duncky, and simply Dodgy. He looks like a man of the mountains, wiry, bearded and full of life, and his boundless enthusiasm both irritated and stimulated those around him.

In April, Terry Nielsen introduced me to John Beecroft, an independent cameraman-cum-documentary-maker. John was just back from filming a remote Indonesian tribe, and living in a jungle treehouse for weeks on end, and was scheduled to be off soon to the Amazon doing something similar. At the time I still hadn't pinned down any major sponsorship, and couldn't afford to pay up front for a cameraman, but John was excited by the whole concept, and in principle agreed to join up without wages, providing we helped with the hire of his camera kit. His appearance was exactly how I would have expected someone of his lifestyle to look: dark T-shirt, dark jeans and hiking boots, with dark, curly, greying hair and matching stubble. John had a difficult job as the official 'fly on the wall' recorder of events; and his personality, and style of dealing with others caused a few sparks to fly, as the unfolding narrative will illustrate. After we had done our provisional deal, John disappeared into the Amazon, and didn't return until one week before my scheduled departure on 22 August, which was four weeks later than his anticipated return. In the meantime, with no guarantee that he would make it back in time, and desperate to get a promotional video done, I decided to find another film-maker.

Terry (again) remembered a student he had met at the Boat Show, who had done the filming on the successful Cable and Wireless sponsored attempt to break the round-the-world powerboat record. Her name was Sarah Aynesworth, and I managed to track her down to a student house in Bristol. She had just graduated with a media studies degree and was looking for another adventure. Within twenty-four hours Sarah had organised the loan of some film camera kit, and we agreed to meet at the beach to do a shoot the next day for my promotional video. Sarah turned up in a Morris Minor, loaded to the roof with expensive camera kit, a bright, breezy, attractive, confident girl always ready to smile, but also to prove tough minded and resilient and very good at her job. Sarah was more mature and worldly than many of her age, but also had that zaniness and sense of fun that tends to wane with age and responsibility. Having Sarah out on the RIB filming was like having a warm coal fire with us. She thawed any cold, frosty atmospheres, and even once had Steve smiling before 10.30 a.m. Sarah also handled all TV and radio media liaison, and worked closely with Duncan on the press side.

When John did escape from the Amazon, he called me up and asked whether there was still space on the trip. I explained that I had needed to find a replacement film/documentary-maker, and told him about Sarah. I also told him that we had been asked by Mentorn, a TV production company, to supply them with video footage for a documentary to be

Clockwise from top right:

Tim the rock, Andy with his anemometer, Steve almost smiling,
Sarah in the galley, Duncan snapping away and Philippe alias
'Wurzle'.

made for the National Geographic channel, and that they were loaning Sarah a MiniDV camera for this task. John suggested that there was still an opportunity to make a second documentary, with higher quality film-making kit, to be sold to other TV channels. He proposed that if I would cover a minority cost of the camera kit hire, he would split any sale or royalty proceeds 50:50. I accepted, so we then had three media types on the team, who became collectively known as the Paparazzi or Paps.

Terry's third referral was a woman of roughly my age, who had been medical officer and galley manager on various ocean-racing and charter yachts for most of the last five years. I met Sophie in March at the Sailboat and Windsurf show at Alexandra Palace in London. She was a highly qualified nurse and hospital administrator who simply loved the sea. Sophie had a perfect background for three of the roles I needed to fill, and a strong systematic personality. She was destined to become medical officer, galley manager and budget manager. I was waiting for her outside the front entrance and knew immediately that the large purposeful woman, clad in a well-worn Musto all-weather sailing jacket, striding up the path 100 yards away, was Sophie. After ten minutes of conversation, I was convinced that her highly organised and professional mindset would nicely complement some of the more errant characters hired to date. I was both right and wrong, and ironically Sophie's big yellow Musto jacket was to be the subject of the fiercest row of the whole trip.

Now all I needed was an equipment manager or caddy, a van driver, a physio, and someone to take on the charity fundraising. We were also still one short of the minimum six able-bodied seamen needed to sail Maiden, and so I actually needed a physio-cum-experienced yacht crew, and van driver-cum-charity fundraiser. With considerable help from Sue Crayfer (who is physio to our Olympic sailors) a Kiwi girl called Denise appeared out of the ether, and agreed to join us for the first three weeks. After that I would have to manage without a physio, and we would have to find some more crew for Maiden. Denise was ever helpful, and particularly adept at brushing off with disdain Gaz's many verbal advances. Along with Sarah, Denise was a vegetarian, and very much unlike Sarah, her system could not tolerate alcohol. Denise had an athletic shape, and was quietly forceful in making sure I did my pre- and post-sailing stretches, and my fifty-minutes evening physio session.

The equipment manager or caddy was effectively to be my personal assistant whilst on the water. Windsurfing is totally different from yachting, in that when the wind strength changes significantly there is no reefing, or changing the foresail whilst still moving under the main. I simply had to stop sailing, have my rig hauled onto the back of the RIB, dismantled, and a smaller or larger variant assembled. This process on a beach takes time and expertise. On a bucking windblown RIB it took great skill, teamwork and considerable strength. I needed to preserve my energy, and often used sail-change time to eat and drink. I also needed the sail to be rigged just right for the conditions, and a caddy who could look at me sailing, and help me fine tune my technique, or the kit set-up, would be an invaluable asset. We also had different boards for different conditions, and on the worst days could have five to six sail and board changes. So I needed a caddy who was an experienced windsurfer, and preferably wind-surf instructor; but also could thrive on a daily routine of seven to eight hours rigging and derigging on a slamming RIB exposed to everything the weather had to offer, whilst watching someone else having fun windsurfing at great speed down the swell lines. Clearly an easy position to fill!

My first call was to Jon White, head of RYA Windsurfing. Jon went off to tap into his own network, and advised me to advertise in the windsurfing press. Despite the attractive spec (?) I only received seven enquiries. The first individual I met looked great for the job, and after a week of pondering accepted my offer. I then told the rest of the team, and my sponsors that the team was now virtually complete, and prepared a press release. Two weeks later this individual changed his mind. I was angry and bitterly disappointed, and running out of time. One of the original seven enquiries was Tim Birkes, a between-jobs geophysicist, who was also a competent windsurfer, and had lived and worked at sea. Tim drove down from the Lake District for a trial session together out on the RIB in late July. He was a thoroughly nice guy, but not the expert instructor type I had been looking for. But he was keen and available and prepared to be the main van driver and reserve caddy. Tim was single, mid-thirties and very much addicted to that 'fresh air thing'. Tim's passions, alongside windsurfing, were climbing and fell running. And his main dislikes were arrogant aggressive bosses, work stress, and being the centre of attention. He was one of the most flexible, effective, accommodating, efficient background operators I have ever known. Others joked that Tim's only personality defect was that he never disagreed with anyone. Tim's appearance and manner were wholly consistent with his character and lifestyle, lithe, lightweight, weather-beaten, bearded, thinning, and with a quiet considered speech. Unfortunately he also had a medical condition which sometimes gave him balance problems out on the wobbly RIB; and when Tim stepped in as reserve caddy, it was not unusual to see others on the RIB grab one of Tim's limbs, as he gave the impression of being about to disappear over the side.

With only three weeks to go to D-Day, I still didn't have a lead caddy. Then the same day I got calls from Russ Kerslake and Jon White, telling me that the perfect candidate, Andy Crocker, had just arrived back in the

UK after a two-year instructors' assignment in Barbados. I met Andy in the pub, and we agreed to go windsurfing together the next day. It was a warm, breezy July day, and Andy was cold! How the hell was this individual going to survive Scotland in October? He was a better windsurfer than me, and built like the proverbial brick outhouse. If anyone could rig and derig a 10.7m sail on the back of a RIB, then Andy could. He also had strong clear opinions on rigging, kit set-up and technique, many of which differed from the advice I had received from Simon Bornhoft. Andy was also an experienced RIB driver, navigator and had crewed on big yachts. At first I had some difficulty following what Andy was saying. He spoke rapidly and used phrases, which seemed half Barbados and half student-speak. Everything was 'pants' which meant nothing to a sensible 41 year old. In appearance Andy was tall, big boned, blonde and muscular, and in manner talkative, colourful and at times a bit bossy. In group situations he sometimes had a tendency to lay down the law, without listening to the views of others, and also regularly irritated me by being slow to get going in the mornings. In retrospect, Andy's job was probably the most difficult of all. He was nearly twenty years my junior, and had to stand up to my burning desire to go early, cut corners and finish late, with rational arguments concerning tides, navigation and exhaustion.

All I needed to do now, to have all the jobs and roles fully allocated, was to give one of the existing team the charity fundraising job. This I decided to defer until we all got together.

During the event, I tended to be very wrapped up in my own success or failure, and sometimes saw the support team as sub-optimal and holding me back. Only I could cover the miles, which was actually quite a lonely existence. I tended to forget that most of them were volunteers, and because there was so much at stake for me personally, I, unlike most of the support team, was not able to relax and take my mind elsewhere. These differences only served to strengthen the 'me and them' divide, and blur my perception of how critically important they all were to the success of the venture. With the benefit of hindsight, I can now see how physically and mentally draining many of the support jobs were, and that I was incredibly lucky to come across a core of truly exceptional people.

So we now had: a retired lawyer, an ex-chip shop manager, two ex-marines, a hyperactive skiing photographer, a tree-house dwelling cameraman, a bubbly media studies graduate, a wobbly ex-geophysicist, a matronly hospital administrator, a vegetarian Kiwi physio, and a fast-talking, jargon-bound windsurf instructor. Sociologists would have had a field day observing this lot interact! Even worse, the guy who they were all there to support, the nutter who wanted to windsurf 2,000 miles, was also the guy who had to manage and coordinate this disparate, colourful bunch.

His background as a biotech business manager had given him absolutely nil experience with ex-marines, media types or in fact any of the above. Taking into account that well-worn business dictum, that the only inevitability is change, we subsequently added to this list: a hard-drinking, arty, RIB coxswain (Philippe), a one-legged Irishman (Damian), and two more windsurf instructors hired to crew on Maiden (Peter Head, who amazingly joined us the day we ran into Peterhead in Aberdeenshire, and Lindsay Porter who joined us at Wells-next-the-Sea).

In parallel with all my ferreting around for crew, during the February-August period, I spent twenty to thirty hours per week either fitness training, or out on the water improving my windsurfing abilities. The next chapter charts the mental and physical hurdles which at times brought me crashing down to earth, but also gave me a great sense of achievement when cleared.

Chapter IV

Fitness and Preparation

*F*ollowing on from our pre-Christmas discussions, I agreed to meet Simon Bornhoft on 28 February at West Wittering Yacht Club, for him to have a look at my windsurfing ability, and propose the way ahead (or not as the case may be). I didn't tell him that I had entered a charity race at Burghfield Sailing Club in October and come last out of a field of 15!

It was a cool, sunny, blustery day with an offshore wind. He watched me rig my old 6.9m Tushingham sail, and plug it into my trusty 2.80m slalom board. I then carried the said kit to the water's edge, and proceeded to fail miserably to get out through the windshadow. I must have looked like an absolute beginner, falling in, taking several attempts to waterstart in the light fluky winds, falling in again, and eventually swimming the board back to shore. The conditions were difficult, but I have handled worse, and for some reason, my forearms failed to deliver any useful grip after about ten minutes of this hapless, hopeless display. To add insult to injury Simon then proceeded to radically change the set-up of my board and sail, and balance out effortlessly through the windshadow and into the solid F4 and 5–6 ft swells beyond. I thought to myself that he will humour me by us having a sail together, and then carefully and politely tell me afterwards in the bar that my windsurfing was simply not up to it.

We did have a sail together, he on his kit and me on my retuned apparatus; and this time I did manage to get out through the gusty windshadow without a dunking. Simon's instruction was 'to follow him' which was far easier said than done. The wind had picked up a notch to a good F5. I was overpowered, my forearms were burning with fatigue, and following Simon meant bearing away onto a fast and frightening broad reach over a significant swell. I had never sailed so fast, so close to a horrendous catapult fall for so long before. Through what I can only guess was divine intervention, or the input of my live-that-dream fairy god-mother, I stayed broadly in touch with Simon, and even managed to successfully complete some ungainly carve gybes. His verdict later in the bar was that I had good board speed (I had never been that fast before!), but that there was a huge amount of work to do on my gybes, my stance, my downwind technique, and on rectifying a whole directory of other windsurfing abnormalities. Surprisingly he did not suggest major surgery to re-engineer my weedy, dysfunctional, 41-year-old frame.

Anyway at least I had 'good board speed'. Contrary to my earlier worry, and his list of terminal deficiencies, Simon's conclusion was that the basics were good enough, and that he would put together a technique improvement programme for me, to be implemented over the coming five to six months. I never got him to explain what he meant by the basics being good enough, but in hindsight I feel that he was probably referring to the fact that I had two legs, two arms and a strong determination to improve.

The specifics of Simon's improvement plan fell into five main areas. First I had to have a reliable transition technique for all conditions, meaning big changes to my self-taught methods of tacking and gybing. Secondly I had to get much better at sailing upwind (beating/closehauled) and downwind (broad reaching/running) in heavy seas, as this is what the proposed journey would often entail. A normal day's sailing across the wind (beam reaching) and back, on inshore waters would be next to useless preparation. Thirdly, I would have to get my body accustomed to sailing six to eight hours per day, day after day. A normal long Saturday session, followed by seven days to recover was 'not applicable'. Fourthly, I needed to go from a score of 2/10 to at least 8/10 in understanding how to optimally set up my board and sail for the prevailing conditions. This latter point would be the key to preserving my very much limited energies in difficult conditions. Lastly I needed to get out there and give it a try doing some long-distance jaunts with a safety boat, such as around the Isle of Wight.

To implement this five-point plan over the next few months, I would need to spend an average of ten to fifteen hours per week windsurfing, and organise three to four weeks away, in predictably windy locations (not the UK), where I could concentrate upon nothing else except windsurfing every day, and taking on board the advice of Simon and other experts. Simon recommended spells in May and June away in Egypt and the Dominican Republic, the latter of which was to tie in with one of his coaching packages out there. My wife was going to love this. I was scheduled to give up work on 1/6/99, only to disappear for two weeks to the Caribbean 'training'.

In parallel with my link to Simon, I had also sought the help of experts to build my overall fitness, stamina and resistance to injury. Jon White at the RYA had put me onto Euan McGrath, who I visited at the Southampton Institute in early February. Euan was as helpful and supportive as they come; and made me feel good about the above-average results I achieved across a battery of fitness tests in their gym. I had kept a reasonable routine going over the winter, with three to four training sessions per week, either running, cycling, swimming or in the gym, adding up to about four hrs/week. Euan's main focus was to set a programme which would significantly improve my stamina or in the jargon, my VO2 max (the body's ability to transport and use energy-giving oxygen); and to work on improving my overall flexibility and resistance to injury. I also started to read up on how the body works, in burning its food fuel and oxygen to give energy for physical exertion; and how the removal of waste products of this process is so critical. Euan also told me to forget about running, and focus more on the dreaded Concept II rowing machine. This would give me the VO2 max improvement, whilst exercising a broader range of muscle groups, including arms, back and stomach, which are critical for windsurfing. In addition to specific advice, Euan also gave me discipline. I was still at work, and trying to be a half-decent husband and father, so most sessions were either early morning or late at night when readiness to 'take some pain' is minimal. There is no way I would have stuck to the programme without the thought that on Sunday night I would have to e-mail my weekly training report to Euan (example training report – see Appendix I). He was giving his time to help me, and something in my psyche would not let me accept my own (often quite reasonable) excuses for falling behind the programme. Whilst travelling on business, I often structured my appointments to ensure there was time to find a gym somewhere. Perhaps my most ludicrous training session was a hard 1.5-hour stint in my sleeper cabin on the Helsinki to Stockholm ferry, doing endless sit ups, press ups and stretches in a space where there was not enough room to pick a cat up never mind swing one around.

Euan also drilled into me the importance of refuelling and rehydrating during and after exercise. Apparently if you exercise heavily and use up all the glycogen stores in the muscles, you have a maximum of four hours to replenish those stores. If the tank is not refilled within four hours, it can take two to three days to 'get your energy back'. The body is like a sponge with a half-life. The sooner the refuelling happens the better, and preferably within two rather than four hours. Euan showed me which energy drinks to buy and how to use them. I then always made sure I was adequately refuelled and rehydrated. We also talked about how to monitor level of effort whilst training. Fortunately, I was already a heart rate monitor user, and was familiar with the modern training philosophies of setting a level of intensity based on heart rate.

Jon White had also put me in touch with Sue Crayfer (physio to our Olympic sailors, and recommended that I spend £100 on one of Sue's famous 'musculoskeletal screens' so I travelled down to her Southampton surgery at the end of February. Coincidentally, Sue shared a house with Simon Bornhoft, and was thus well aware of my crazy scheme. Sue struck me as a fit, wiry, highly talkative and energetic individual with a ready and infectious laugh, and blatantly obvious passion for her work and the whole sailing lifestyle. Sue was full of advice, ideas, and contacts and, if I could have remembered 10 per cent of the quickfire points of wisdom she dispensed whilst bending, poking and trying to align my worn-out limbs,

I could have probably presented a physiotherapy paper at a sports medicine conference the next day.

After reading Sue's three-page report on my body, it was clear that she had been screening for normalities, rather than abnormalities, without success. Her report read like that of a structural surveyor who has just examined the house of your dreams, and given it the 'no-one will ever lend you money to buy this' verdict.

I quote and translate:

'Anterior tilted pelvis, lumbar lordosis, thoracic kyphosis with protruding neck' (meaning horrible posture, and a spine that bends in the wrong places and is rigid elsewhere).

'Hyperextended knee joints, and tight hamstrings, calves and hip flexors' (meaning wobbly unstable knees, and leg muscles ready to twang under only moderate stress).

'Ankle range inversion restricted + ligament adhesions' (meaning very stiff ankles).

'Elevated left shoulder girdle, and protracted right shoulder girdle' (meaning one shoulder much higher than the other, and the two shoulders bend in two completely different abnormal ways).

'Right sided dominance illustrated by differing muscle sizes'.

'Numerous fractures (arm, leg, face, nose etc.) from Rugby, Football etc.'

'Unable to squat due to locking in flexion of right knee'.

Sue's conclusion was that I was a bit lopsided (the understatement of the decade), and that I would need to become much more balanced and flexible if I was to avoid repetitive stress injury. She also warned me that taking on a totally unnatural activity such as windsurfing for seven hours per day for eight weeks, and living on a cold damp yacht could give me some serious problems later in life, such as rheumatoid arthritis. Despite this wonderfully optimistic prognosis, we had a good laugh, and Sue accepted my excuse that normally I was quite normal, and all these abnormalities were due to the fact that I had two hours earlier stepped off a ten-hour flight from California! My take-away from the session with Sue was a very specific series of exercises to address my musculoskeletal deficiencies, and a referral to another physio, Sue Cotgrove, who lived nearer to Marlborough, and who I could get ongoing treatment and guidance from. The two Sues between them set me a programme of pre- and post-exercise stretches, to reduce risk of injury, and enhance muscle recovery.

The links to valuable people were set to cascade further, as Sue Crayfer recommended I see Pete Cunningham, who was the fitness coach to our Olympic sailors and windsurfers, and to various premiership rugby clubs. I mentioned Pete's name to Euan, who was immediately supportive, on the basis that Pete had access to a much more sophisticated battery of tests and measurements, and thus could be much more targeted in his programme recommendations.

I booked a slot to see Pete in early March, and had quite an audience with Euan, Sue, Sue and Simon all showing up at Pete's Winchester lab/gym to see how the monkey performed. There were three main measurements, and a whole series of other blood and fitness and metabolic checks.

Test 1 put me on the rowing machine. Blood samples were taken every few minutes, as the speed and thus resistance were incrementally increased, to give a measurement of the 'Onset of Blood Lactate Accumulation or OBLA'. This basically tells at what level of effort (measured as heart rate or rowing power) my muscles were starting to seriously tire. When blood lactate starts accumulating, it is only a matter of time before the muscles say enough is enough. Endurance athletes thus logically focus on pushing up their OBLA, which can be partly achieved by training close to heart rate at OBLA. Pete and Euan thus gave me one hard OBLA session per week, where I had to row for thirty minutes on the Concept II with my heart rate average around 160 beats per minute. Compared with the rest of my training this was an absolute killer, and the dreaded OBLA session would always be postponed until later in the week if at all possible. For those with any experience of a Concept II rowing machine, Appendix I contains full details of my test and training results. For those with no experience of the Concept II rowing machine, my advice would be not to get any, and certainly not to do a thirty-minute OBLA session on it. Pushing myself to the limit, running, swimming or cycling just seemed to be so much easier, and less unpleasant. Having said that, and falling into line with the well-treasured 'pain=gain' philosophy, I am convinced these OBLA sessions did me the world of good, as the results described later in this chapter illustrate.

Tests 2 & 3 were also on the rowing machine, but with a face mask over my mouth and nose to enable analysis of inhaled and exhaled gases. Test 2 took me incrementally up to my absolute maximum effort level (heart rate around 170), and gave a VO2 max value of 55 ml/kg/min, which was apparently at the average test level for our Olympic windsurfers, and not far short of the average professional rugby and soccer player tested. For Test 3, I did nothing. The lab wizards measured the proportion of various exhaled gases (carbon dioxide and oxygen, I guess) and gave me an RER value which apparently tells whether I was burning mostly fat or mostly carbohydrate. Good endurance athletes are good fat burners. Fat contains much more energy than carbohydrate, but takes more oxygen to release that energy. Thus, providing an athlete's oxygen supply system is good enough, he or she will keep going much longer if burning more fat than carbohydrate. I was burning predominantly carbohydrates, and Pete's prediction was that if we didn't improve this ratio in favour of fat burning, I would simply not be able to get enough carbohydrate derived fuel into my system on the very demanding days, and would then be knackered for the next two to three days, until the tanks had gradually refilled.

The training to coerce the body into being a better fat burner was simply lots of time at medium levels of effort, which for me meant one to two hours non-stop at a heart rate of around 140 bpm. This I did either on long (30-mile+) bike rides, or in the gym where I would do 25 mins on the bike, followed by 25 mins on the Concept II, followed by 25 mins on the stepper, followed by 25 mins on the treadmill. These three to four times per week fat-burn sessions were mind-blowingly tedious, but according to the machine had me burning 1,500–2,000 calories over 100 minutes. I was certainly very thirsty and very hungry afterwards! In parallel with my challenges, my wife found that her normal food shopping was no longer sufficient. I was eating at least 50 per cent more than normal, but still noticed that my body fat (measured at 16 per cent in March) was decreasing.

Unfortunately, it wasn't always easy to find three or four two-hour slots per week, so encouraged by Euan and Pete, I would still fit in some shorter sessions where I could, as for example, do a 50-length lunchtime swim or 40 mins weights session or 30 mins sit-ups in a hotel room. I also often found myself in an empty gym on Saturday nights, which was a particularly lonely feeling knowing that most of my friends would be out at the pub having a good laugh. After the test with Pete, I effectively stepped up to around nine to ten hours per week of serious fitness training, with each session starting and ending with ten to fifteen minutes of Sue Crayfer specified stretches. When I couldn't do the aerobic training I would still do the stretches, and also I took on board advice from the two Sues to exercise my smaller internal muscles, whilst working at my desk or driving. Anyone watching me at the traffic lights, doing neck muscle and pelvic floor exercises to the easy rhythms of Classic FM, tended to either laugh, or get on their mobile phone to inform the authorities. To complete the spectacle, Sue Cotgrove gave me a wobble board and gym ball, to respectively improve my ankle flexibility and strength, and what she called general balance muscles. Apparently there are lots of smaller internal muscles which can be trained to enhance balance and stability. Either I was born without any of these muscles, or they were a lazy good-for-nothing group of useless lumps of meat, because my balance was appalling. Dog walkers passing our house in the late evening would occasionally be treated to the ridiculous sight of me either trying to stand on one leg on the wobble board for more than five seconds, or sitting on the gym ball with only one leg on the ground, whilst throwing a football back and forth off the wall.

From early March until mid-July, I worked harder, and became fitter than I have ever been in my life. Over March, April and May, whilst I was still at work, it was particularly draining, but still highly satisfying, as I was able to measure improvements in performance almost weekly. During June and July, I felt like a professional athlete. I would be down at the coast windsurfing two to four days per week, and working hard on one or other elements of the fitness programme virtually every day. The flipside of this athletic existence was that I apparently became quite anti-social. I would resist going out more than once per week, and even then drink carefully, and be grumpy if we were still out after midnight. This was totally at odds with my normal behaviour, and therefore worthy of significant stick from wife and mates. By mid-April I had been down to the coast a few times, with Simon or another coach Dave Thompson, helping me improve my technique. I was starting to feel better about my windsurfing. My training reports to Euan were also starting to show some improvements. It was time to get some long-distance experience under my belt.

It was 6.30 a.m., Tuesday, 20 April. Today was the first real test of my windsurfing ability. I had booked IRS to provide a safety boat, and hired Dave Thompson (an RYA coach) for the day. My main coach Simon Bornhoft was away teaching in the Caribbean. We were to leave from Lymington at 9.00 a.m., to attempt to windsurf some 60 miles around the Isle of Wight. This had been done by several other windsurfers in the past, and getting round would give me a huge boost of much-needed confidence. The previous night's forecast was broadly favourable, with F4/5 south/south-west winds, but I still drove all the way from Marlborough to Lymington with a queasy knotted feeling somewhere deep down in my guts. How would I handle the wind-over-tide conditions off Hurst Point, and St Catherine's Point? Would I be able to handle the dreaded downwind sections? Would my fitness be good enough? What would the IRS attitude be if I failed? Would they decide to pull out of our cooperation?

I met Steve, Russ and Dave at the Lymington marina, and after looking at the 15–20 knots of southerly wind (F4/5) whistling around the clubhouse weather vane, we decided to rig my 6.9m sail, and set off with the 3.05

early planing board (Katie). A good upwind combination, which should work well for the first half of the journey going south-west out of the Solent, and then south-east down to St Catherine's Point. It was a cold day, and I donned my wetsuit, with neoprene undervest, and smeared vaseline around the neck-seal to prevent chaffing. This was it. Steve took the RIB out of the river estuary, and Richard Cooper, with board and sail, was dumped over the side into the yellow murky Solent to show what he could do.

In this wind direction the sea surface was nice and flat, due to the sheltering effect of the IOW land mass, making for easy starting conditions; but I had managed to smear vaseline all over my hands, and get the harness lines too far back. I was thus using far too much energy to grip the boom and control the sail, and my forearms started to burn after less than 40 minutes of sailing; not a very professional start for a man about to try and sail around the British Isles! After degreasing my hands, and getting the lines correctly positioned, life became easier as I planed towards Hurst Castle, which overlooks the very narrow channel between the Isle of Wight and the mainland. Everyone I had spoken to had warned me of the fierce tides, currents and overfalls in this channel. We were riding an outgoing tide against a southerly wind, and I was told that at Hurst Point itself, two strong tidal streams meet to throw up a confused melee of white water, eddies and mini whirlpools. As I approached this danger zone sailing over a glassy flat sea, I could see a line of white water, running straight across the channel and looking from a distance like 3–5 ft waves breaking on a beach. My heart raced as I came closer and closer to a patch of wild water that looked like the surface of a giant cooking vessel, just brought to a furious boiling state. Once into the chaos, I could only think about staying on my horrendously buffeted board, and that this was what it must be like to try and windsurf in some giant washing machine. The good news about these tidal confluence zones, is that they are often only 100–200 metres wide, and somehow I emerged exhausted but unscathed, technically out of the Solent, and on my way towards the famous Needles lighthouse. The beat south/south-west was fast and relatively comfortable, but my arms were seriously tired. I also made an elementary mistake of sailing in too close to cliffs, just before the Needles rocks, and got myself into a horrible windshadow area, with 90-degree direction shifts and wind strength from F1 to F5. Falling in, unhauling, falling in again, waterstarting, falling in again. What a plonker I must have looked to Steve and Russ. After twenty minutes of struggle and becoming seriously exhausted, I gave up and climbed into the safety boat, and they towed my board and sail out of the windshadow. Their thoughts were difficult to read from their military-trained deadpan exteriors, but 'This guy can't be serious' had to be in there somewhere.

Following a twenty-minute coffee break, I was turfed over the side again to remount my awkward steed, and pointed it south-east past the Needles. Once out onto the open sea, the wind strength and direction steadied to a solid F5 from the south-east, meaning I had about a 15-mile beat into wind and tide to reach St Catherine's Point. This was a challenge I think I could have handled on inshore conditions, but the sea state was something I had never experienced before. The 6–8 ft seas were very confused and steep. There was no swell line to push me upwind, and I had difficulty from keeping the board from screwing into wind every time it became airborne off the top of a swell. After a good hour of toil, falling in and exhausting restarts, to cover only 2–3 miles, I climbed into the RIB, and encouraged by Steve Russ and Dave, decided that we didn't have a hope in hell of making it round in these conditions. The only option was to turn around and head back into the Solent. I was physically shattered, and realised later that I had gone into 'energy deficit' where there was simply not enough fuel in the system to sustain the required level of effort. I had burnt myself out, and the more tired I became, the greater the deterioration in my windsurf technique, which in turn meant more falls and more exhausting restarts. A vicious circle which, without a safety boat, could have had dire consequences.

After an abortive try to sail downwind in these conditions back round the Needles, I gave up for the third time that day, and the RIB eventually deposited me and board onto the flat friendly water inside Hurst Point back in the Solent. I was determined to show my potential support team that I could windsurf in 'normal' conditions, and the strong offshore wind and flat water gave me the longest, fastest beam reach I had ever done. Within an hour I had virtually sailed the inside length of the Isle of Wight, touching 30 knots at times according to the RIB speedo. My confidence was partially restored, but I knew in my heart that the outside section (where I had failed miserably) was going to be more 'normal' going round Britain and Ireland, than the friendly Solent.

The wind picked up further in the afternoon to a F5–6, and we managed a clumsy sail change to the 5.4m version, on flat water, sheltered from the wind under a cliff. How could this be done on a big rolling sea in a gale? To sail north-west back to Lymington meant I had to do a series of downwind broad reaches, over a sea that was getting increasingly choppy as we moved away from the Isle of Wight. Again I failed, and had to give up after a frightening high-speed catapult fall, which left me with a painfully stiff neck for days afterwards.

Sitting in the Lymington Yacht Club bar afterwards, Russ, Steve and Dave could see how utterly beaten and dejected I was. It was very simple. Unless my fitness and windsurfing ability improved immeasurably, then there was no point setting off anywhere on 22/8/99, let alone getting all carried away with media coverage, sponsorship and charity fundraising. If I didn't get my act together, my dream was likely to evaporate in a cloud of withering embarrassment. I had talked to so many people about this dream, sceptics and supporters. I had to both prove the sceptics wrong and justify the belief of my supporters.

Dave Thompson let me have a couple of days to calm down emotionally, then gave me a call, where we rationally analyzed what had gone wrong. He stressed that the conditions on the outside had been difficult, but that a fresh Richard Cooper could have handled it. Something had gone wrong with my energy supply system. The two hours hard graft getting to the Needles had obviously drained my reserves, but the tank had maybe not been full enough in the first place. I had also done a hard (OBLA) gym session the night before, which Dave said was a far from ideal preparation. He also stressed that on the journey itself, if I had a situation where I was tiring, and having to beat against wind and tide, I should simply jump onto the safety boat, motor into shelter, and sit it out until either the tide turned and/or the wind direction shifted. We also rationalised that I still had some four months more to improve my fitness and my windsurfing; and that with time and the right focus, I could still achieve some real step changes in ability. With the benefit of hindsight, my Isle of Wight failure was probably the perfect tonic. If I had cruised round in ideal conditions, I would not have subsequently worked so hard.

By May I had effectively handed over to my successor at work. He liked having me around as a sounding board, but we both realised that the staff were still coming to me on certain issues, and it would be easier for him if I was out of the way. I thus agreed with my boss that I could take some extra holiday in May, and managed to get down to the coast one or two days per week. I also booked a one-week trip to Moon Beach in Egypt with Club Sportif/Gybemasters.

Leaving for Gatwick en route to Egypt was a strange experience. Apart from the odd lad's golfing weekend, it was the first time I had left my family to 'holiday' on my own. I remember being close to tears leaving my busy, tousely blonde two-year-old Amy playing on the kitchen floor. The three older kids had mixed feelings about the whole thing. They were all excited by the adventure of it all, and keen to tell their mates, but my five-year-old George was convinced I would be eaten alive by sharks or killer whales. Seven-year-old Jack and nine-year-old Rosie were more prag-matic, but still emotional when I left. My wife Mandy was similarly pragmatic. She did not like the idea that I would be away enjoying myself on the Red Sea whilst she was stuck with the arduous domestic routine of looking after four kids; but she also acknowledged that if I was going have a go at this crazy scheme, I might as well prepare thoroughly. I didn't see it as a holiday in the normal sense of the word, but I was looking forward to being able to windsurf every day, with reliable winds on a warm clear blue sea. I had also lived in Egypt for two years in the early 1980s, and still had a vivid picture in my mind of all its competing charms and ugliness.

I could have been led blindfold into Sharm El Sheik airport and immediately recognised it as Egypt. It is a difficult smell to describe. There is a pungent mustiness about the air, with a shifting tint of either urine, body odour or cooking spices, depending upon the immediate environment. That smell was like suddenly hearing a long-forgotten record, which my brain identified with a passionate but ultimately doomed love affair. Certain days, places and people started flooding into my consciousness. It was like opening the dam gates of my mind, and being smothered in long-forgotten memories from another era.

I arrived in the resort after a four-hour taxi ride at 2.00 a.m., still bubbling with nostalgic thoughts. The sum total of punters and instructors in residence at Moon Beach that week was 8, symmetrically split into 2 groups of 4. There was nothing consistent about the make-up of either of these groups, particularly the punters. In addition to the nutter training to sail around the British Isles, there was Bob, a 75-year-old, retired civil engineer from Wimbledon, whose windsurfing ability relative to age was unbelievable. Big Al was a typical big Al: a strong, fit, sincere, clumsy, hard-drinking, enthusiastic, talkative ex-marine, who was studying to become a software engineer. Doug, a high-flying IT marketing executive from Singapore, completed the picture. Phil, the captain of the instructors' team, was a typical laid-back, compact, muscular, good-looking, lifetime windsurf addict, but also an excellent teacher, and more interested in the outside world than some of his ilk. Phil's girlfriend, and general admin manager, Polly, was a good-looking marketing graduate, always helpful, and with a keen enough wit to be more than a match for any drunken lewd chat from the lads. I could easily have swapped bodies with Phil. He would hopefully have enjoyed learning to be a hot-shot windsurfer all over again, and I would certainly have enjoyed learning to cope with Polly's amorous advances. Phil's team of instructors comprised the lithe, arty, and totally off-the-wall graduate Jay, and the very porky, considerably older windsurf bum Bindy. Without their normal compliment of fifteen to twenty punters, Jay and Bindy were free to focus on seriously depleting the beach bar's stocks of anything and everything every night.

I had seven great days sailing at Moon Beach, and on a scale of 1 to 10 took my general ability from a 5 to a 7. The conditions were near to perfect with generally a F3 in the mornings and F5 in the afternoons, and flat water on the inside running into regular gentle 3–4 ft swells on the outside. I worked hard on improving my transitions, and in particular on cracking the step gybe. I also did a lot of upwind and downwind sailing with a bigger sail and board in the morning. For the first time in my windsurfing life I became almost comfortable sailing very broad and very fast (up to 30 knots) in choppy F5 conditions. For the non-windsurfers, this is akin to riding a bike with no breaks down a steep hill at 45 mph. The acceleration is beyond your control, and you know that if you make a mistake with the steering, the bike will decelerate rapidly, the rider will fly over the front and sustain some messy injuries. Windsurfing in any wind strength above F2 is generally done with the help of a harness, enabling the rider to hook onto a loop of rope suspended from the boom, and take the pull of the sail with body weight rather than biceps. The only downside of using a harness is the dreaded catapult fall. When sailing on a beam reach or beat, the rider's weight is pulling more laterally against the sail, and the body is out over the windward side. If anything goes wrong, the board normally screws up into the wind allowing the rider a relatively slow, soft dismount. When sailing off the wind or broad, the sail is more open or perpendicular to the board (see Fig 1), and the body weight more over the board. Thus if anything goes wrong, and the board comes to a sudden stop, the rider (who never has time to unhook his harness) is catapulted at great speed, normally into the mast or boom. Cracked ribs, twisted necks, and broken noses are the most common outcome.

During my time at Moon Beach I also started to feel more comfortable controlling the board in the air; and went looking for rather than avoiding steep swell faces which would lift me 6–8 ft into the air, and allow me the satisfaction of a smooth sail-away landing, rather than my traditional splat and waterstart. Perhaps most important of all, I became much more competent in the selection, set-up and tuning of my kit for different wind strengths, sea states, and points of sailing. Moon Beach was also an acid test of whether my recently tuned up body would be able to handle consecutive days of five to six hours hard sailing. The said 41-year-old frame did in fact hold out quite well, apart from some minor tendonitis in my arms, and the skin on my hands starting to disintegrate towards the end of the week. I diligently did my Sue Crayfer stretches before and after sailing, and also found time for two or three long-distance swims or runs along the beach. In line with my new 'captain sensible/professional athlete' mindset, I resisted the temptation to join the others late into the night at the Spreader Bar, and would coyly slope off to bed, often before Bob, our resident pensioner. I really was becoming a 'boring old fart'.

Apart from the ever-present smell of Egypt, the warm and colourful Gybemasters characters, and the progress with my windsurfing ability, I will also treasure the memory of sailing with playful dolphins cavorting around under my board. This was the bit that my kids of course found the most exciting, and an experience I would love them to have at some stage in their young lives.

I was only back in the UK for a week before my scheduled two-week trip to Cabarete with Simon Bornhoft came around. A week in Egypt was one thing, but taking off eight days later for two weeks in the glorious Caribbean was a completely different kettle of fish. I tried in vain to explain that Cabarete had the guaranteed winds and waves, and a resident coach, that I simply could not get at this time of year in the UK, but friends and family did not take this explanation at all seriously. The timing was also made worse by the fact that the week in between the two trips was my last week at work after twelve years, with a whole series of dinners and parties in Finland and Marlborough. I was perhaps blinded by my own sense of purpose at the time, but looking back I can see how, surrounded by humorous 'what a life' jibes from friends, my wife was not at all happy when I left for Heathrow on 1 June bound for Cabarete. I also felt guilty and selfish, and did not relish the prospect of being away from my kids for another two weeks. Although there was much more going on in Cabarete, it was somehow a quite lonely experience for me, with a lot of the non-sailing time spent worrying about how my wife was coping. I was with nice, friendly, bubbly people much of the time, but whilst with them I was somehow still on my own. My very different reason for being there was also highlighted by the serious party town character of Cabarete. Going to bed early in desolate, isolated Moon Beach was one thing, but here it was tantamount to lunacy. I very much started the two-week period in Captain Sensible mode, but my fellow students were a very lively, persuasive bunch, and on the last night I was unable to resist a serious cocktail frenzy, and was apparently seen dancing on a table, and playing spoof to determine who would be next to be pitched fully clothed into the pool.

A fellow vacationer at a Club Mark Warner resort in Greece once said to me that the key to relaxation on holiday was to develop a predictable routine. Too much unpredictability meant too much decision making which was inherently stressful. I'm still not sure I subscribe to this philosophy, but in Cabarete I did develop a so-called stress-busting routine. I would get up around 7 a.m., wander down onto the deserted hotel lawn, and do forty to fifty minutes of stretches and sit-ups. I would then shower and join the others for breakfast by the pool, taking up to an hour over a meal which at home would be defined as abject idleness if I were allowed to sit down at all. After phoning home at around 11 a.m., we (yours truly + ten to twelve other participants in the Simon Bornhoft technique clinic) would wander down to the beach, and listen to Simon's plan for the day for each of us. Wind permitting, I would eagerly get out on the water and diligently work on implementing Simon's instructions. I would lunch on three or four bananas, a sandwich and gallons of water; and continue trying to improve through the afternoon, giving up normally around 5 p.m. when the wind died. After my cool-down stretches, and sometimes a run or long swim, I would shower, read for an hour or two, then wander down to the bar, down a couple of beers, and lots of black olives. After dinner out somewhere with the other windsurfers, I would retire to my spartan room, read for a while, sleep, and wake at 7.00 a.m. the next day to repeat the process. Routines are of course a valuable motivational tool as they do take away objective decision making. I could easily have rationalised that getting up at 7.00 a.m. to pulverise my stomach muscles for forty minutes was not necessary, but once it became part of the routine, its validity was never questioned. So much of getting fit, and staying fit, is about creating sacrosanct routines, and it's nearly always the starting rather than the doing which is the difficult bit.

The punters on Simon's course that fortnight included a doctor, a dentist, a nurse, an osteopath, a retired IBM executive, a millionaire derivatives trader, a top fashion designer, a couple of management consultants, a children's book publisher, a professional rugby league player, and an odd Canadian couple who were intent on adopting (for taking home to Canada) any mangy stray dog they came across on the beach. Perhaps more so than most other sports, keen windsurfers cannot be classified into any preconceived stereotypes. Individuals from all walks of life give it a try (often on holiday) and some simply get the bug, and can't live without it. The personalities within this group are too many to describe in detail, but I really enjoyed my breakfasts with Kevin (the dentist), Red (the IBM retiree), Simon, and Sarah (the publisher).

The Dominican Republic very much reminded me of Costa Rica, where I had spent a year completing a master's degree thesis in tropical agriculture in 1980. It was all wet tin roofs, banana leaves, fruit cocktails, and friendly noise. The highlight for me was walking in the forest after a heavy rainstorm. The cacophony of crisp pure sounds and amplified sweet earthy smells is just magical. Cabarete was the Dom Rep's equivalent to Spain's Tarifa – a tourist town thriving as one of the world's most popular windsurf destinations, full of young bronzed beautiful people from Europe, Asia and the Americas. Like Tarifa, Cabarete attracted the cool set, and had a characterful old town, and gaudy, misplaced new buildings. Like Tarifa, there was music everywhere, some great and some not so great eateries, and an overall cosmopolitan buzz about the place. I really liked Cabarete, and would readily come back, if I could persuade my family that they would also like it!

The statistically reliable winds predicated for this time of year decided to have their one year in ten off in 1999. Cabarete is also renowned for having a fairly significant reef break (up to 10-ft waves, breaking on a rock/coral ledge about 400m off the beach), which was one of the main reasons I had come. Training in the Solent and at Moon Beach, had given me zero experience of sailing in big breaking seas, which we would certainly encounter off Britain and Ireland.

So here I was in famous Cabarete, ready to learn how to handle my board and sail in strong winds and big breaking seas. During my two-week stay, we only had three days of decent waves and fresh to strong winds (F4–6). We had three or four almost completely windless days and the rest gave three to five hours per day of moderate (F3) conditions. I did, however, further improve my light wind technique, and with Simon ever present, was able to suck him dry of wisdom, on kit set-up and tuning. Physically, I didn't have any problem with the average four hours per day sailing, but again patches of skin on my hands blistered and peeled like layers of decaying onion. This worried me, but Simon was relaxed. Apparently the warm, salty, bacteria-laden, tropical water is much worse for the hands than cooler climate seas, and he predicted that by sailing two or three days per week when I got home, the skin on my hands would harden and thicken in time for the main event. Looking back, my trip to Cabarete did serve a purpose as part of my overall preparation, but my wife didn't see it that way; and with a previous existence characterised by having far too little time to share with my growing kids, the hours of down-time waiting for the wind to blow, seemed such a painful waste.

For the next six weeks, during June and July, I worked very hard on my fitness and windsurfing technique. I had four or five days out with Simon, and made one further attempt to sail round the Isle of Wight. This time I was beaten by lack of wind! I also had two separate runs from Lymington in the Solent down to Swanage, a distance of around 25 miles. The first run was mostly a F3 beat against wind and tide, and then a series of broad reaches back. I felt I was sailing quite close to my best, and it was very comforting to get comments from Simon and Russ in the RIB, that I looked like a completely different sailor compared with four months before. To point Katie as high as possible into wind, I was following Simon's instructions to skew my body weight as far forward as possible, whilst raking the rig as far back as possible. At first I concluded that the only way to comfortably hold this position was to have my body re-engineered, such that ankles and hips were both capable of frictionless 180-degree rotation. After a while the discomfort became bearable, but my ankles in particular could only take 2–3 miles on one tack. How the hell was I going to cope with days which required 50 miles on one tack, pointing as high to the wind as possible? The second Swanage run was my nightmare scenario –

dead downwind sailing, in light winds, and a choppy sea. To get any sort of forward motion I had a huge, heavy 10.0m sail, but there was still not enough wind to hang against and therefore use the harness. Standing with both feet pointing towards the nose of the board, I had to anticipate and react to all the rolling undulations of the sea. It was like being stood on the back of an unpredictable circus horse, with only a limp rope for stability. After 10–12 miles my back and shoulders were aching for Britain, and I was starting to fall in regularly, as my powers of concentration waned to nothing. After one embarrassing plop into the water, as my balance failed me again, I looked up at the RIB some 20 yards away, and a huge bottle-nosed dolphin jumped clear of the water about 15 yds behind them. I had never seen a dolphin in UK waters before, and certainly didn't expect to see any in the murky English Channel off Bournemouth! I took it as a good omen for our pending little adventure, and of course reported the sighting to the Marine Conservation Society. They confirmed that there was a resident group of bottlenoses regularly reported in this area, which somewhat took the gloss off my sighting. To me, a sighting such as this is twenty times the thrill when totally unexpected.

By mid-July my windsurfing had come as far as it was likely to get. I kept sailing two or three times per week up to D-Day, as much as anything to toughen up my hands. My final session with Simon was actually in a park at West Wittering where we layed out and marked up 10 sails, 8 masts and 8 booms. I was also due a re-test with Pete Cunningham in mid-July, to see how far I'd come on my fitness. I was optimistic the results would show some improvement because I'd been working hard, and had myself been gradually improving bike and rowing machine test times. One week in late April, I had a go at beating my record over a hilly 18-mile road bike circuit that I had used regularly over the last three years. My best time ever was around 54 minutes, and my average around 56 minutes. I was absolutely gobsmacked when I came in in just over 51 minutes. It was a very significant private achievement which told me that the way my body worked had changed big time. In true fitness anorak tradition, I entered the time in my log book + asterisk and the PB abbreviation in brackets. Someday I'd like to read up and try and understand the psychology of fitness training. It was a way of life for me during that February to July period (the scheduling, the execution, and of course the recording and reporting), and to a certain extent took over from work and family as my main source of achievement and satisfaction. It was very very hard at times to turn down the chance of a kickaround with my two sons, in order to pound away in the gym for two sweaty hours. At least for me, putting so much time and determination into training would have been impossible without a bigger vision to drive me on. I also cannot deny that I enjoyed seeing my body shape change. My arms felt more muscular, and for the first time in my life I had discernible stomach muscles. It was perhaps a 3-pack, rather than the ubiquitous 6-pack, advertised so regularly on the front covers of men's magazines. My wife seemed barely to notice, but what the hell, hopefully this would mean that she would also not notice if I went into serious 'spreading' mode post event!

On the day of my fitness re-test in late July, Euan and Pete were waiting for me at Pete's Chichester base. Their first comment was that I had lost weight, but put on muscle bulk, particularly my forearms. The scales confirmed their observation. Compared with my March test, I had dropped from 86kg to 82 kg, and my body fat had dropped from 16 per cent to 12 per cent. I then went through the full range of tests, and it was clear that the improvements were way ahead of Pete's, Euan's and my expectations. On most of the major parameters I was showing 10–15 per cent improvements, and my Vo2 max had gone up from 55 to 63 ml/kg/min. Pete's report noted that 'Your present fitness level is quite similar to our best Olympic windsurfers, and they are on average 20 years your junior!' I drove home on a big high, feeling very pleased with myself – almost forgetting about the minor issue of 2,000 miles to windsurf. I had applied myself diligently, pushed myself very hard and had gone way past the expectations of my coaches. Maybe I should quit now while ahead! Feeling good but pragmatic the next day, I rationalised that I had only improved various gym test results. I had not won or done anything significant; but I was fitter than I had ever been before in my life, and my windsurfing ability had also taken a big leap forward. I was as ready as I was ever going to be. To a certain extent the favourable test result was an end in itself, and I definitely eased off on the training over the last few weeks. I was anyway absolutely brimful of other last-minute tasks, wanted to spend more time with the family, and maybe it was no bad thing for my body to experience a lull before the storm.

Chapter V

The Catch 22, Money and Media

Sitting at my desk in January I reasoned that it surely wouldn't be as difficult as everyone had predicted. I had a wide network of friends and business contacts in senior positions, across a wide variety of companies. We would almost certainly get excellent media coverage, and there should be no shortage of companies wanting to align with such an epic, photogenic, exciting, environmentally aware event (what a naïve, arrogant attitude!). I did some preliminary sums, estimating that the total costs should be around £85k, made up primarily of Charter Fees/Fuel for RIB and Maiden (£45k), Crew Expenses (£10k), PR/Website/Brochures (£15k), Training/ Consultancy (£5k), Sponsorship (£5k), and Land Support (£5k). From the start I made a brave assumption that I could persuade the windsurfing equipment manufacturers to loan me everything I needed, otherwise I would need to add a further £20k on to the above total. I also assumed that we would not need to hire a PR agency (another £10k), and could handle the media side ourselves. The experts generally felt I had under-budgeted.

Right from the start I came face to face with a perfect Catch 22. The potential sponsors were highly reluctant to commit without guaranteed media coverage, and the media didn't want to give pre-publicity to anything likely to be aborted due to lack of funds. There seemed to be two ways around this conundrum. The first and most used technique is to bullshit, meaning telling the sponsors that a, b and c media had all agreed to cover, and telling the media that x, y and z sponsors had already agreed to back. This is a dangerous technique, as any unfulfillable requests for proof would completely destroy all credibility. My preferred solution was to use some defensible poetic license, and follow a stepwise approach, first getting smaller media and smaller sponsors (who didn't necessarily follow the Catch 22 behaviour pattern) on board, and then using these successes to pitch to the next level. In essence the media and sponsorship jobs were highly interrelated, which is why the rest of this chapter oscillates between the two topics roughly in chronological order.

Coming from a marketing background, I reasoned that a key issue in attaching media attention and sponsorship would be the branding of the project. It had to appeal to a broader audience than just those interested in windsurfing and round-Britain adventures. I needed an easy-to-remember project label, and after two hours of looking for word combinations, and acronyms from multifold combinations of Round, Circumnavigation, Britain and Ireland, Windsurf, the British Isles etc., I gave up, and came at it from a more human personal direction. What I was actually doing was attempting to live my own Dream. I was a typical mid-lifer, looking for something more; a 41-year-old father of four with a steady, normal, predictable existence, stepping out into the unknown. Surely there were millions of people out there who would identify with my situation, decision and emotions. From this standpoint it didn't take long to arrive at the 'Live That Dream', project title or brand. It also helped that Livethatdream seemed to be the only combination of the words live, and dream, that was available as a web site domain name. Just as most people feel it essential to wear underwear, it was obvious that if I was to be taken at all seriously I had to have my own website. An epic adventure without a web site would be akin to an England football team in love with the tabloid press.

A helpful, confident girl called Claire, who worked for Susan Preston-Davies' MPR public relations business, suggested I call Ben Hextal, who had designed and run the web site for such as Mike Golding, and his Group 4 round-the-world racing team. I met Ben in mid-April, down at his Ocean Web office in Port Hamble, overlooking a marina full of very expensive-looking hardware. Ben was a young, round, computer buff, who had come into marine industry web sites via diving and diving photography. He was friendly and constructive, and played to my ego by getting very excited by the livethatdream domain branding. Over several telephone calls and a second meeting, we negotiated a deal whereby I would pay a certain amount for the pre-event design and set-up, and a per-update fee thereafter. I wrote the text during May and June, and provided some of Duncan's photos, and then Ben loaded it all up. Due to the ever-expanding list of pre-event tasks on my mind, my contribution to the web site was delivered late and in bits, which apparently took more of Ben's time than he had anticipated. Without warning he sent me a bill for an extra £600, on account of his 'extra work'. Reminding him that our agreement was a fixed fee for the design and set up, rather than time input based, I refused to pay. Ben sulkily accepted my position, and I assumed that he would put this little tiff to the back of his mind, and get on with optimising the function of my web site, which with 'designed and managed by Ocean Web' on every page, would also be good publicity for him. This was a bad misread. It was far too late in the day to switch to another web site manager; and with hindsight it is clear that Ben, knowing that we were trapped, had decided that we did not deserve a good service. The whole point of the web site was to give the world at large an up-to-date view of how we were doing. I wanted to use the web site to drive charity fundraising, but this was compromised by long delays in Ben loading a sponsorship form. We had also planned to download digital pictures, which could be used by the press, within twenty-four hours of the photographed event happening. In the end, we had to do this via the Classic FM web site. Lastly, and perhaps most irritating for me, whilst we were en route, and sending in regular web site updates, the feedback I was getting from followers was that compared with Classic FM's daily livethatdream news, the web site was sometimes as much as one week behind. Immediately after our arrival back on dry land I decided to transfer the web site hosting to another operator. This whole debacle had a clear lose-lose outcome. I had let pride and principle override common sense, and should have given Ben a face-saving compromise. I was still operating the way I would have expected to be treated in my business life, i.e. if its not in the agreement, then we don't pay. Ben had let his emotions override business sense, and maybe his take-away was that revenge can often hurt the avenger more than the target.

The whole sponsorship-seeking process was a very humbling and at times demeaning experience. I started in February with a two-page fact sheet, e-mailed to my network of mates and contacts. Some responded positively, promising to take it further within their organisation, some were honestly negative, and some never responded at all until chased. I kept the encouraging prospects from this personal network trawl alive with hassling phone calls and presentations, but during March I also decided to produce a more professional sponsorship prospectus, and to pitch (cold call) more widely. I also hired a sponsorship agent who had previously raised £millions for the BT Global Challenge. With the benefit of hindsight, I was six months too late getting this prospectus out, and hiring the agent. I desperately needed something visual for the sponsorship prospectus, and Duncan my photographer wasn't going to be back from the Alps until April. Trawling through old photo albums, the only half-decent windsurfing picture I unearthed was of me blatting across azure blue waters off the Greek Island of Kos, wearing a vest-like excuse for a wetsuit. This would of course be totally compatible with the concept of a man covered from head to toe in neoprene labouring his way around the cold grey seas of the British Isles; but it was all we had! To soften the incompatibility, the picture was severely tampered with and stylised into a logo ... but at least it was me. However, for the brochures, face-to-face pitches to sponsors, web site and press pre-publicity we needed something a tad more professional.

Right from the start, I had this vision of being able to get that one-in-a-million photo that the national press would just have to use. Maiden was a big, beautiful, famous yacht, and surely with good weather, and enough set-up time, we could get a shot of me leaping off the top of a swell line, framed against Maiden's sails, and the Needles lighthouse in the background. Such an image would both overcome the aforementioned Catch

22, and kick off our publicity campaign in style. Potential sponsors would be queuing up to get their logos onto the next award-winning photograph. As soon as Duncan was back from his wintersports photography season in the Alps, he was collared to be down at Lepe Beach, Calshot in early May. Maiden was to meet us out in the Solent at the East Lepe buoy. Russ and his RIB were to collect Duncan and his many cameras, and I was to sail out from Lepe beach to meet them. It was a blustery day with that well-known coverall weather forecast of 'cloudy with showers and sunny periods'. I remember dashing nervously around the beach like a headless chicken, trying to decide which sail to use in an unpredictable gusty wind. Too big a sail, and I would not have the control to manoeuvre into the right positions; too small and I would not be able to give Duncan any decent fast-moving action to capture. In the end I chose a 7m sail and my 3.05m early planing board (Katie). The sail was too small most of the time, and we never came remotely close to realising that 'one-in-a-million' shot. Maybe I now understood that one-in-a-million shots normally take a million attempts. Most of the time I was either much faster, or much slower than Maiden, whose range was restricted by sandbanks, meaning she was mostly either beating upwind or running downwind, points of sailing which were very difficult for me on the kit I had so carefully selected. At times we were more than half a mile apart, and locational coordination was not helped by the fact that our only functioning three-way means of communication was shouting at each other! If we'd had a mathematician with us well versed in chaos theory and probability law, I'm convinced he would have concluded that the statistical probability of getting the three of us in a line, at the right distance from each other, during a brief sunny period, with the Needles as backdrop; would have been similar to winning all the world's major lotteries on the same day with the same numbers. Another big Cooper vision destroyed by the boring practicalities of the real world. In the end we laughed a lot, and Duncan at least got some pics of me sailing, which were good enough for the brochure.

Talking to people in the media forced me to reconsider the newsworthiness of this whole venture. I had based my optimistic prognosis on the fact that the adventure stories that had made front-page news seemed no more adventurous than my little journey, and in most cases much less photogenic. I had not factored into my thinking the random time and people element. For every adventure covered, there were probably at least ten equally valid stories binned, because something else more important took the space; or the hungover editor was not in an 'adventure-story accepting' mood, and had forgotten how charming the blonde PR girl had been when priming him last week over lunch. But perhaps this was an over-cynical view. Surely with top-class photographic images and film footage, and a captivating story of a normal bloke who'd packed it all in to take on one of the toughest unconquered sailing adventures, we would at least get a mention. On the other hand the media attitude could be that 'windsurfing is a marginal niche sport, and even if this nutter does get to the start line, eight weeks is longer than the Tour De France. We can't start with a big splash, if we can't justify regular updates. Maybe we just wait and see if he makes it round and then cover at the end.'

Another common-sense hypothesis was that newsworthiness was more about who else was covering than the topic itself. Perhaps the old marketing adage of drip, drip, drip until suddenly the cup overflows was applicable here. With an aggressive, persistent, well-resourced PR agent, it should be possible to get plenty of regional press, TV and radio coverage, thus reaching a critical mass which the national media couldn't afford to leave alone. My problem was that I couldn't afford the aggressive, persistent, well-resourced PR agent in the first place.

At one stage after a series of media rejections, I briefly considered bowing to the tabloid ethos, and fabricating a story that I'd once slept with Princess Margaret to generate headlines such as: 'Randy Richard, the Wandering Windsurfer Rogered Royal Recluse' or maybe I should go all the way and allude to a homosexual affair with Tony Blair giving 'Round Britain Boardsailor Bonked Blair'. No, my mum wouldn't like it, so my first press release sent to windsurfing and yachting mags was titled 'The Toughest Windsurf Challenge Yet'. *Boards* magazine gave me a few column inches and a photo, but *Windsurf* could only accommodate three small typeface sentences in their catch-all Industry news section which read 'There's another "Round ..." windsurfing attempt being planned. This time the proposal is to circumnavigate the British Mainland and Ireland. Tim Batstone took 6 weeks [wrong it was 10] to sail round the mainland so we reckon if this guy is back by Christmas he'll be lucky, and so will his wife and 4 kids!' The yachting press just ignored our release, ostensibly because it was windsurfing, and thus nothing to do with proper sail-powered journeys. This lack of recognition hurt me, and by the end of April I still had no decent pre-publicity to show potential sponsors.

It would not serve any useful purpose to name the sixty or seventy companies who turned my sponsorship proposal down, but one story was indicative of the procrastination, indecision and at times fabrication that I encountered. I had offered to Plymouth, Gosport, and the Millennium Dome Co., the opportunity to host the start and finish for a cash contribution of £5k. Plymouth were very keen, but slow to come back with anything firm. The Millennium Dome people were also keen, but starting on the Thames would have been horribly impractical for me. After many phone calls, and a meeting with my contact at Gosport Borough Council to go through all the details, he came back to me with an offer of £3k. I was disappointed, but accepted, as I was desperate to firm up the start point for press releases, and Gosport was my first choice for logistical reasons. One week later after I had done the press releases, and sent promotional brochures to print, I received a sheepish letter from my contact, informing me that he had discussed the topic with his new Chairman, and the news was not good. The individual had earlier stressed that it was his budget and his decision, but didn't have the balls to pick up the phone to me and admit otherwise. I was now trapped into a start from Gosport, and had to close down options for other start/finish sponsors.

People from many of the targeted sponsorship prospects would tell me that my venture had been discussed internally, and they were keen for me to present my pitch, and then always be out when I called. Somehow the young professionals, who I'd often pitched to and who liked the idea, couldn't face telling me that their bosses had rejected it. In my old job I had become used to people being straight with me, and generally delivering what had been promised. This was very much my way of working, and it was a humbling and perhaps revealing experience to be a lowly outsider asking for money, and to be treated very differently from the valued client. I will always remember those companies who treated me fairly and honestly, and those who didn't. Memories are long and the world is small, and there must be many companies out there who have come to seriously regret having treated the lowly outsider badly. To me it is also highly indicative of an overall company culture, which either doesn't care if you are not important, or acts on the basis that everyone internally and externally deserves a prompt, honest and fair treatment.

In the end most of my sponsorship successes came from my own personal network, and from those in the windsurfing industry who were keen to see me succeed. My biggest cash sponsor ended up being the radio station Classic FM. I knew some of the senior managers of the GWR group, who own Classic FM, and they passed me on to its London-based MD. At first the concept was that Classic FM would take the whole £85k event, and sell the sponsorship on to their big corporate clients. My optimistic nature, together with encouraging noises from my contacts, gave me the feeling that this was virtually a done deal, and therefore while the pitches to their clients were ongoing, I eased off on other hot sponsorship prospects. I also (stupidly) told most of my support team that we were very nearly there with Classic FM as title sponsor. In the end they did not succeed in selling on the sponsorship, but decided to offer a much smaller but still very valuable cash contribution, in return for becoming the exclusive national radio partner. They also effectively became our press office, which seriously enhanced overall coverage, and saved us money; and they ran a big livethatdream theme, built around my exploits. Listeners were invited to talk about their own dreams, and Classic FM helped some of them implement these ambitions.

The livethatdream message also appealed to my second cash sponsor, Chelverton Asset Management. The main shareholder in this business had packed up his highly salaried city existence to set up an Investment Trust focusing on companies capitalised at under £15 million. He believed that this was an under-represented segment of the market, and as an individual, had experienced the pain of having to jump through higher and higher hoops, to get his dream off the ground. He felt that his now satisfied clients would also identify with this adventure.

All other sponsors provided non-cash contributions. Tushingham Sails were certainly the biggest and most responsive of this group, and in the end gave me 10 brand-new state-of-the-art sails, 8 masts, and 8 booms. Dave Hackford and Roger Tushingham who run this business are both former Olympic sailors, and they immediately identified with the epic, pushing-back-the-frontiers nature of this project. The 3 boards, 20 fins and 8 mast extensions I needed were loaned from Whiteboarders, the F2 importer, who were equally supportive but with a very different style. One morning in April I had arranged to drive over to their offices and warehouse in Brightlingsea, Essex. It was a long drive from Wiltshire, and I wanted to make sure everything would be ready for collection, so I confirmed the agreed 'order' by e-mail and over the phone, and agreed to be there at 9.00 a.m. I arrived at 8.55 a.m., to a deserted Whiteboarders site. The first employee arrived at 9.30, and it was immediately clear that nothing was ready. This was a 'surf culture' where everything was cool and possible, and work was a flexible, overrated interlude between getting stoked on the water, and partying afterwards. The fact that nothing was ready was in no way indicative of lack of commitment. Whiteboaders dug around in their stores, and probably cannibalised real orders, to loan me a brand-new 3.80 raceboard (Big Bertha) and two ex-demo smaller vessels.

Neither Dave Hackford of Tushingaham, nor Dave White of White-boarders needed any form of contractual agreement over the 000's of pounds-worth of their equipment I was taking away. They respected what I was trying to do, knew many of the people I was working with, had met me once, and trusted me. My third port of call for windsurfing kit, was Ultrasport, the importers of Neil Pryde wetsuits and harnesses. After a wasted three weeks waiting for their sales manager to return my calls, I got through to the boss Gordon Way. He had been part of an attempted windsurf relay around Britain in the 1980s, and was immediately supportive. Ultrasport sent me four wetsuits, two harnesses, and a plethora of boots, helmets, neoprene vests, gloves etc. Finally Sportif International, who specialise in windsurfing holidays, gave me heavily discounted training trips to Moon Beach and Cabarete, and Noble Marine Insurance covered the hefty premium to insure all this kit.

Duncan, though experienced in working at altitude in the snow, was not at all well equipped for wet and wild sea adventure photography. He thus approached a company called Cameras Underwater who were immediately supportive in providing an excellent series of waterproof housings for his treasured Nikon cameras. Nikon also loaned Duncan a 950 Coolpix digital camera, which turned out to be a mainstay of our press campaign, enabling high-quality action shots to be clipped to an e-mail, and sent to the press within hours of the event.

Windsurfing is a sport where its participants talk endlessly about the merits of different sails or boards, and derive great pleasure from owning, touching and faffing with 'the latest' or in an individual's opinion 'the best'. In my pathetic early windsurfing years, whilst recently married and living in a two-up two-down in Twickenham, the only reasonable place to keep my custom-finished waveboard was lashed to the outside of the stair-rail. It didn't fit easily in the double bed between us, so this was a fair second-best option. I could gaze at its sensuous curves, and exciting radical artwork, whilst eating my meals or watching TV. If I hadn't been able to go out at the weekend and bond with my baby on the water, I would take it down from its lordly position, and needlessly polish its pristine underside for far too long. People who become obsessed in the same way with the beauty, form and function of a car, or a model airplane, are obviously pathetic, sad individuals. Windsurfers are clearly different. Now I had more new shiny kit in my garage than in my wildest dreams. It must be something like being locked in a toilet with six naked, willing models; and being so excited that I couldn't decide which bits of which girl to fondle first.

There are two very distinct classes of windsurfer: minimalists, and maximalists. You either take only your waveboard and wavesail to the beach regardless of conditions, but at least look and feel cool and minimalist on the four out of five days when there is not enough wind; or you take everything you have regardless of the forecast, to make sure that you will get a fix whatever the conditions. Maximalists enjoy loading the patently unsuitable family car in a tidy, efficient, but time-consuming way, whereas minimalists squeeze the board through the tailgate of their scruffy old hatchback, and drive to the beach with an epoxy rail rubbing against their left ear. I guess I had been somewhat bi-sexual, going through periods of minimalist and maximalist behaviour, but now I had to be ready for whatever the wind gods threw at me, so it was Richard Cooper, big-time maximalist. Thinking about other sports, I also know minimalist golfers who derive most pleasure from bucking the trend and using a half set of twenty-year-old irons, to irritate the maximalist, who even carries three different ball types for different conditions. Another parallel is packing to go on holiday. I (and most males I think) feel the holiday was a success if the one sweatshirt packed was used every night for two weeks during the cooler-than-expected evenings. Without going into details, my wife is somewhat different.

Unfortunately our family car could not quite take three boards, and ten sails, so I urgently needed a 'big white van', both during the training period, and to be our land support for the main event. Fortunately my brother-in-law, Geoff, worked in the big-white-van leasing industry, and he and I persuaded Fiat that they would derive immeasurable promotional exposure from loaning us a Fiat Ducato 2.5 TD Maxi. It was a surprisingly easy vehicle to drive, and once liveried up with our lovely Livethatdream logos, felt as cool, and credible as a Porche in Chelsea.

One major chore during this sponsorship and media-courting period was to get logos, prospectuses, and brochures designed and printed. Fortunately (again) my best man Phil had his own PR and design agency. We had been committed academics (?) together at Reading University studying Agriculture; and bestowing our loud drunken northern charm on a variety of unsuspecting and always unimpressed southern belles. I had anyway forgiven him for his 1988, 55-minute wedding speech extolling my lack of virtue to all my farming relatives from Lancashire, and my wife's professional brethren from deepest Wales. Phil and his colleagues took the project to heart and saved me thousands on the design and printing of everything we needed.

The whole sponsorship experience was one I felt I could do much better next time (if there ever is a next time), but I also came to the conclusion in late May that I could either spend most of my remaining time chasing sponsorship, or on continuing the heavy focus on further improving my fitness and my sailing. I could not do both and still have some time for my family. I reasoned that if I was not in good enough shape, then I would reduce my chances of success, and waste all the humungous efforts and inputs of all involved so far. I also reasoned that I could borrow money to fund any cash shortfall, and pay it back from TV documentary and book royalties afterwards. With my ridiculously late start, and lowered priority on the sponsorship game, it was not surprising that I came up short. The total cost of the project could have easily been over £100k, if not for the flexibility of my main suppliers, and efforts and generosity of all those and more listed above. In the end the cash expenses element was around £55k, more than half of which I had to put in myself.

Logically my media exposure started to pick up when Simon Bornhoft, my windsurf technique instructor, became involved. Simon is one of the

UK's most filmed and photographed windsurfers, and he gave me two ultimately very fruitful contacts. Simon had already briefed Sally Simmonds of Meridian TV before I called. Sally was the leading sports presenter/reporter for Southampton-based Meridian, who also happened to be a keen windsurfer, and had attended one of Simon's technique-improvement clinics. The conversation was short and successful: 'Hello, my name is Richard Cooper.' 'Oh yes I've heard all about you. We would like to fix a date in July to come out on the Solent and film you training for a regional news piece.' 'OK, I'll get back to you with a date.' A date of 17 July was later agreed; but to avoid unnecessary simplicity, I also booked Duncan to be there to get some better shots for pre-event press releases, Simon to be out on the water with me, and Sarah Aynesworth to take film footage which we could use to produce a short promotional video to send to other TV companies (something else I should have done six months earlier).

After our hopeless earlier photo shoot, we put a bit more thought into how to manage my first day as a film star. I was desperately worried that the Meridian film crew would spend most of the afternoon cruising up and down the Solent on Maiden scanning the horizon for a lonely windsurfer and his trainer. The weather gods seemed to be in a good mood, and we had sunshine and moderate (F3) westerly winds forecast. The day started with myself and Duncan on Lepe beach, for a shoot with me fully clad in wetsuit, harness, boots and Classic FM cap, standing over all my logoed-up boards and sails. Sarah and the RIB then arrived, and she collected the beach-based and RIB-based footage she needed. I felt quite relaxed at this stage blasting in, and carving powerful gybes as near to the beach as I dared in front of Duncan and Sarah's various lenses (poseur). A stationary Maiden was to be the main filming platform for the Meridian entourage; and my nerves took a severe turn for the worse, as I approached at speed and ended my first gybe in front of the Meridian cameraman, in a big pile of spray, tangled limbs, and windsurfer parts. I had gone from poseur to plonker in a matter of minutes ... something about pride and a fall? Simon calmed me down, and made sure I was in the right place for the cameras thereafter, and apparently they were extremely pleased with the footage. I also had to climb on board Maiden for an interview with the lovely Sally. Duncan was feverishly snapping away, looking for the perfect shot of me being interviewed (I think!). All in all 17 July ended up being a very successful day. Meridian got some very good footage, Sarah and Duncan got what they needed, and I emerged from my first day in Holywood relatively unscathed. The Meridian footage would apparently be made available to any sister (ITN) regional channels who were interested, and Sarah's excellent promotional video was sent to BBC regionals, Channel 4 and various other TV production companies.

Simon's second media lead was a friend of his and fellow windsurfer named Jonny Clothier, who was a big noise in the TV production company Mentorn. Somewhat fortuitously Mentorn had been recently commissioned to make a series of adventure documentaries for the National Geographic channel. A meeting was fixed with Jonny and colleagues, and one day in late July I found myself on the Swindon-Paddington train, silently going from one grey featureless face to another, and feeling so alive and privileged, with the start of my wonderful adventure just around the corner.

Jonny was a scruffily dressed, informal, fast-talking, fast-thinking media type. The meeting was held in a dark cluttered room full of worn sloppy armchairs. The white-shirted, grey-suited, National Geographic executive who came in with Jonny looked totally out of place, which probably accounts for the fact that he stood up throughout the one-hour meeting. I was also a long way from home, if home was the austere, pine-decked, light-filled conference rooms of my former employer, but I felt relaxed and confident with my pitch. In response to Jonny's position that they definitely wanted to make a documentary on my project for the Nat Geo Explorer's Journal series, I explained that we already had an experienced cameraman (Sarah) on board, and that exclusive rights to the footage were available at a price. Jonny responded with a view that my key sponsors should be orgasmic with the prospect of their logos being beamed into so many million households in more than twenty countries, and that it was highly unusual to have to pay for footage such as this! My easy counter was that I didn't have a title sponsor, and that my model for paying off my debts was via royalties from book, video and documentary. The white-shirted Vice-President interjected that the project might be special enough to qualify for National Geographic funding (and branding). He then picked up the phone to Washington DC, and within twenty minutes his people had looked up my web site, and called back with 'very positive indications' of a contribution up to $10k.

I left for Paddington very excited. Not only could I get back to the sponsorship agent and give him more 'guaranteed media coverage' to use with wavering sponsors, but I also had the massive credibility boost of backing from the world-renowned National Geographic organisation. With a lot of help from Simon, and my friends at Classic FM, I had come a long way from that dismissive first mention in *Windsurf* magazine. The final approval from Washington DC would apparently take two to three days, but it was pretty much a rubber-stamping exercise ... apparently. Not for the first time, my white-shirted Vice-President was clearly a bit more vice than the rubber-stamping Vice-President, who did not think this project was special enough for their backing. Yet another false dawn and slap in the face. The Mentorn people were very apologetic, and explained that they simply didn't have any budget to pay for the exclusive rights to our footage, so we ended up with a non-exclusive deal, and Mentorn lending us the mini DV camera kit, which saved me another £2–3k. They also came down, some days before D-Day, and did a whole series of filmed interviews with crew members on Maiden, and with me on the beach surrounded by all my equipment. The plan was that Sarah would chronicle the journey on her mini DV camera, and then the Mentorn film crew would do the pre- and post-event background, and the setting sail and welcome back scenes. They also talked about hiring a helicopter to film us sailing round the north coast of Scotland.

All this media attention had clearly gone to my head, and I was on a roll. The next call was from Channel 4's *The Big Breakfast*, which apparently had an audience of 3 million. I had never watched breakfast TV, and assumed it would be something like a morning version of Jeremy Paxman's *Newsnight*. I was quickly corrected, with recourse to graphic descriptions of Sarah Cox, and how the only thing she had in common with Jeremy Paxman was their prehistoric ancestry (and that even this was in doubt). Some dotty production assistant kept ringing me up with instructions, and even sent me a rough script, so I could prepare my answers. I was to bring my board and sail, and wear a wetsuit and all my kit. I was told I would be on between 8.00 and 8.45, and excitedly told all my friends and relatives. I drove up to London the night before with my two sons, didn't sleep much, and was herded into a waiting room with other live guests on arrival. My three-minute slot was as chaotic, manic, and completely of the wall as warned. I strode onto the living-room set with all and sundry whooping and shouting and slinging high fives at me. Everyone in the room had also been primed to shout 'extreme' if at any stage of the interview I or Sarah used words like fast, big or dangerous. The camera work was, to put it mildly, unusual; and their erratic in-your-face-and-out-again style had to be ramped up another notch on the chaos scale every time the extreme chorus was called for. They didn't ask the questions I had wanted to answer, but they did use some of Sarah Aynesworth's promo video footage; and although to an older audience I must have looked like a right pillock, my eight- and six-years-old sons, who were part of the on set rent-a-crowd, said I looked cool. This was the ultimate accolade. My father on the other hand was hopping mad. The dotty production assistant had informed me at the last minute that my slot had been moved forward to 7.45, giving me no time to warn anyone. My father, who only uses television for *Coronation Street* and sport, had got up early to do his farm chores, and come in to plant himself in front of channel 4 at 8.00 a.m. He sat through ninety minutes, of what to him was puerile, mindless trash, without seeing even a glimpse of his wetsuit-clad son.

I don't think we would have got either the Mentorn/Nat Geo deal, or the *Big Breakfast* coverage, or some of the other regional TV without Sarah's three-minute promotional video. Sarah also became my PR agent for all media that Classic FM couldn't reach, like competitor radio stations. Probably the single most enjoyable radio interview I did was with Ocean FM in Portsmouth, who on air had me teaching their young female DJ how to windsurf using an ironing board as a substitute windsurf board. If their listenership found it half as hilarious as the three of us in the studio, then it was good entertainment.

In the final few days before departure I did a whole series of radio and press interviews, which made it seem like most of the last three weeks had been media driven, and which brought me back to an earlier conversation I had with an individual named Richard Clifford. Richard had a high-ranking ex-naval background, and now had his own business in the areas of survival training and marine industry consulting. He had also been the Safety Officer on the 1998 Transatlantic Windsurf Race (which was something of a misnomer, as the participants only sailed a series of staged race legs, rather than the full transatlantic distance). I had primarily called Richard to get his input into my safety and logistical plan, but he had forced me to first come clean on my real motives. Was I doing it to set a record and push myself to the limit, or was I looking to maximise media coverage? I realised that my main motive was the former, but I still very much liked the idea of being the 'and now for something completely different' slot on News at Ten, or even more ridiculously being a witty personality on Clive Anderson's talk show. As it transpired once we got underway, it became either we cover the miles or we maximise media coverage, and several times we turned down regional TV coverage, because it would have held up progress, and thus reduced long-term probability of success. All this late-stage media coverage made existing sponsors happy but it was simply too late to help win any new funding. There is always some good from bad, and with hindsight, having to pander to the media needs of a demanding title sponsor could have significantly slowed progress, and ultimately killed the chance of getting all the way round. So maybe the Catch 22 acted in my favour after all!

Chapter VI

The Day of Reckoning

Two roads diverged in a yellow wood,
And sorry I could not travel both,
And be one traveller long I stood
And looked down one as far as I could
To where it bent in the undergrowth.
I shall be telling this with a sigh
Somewhere ages and ages hence:
Two roads diverged in a wood, and I
Took the one less travelled by
And that has made all the difference.

Robert Frost

*O*n Saturday, 21 August, I was up and busy loading the van by 6.00 a.m., thinking that for at least another eight weeks I would not be woken by the gorgeous, wriggling form of my three-year-old daughter squeezing

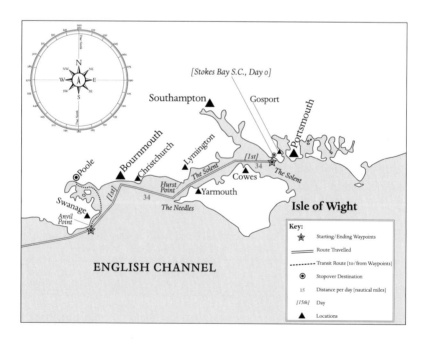

Above: The motley crew assembled, clockwise from bottom right: Tim, Steve, Gaz, Andy, Sarah, Richard, Sophie, Denise, Terry, John and Kevin.

Below: Day 1, blasting past *The Needles*.

into the space between myself and my wife. I had spent the last six months trying to think of everything, but even now at this late stage, my brain was mechanically going through a whole library of checklists. Still there were seven or eight ticks missing. Some could be sorted today. Some we would just have to give up on. I would see the family later today, and tomorrow on the beach before taking to the water, but leaving my house and home comforts behind, for a totally different existence, was still a big emotional wrench.

With the day of reckoning almost upon me, I felt like I was stewing in a pot of self-doubt. It was all fretful, ridiculous worrying and thinking about why I was doing it, and how I would handle myself if it all went pear-shaped. I also worried about sleeping and calls of nature. I had always been a dreadfully light sleeper, and irregular bowel mover. How would I feel trying to windsurf every day after two or three hours of fitful sleep, in a noisy crowded cabin? There was no toilet on the RIB. How would I cope if my system decided that I had to go at 3.15 p.m. precisely, whilst we were fighting our way through a horrible tidal race? I also started to ponder on the difference between winning and giving it your best shot. Friends at home had said that giving it everything I had was more important than getting round. The theory was good, and very much in line with the values I had tried to give my kids; but (typically British) glorious failure sounded very unsatisfying and emotionally painful to me. I wondered whether I had stuck my neck out that bit too far. I had talked so confidently of success, and managed to carry many others along on my own hype wagon, but then without confidence in my own ability nobody would have backed me. I had always had a tendency in business to tell what I intended to do before I knew how, and on most occasions the dreamer's vision had been realised. There were of course also some crashing failures. God forbid that this would be the biggest one of all.

Tim drove the big Fiat van down to Lymington, whilst I made a series of phone calls, and did a couple of radio interviews on the mobile. We were to meet up with our big yellow RIB at the Lymington marina, and transfer all the boards, sails, masts, and booms from van to RIB. Engine spares, and various oils for the RIB, and boxes full of windsurf spares would stay in the van. Then we were going out into the Solent with Andy to practice sail and board changes. Because Andy had joined so late, and neither I nor the RIB had been available for the last ten days, we had not had a chance to get out on the water and run through board and sail change routines with Andy, whose main job was precisely that. To my mind it would be ludicrous to set off with a caddy who had never rigged and derigged a sail on a RIB; but on arrival it was clear from the faces of Steve, Gaz and Philippe that some major technical hitches had arisen, and there was no way the RIB would be going out on any last-minute training runs today. The RIB had only done its first major sea trial some days before and had just come back from having a whole series of structural reinforcements completed. They were still drilling out the holes into which the lifting brackets would be fitted when we arrived, and there were still some outstanding electrical faults. I had also provided two big Quiverack top boxes, which were to be bolted to the rear of the RIB over the engine cover, as secure stowage for masts and sails. They apparently could not now be bolted to the engine cover for technical reasons, and were lashed incongruously to the sides of the rear-seat frame. This set-up did not look stable or practical enough, but I was the client not the engineer, and deferred to greater technical wisdom. Before leaving Lymington, I did a radio interview with BBC Radio Leeds from a portacabin phone on the dockside. This was the first of a whole serious of unusual radio interview locations.

I grumpily gave up on the RIB being ready before late p.m., and we drove over to Moody's boatyard on the River Hamble, where Maiden was moored. After the tense frustrating mood at Lymington, there was an equally tense but uplifting atmosphere of anticipation aboard Maiden. I packed my very limited expedition clothing into a locker, no bigger than my sock drawer at home, and got everyone together for a final briefing. This was the first time many had met, and my last chance to set out the rules of the road. I went round everyone, and asked them what they were expecting to get out of the project. The answers were dangerously varied, but not out of line with my expectations. Terry was looking forward to taking Maiden where she had never been before, but more than that, he needed the venture to be a big media success, and thus give Maiden the publicity he needed to boost his charter business. Duncan wanted to get valuable experience and sea miles towards his yachtmaster qualification, and extend his photographic reputation into the yachting/watersports arena. Sarah was just thrilled to bits with being part of such a wonderful adventure, but as a recent graduate, also knew that if she did a good job with the video chronicle, and media liaison, it could well open up job opportunities. Andy was also doing it partly for career reasons. As a top windsurf coach, being part of the first ever Round Britain and Ireland windsurf would be good on his cv. Kevin was there to have a great sailing journey and make history in the process. Sophie was looking forward to being at sea on Maiden, and making history. Tim was there to start living again after recent work and health traumas. John Beecroft was there to make a top-quality film of the whole adventure. I ended by saying that I was there to set a record that would be difficult to beat, and that any other needs such as maximising media exposure and charity fundraising would have to be secondary to this overriding goal. At the time everyone agreed that this made sense, and that the media story and documentary value would anyway be much reduced if we didn't finish. Despite this pre-event buy-in, there were still any number of conflicts as we went round, between those who wanted to maximise media exposure, such as Terry and Duncan, and those who were only interested in progress, such as Steve and Andy. My final comment was that there would be twelve of us living together in a cabin smaller than most of our living rooms, and that tensions and conflicts were inevitable. We had to be sensitive to the needs and values of others, but also practical as to what was and wasn't possible. Openness was absolutely critical. Growing, festering frustrations would only make matters worse. If anyone wanted to leave, then I would expect one week's notice. If I decided that someone had to leave they would get one week's notice. We also talked about roles and responsibilities, and I asked for a volunteer to be the MCS fundraising champion. Several said they would think about it, but no-one volunteered, and not pushing this issue to a conclusion ended up being a big mistake.

Later that afternoon, everyone's families and partners arrived en masse. My wife was in a bad mood, having got seriously lost trying to find Moody's boatyard, because of my inadequate directions. My parents were there. My in-laws were there. My four kids were wild with excitement tearing around Maiden's freshly scrubbed decks, and hanging over the bow, arms aloft *Titanic*-style. It was all too much. I was stressed, because I still had a brain full of last-minute problems, and my kids were stressing everyone on Maiden. My wife and in-laws were stressed by the fact that the probability of one of my four children disappearing into the dock was increasing exponentially, as they had for twenty minutes already been hanging off, and pushing each other around any piece of rigging they could find. It was simply a matter of time. My parents were stressed because everyone else was stressed. We decided to make a mass exodus, and find the kids a nearby beach, where they could burn the appropriate amount of energy without risk of damaging either themselves, their immediate environment, or the sanity of those around them.

That evening we all gathered for a pub meal in Bursledon. I was late arriving, but the alcohol-induced bonding had already started. It was a good night, but I was preoccupied with my wife's general unhappiness. She was not looking forward to eight weeks on her own with our four demanding offspring. I was going off on my wonderful adventure, and she was stuck at home doing shopping, cooking, ironing and school runs. Everyone else was getting all wound up and excited, and I was the centre of attention; but she was the only one who would actually suffer as a result of me living my dream. I had no answer, accept to agree and repeat my heartfelt appreciation that none of this would be possible without her support. Friends and relatives were all earmarked to help in various ways. I would call every day. We would try and meet up en route where possible. Mandy and the kids were of course proud of me, and would be even more so if I made it all the way round, but this didn't take away the pain of being left for such a long time. I didn't sleep much that night, and had to be up at 6.00 a.m. to do a Radio 5 live interview. I then had a radio hook-up with Keith Russell who had just completed the second ever 'Round Britain Windsurf' in sixty-two days. We were introduced as competitors, but I don't think either of us saw it that way. There were many differences between our respective challenges, but the main one was that he had finished, and I was yet to start. I congratulated him, and he wished me luck, and told me to look after the skin on my hands, and never give up.

Walking down the Moody's pontoon towards Maiden, I could see that the RIB still hadn't arrived from Lymington. What the hell was going on? All the careful scheduling of the last two days had been totally kiboshed by RIB problems. I was desperate to get to the Stokes Bay launch site early, get out and get a feel for my board, and make sure everything was properly tuned and ready. I had also picked up that last night's session, had been a long one with copious brandies going down, and in particular going down Andy's and Kevin's gullets. As my equipment manager and caddy, Andy was a key man for me today, and he needed to be at his best. After thirty minutes of irritated pacing around I was informed that they were due to leave Lymington soon! I would be too late to Stokes Bay if I waited, so I had no choice but to drive over, and hope that they would get there in time, with all the right bits on board. My scheduled start was 12.30 p.m., and I had media appointments from 10.30 a.m. onwards. I left Mandy with the kids on Maiden. They were very keen to sail round from Moody's to Stokes Bay, the plan being to then offload them into a RIB, and reunite them with me on the beach at 11.30-ish.

Back in May I had decided that to get any decent media coverage, we had to make my setting sail a real spectacle, and that we should thus invite other windsurfers to join me in a mass start. They could then do a short race, and I would disappear over the horizon. I discussed this with a local windsurf equipment retailer named Andy Biggs, who offered to help, and also put me in touch with Stokes Bay Sailing Club to host the start. For various reasons the publicity for this mass start was far from optimal, and I was desperately worried that there would only be me and a couple of mates who had promised to be there. Three days earlier I had also taken a call from Dave White informing me that he and his Whiteboarders staff would be there, with their F2 promotional roadshow, and ... Karin Jaggi, the current women's world champion. Jon White from the RYA would also be there with his team and van to run the mass start and race. Stokes Bay Sailing Club had provided safety boat cover for the expected 50+ mass start participants. Three TV stations, the *Daily Telegraph*, and a host of local media would be there to record it all. So much could go wrong today. Never mind managing a mass start on my own, what if the wind failed to arrive, and I set sail only to drift inexorably backwards on the east-flowing tide. That would make for some highly amusing but humiliating headlines. My goal for the day was simple. Whatever the conditions, however long it took, I had to get out of the Solent past the Hurst Point tidal race.

This was my FA Cup Final, and as we drove towards Stokes Bay and turned into the car park my stomach was churning like it has never churned before. I then caught a glimpse of some fifty cars already there, and a steady easterly wind lifting the flags. My spirits soared, as I realised that maybe today was going to be a success after all. The beach was already a maelstrom of activity with all the sponsors' vans, film crews, Marine Conservation Society and RYA setting up their wares. The cars were still pouring in, and my friends and relatives were starting to arrive. Everybody wanted a piece of me, and it seemed like I couldn't finish a conversation with anyone. I've no idea what chemicals my body was producing in response to all the emotion and excitement around me, but it sure felt good. I doubt whether my heart rate dropped much below 100 the entire morning, which was a long way from my superfit resting pulse of less than 40. I probably used up a month's supply of adrenaline that day, but I still managed to feel confident and lucid during the many media interviews. For the first time in my life I was really centre stage of a big (for me) public event. With only one hour to go until scheduled departure time, the RIB eventually roared into the bay, and I saw them start to rig my sail. Then they suddenly packed away what they had just unpacked, and roared out of the bay back the way they had come. Oh my God, something had gone seriously wrong. What had they forgotten? It was going to be a disastrous humiliation. Hundreds of well-wishers and media waiting for hours on the beach for the highly professional Round Britain and Ireland team trying to find a missing piece of kit needed to rig the sail. It was then confirmed by Duncan on his mobile that they had left the mast extensions on Maiden. Twenty minutes later they were back again, and hungover Andy, who had never rigged a sail before on the back of a RIB, was going at it like an epileptic whirling dervish, with tremendous haste and much less speed.

The photographer from the *Daily Telegraph* wanted to get out in one of the sailing club inflatables and take some photos of me speeding by. I was just winding down my last interview, and out of the corner of my eye could see Andy checking my hastily rigged sail, by blasting into the shore and doing tricks for the crowds. This was not his job, and with only thirty minutes to go, my earlier euphoria was being replaced by a feeling of hopeless but intense anger and frustration. I had still not been out on my board to check it was all set up right. My family were still on Maiden somewhere, and Andy was behaving like a real pillock. Duncan was ushering me here there and everywhere for 'one more shot'. At one stage I felt like running away to hide in the toilet until I could regain control of myself. Anyway the screams of torment were bottled up, I took the board and sail from Andy, and calmed my nerves by doing a few high-speed passes for the *Telegraph* man. The battery of cameras on the beach were shouting for a close-in pass, so I screamed in and went for the carve gybe. My legs were still like jelly, and did not follow the behaviour pattern conditioned through tens of thousands of similar gybes. The gybe was going badly, but I would simply let it stall, and then uphaul the sail and power away. I grabbed the uphaul, and started to yank the sail into position, only for the uphaul fixing to the boom end to disconnect, leaving me to plop backwards into the water, like some sort of clown who was there to entertain the audience by doing everything possible to look as stupid as possible. I thought about staying underwater and never coming up, but then quickly started to retie the uphaul fixing, and sailed the board back into shore. The crowd didn't seem to be bothered by my gigantic faux pas, and with only fifteen minutes to go it was time to do the round of goodbyes. Most of my family were in tears, as were several friends. I filled up, but somehow managed to arrest the deterioration into a blubbering wreck. To be responsible for such a visible public outpouring of emotion was also a big first in my life, and something I will never ever forget. It was deeply moving, deeply satisfying, but also somehow a huge burden of responsibility. These people (friends, family and complete strangers) were all here to see me off, and wish me well. I would feel a fraud if I didn't make it now. To add to the tension, Maiden had only just arrived with my family, and they were about to be ferried to shore. All the mass start participants were already lined up on the beach ready for the off. On the one hand I was now desperate to get away from all this hullabaloo, and just be alone with my board and sail and the sea, but on the other hand I was going absolutely nowhere before I had given some very big long hugs to my wife and kids. The mass start was delayed, whilst the Cooper family were beached, and tearfully hugged, and then that was it. Duncan's request for one more photo was forcefully denied; I got hold of my sail, jumped on the board, and tracked out towards the press boat followed by my mass start club. Rounding the press boat some 200 yds offshore, I had a quick look and wave back to the crowd, then turned the board westwards. We would not turn to sail eastwards for another 800 miles.

The feeling of release and escape over those first few miles was indescribable. I had been actively planning for this moment for more than eight months, and had become so worked up about everything that could go wrong. I had also just gone through one of the most moving experiences of my life. I was angry, terribly sad, absolutely elated, mentally drained, as excited as a four-year-old on Christmas morning; but also felt like I'd just escaped from Colditz and had to just keep on running until I couldn't run any further. I wanted to be alone with and enjoy my thoughts, but couldn't control my randomly travelling mind. Thoughts, worries and emotions would flood into and out of my consciousness. My mind was like a malfunctioning clock where the hands start to spin faster and faster round the clockface. I was almost in a trance, and very much doubt whether I would have heard anything if anyone had tried to speak to me.

The hands on the clock eventually slowed back down to normal, and I realised that I had sailed about 10 miles down the Solent without seeing anything. I also realised that my rig set-up was a mess. The adjustable outhauls were OK to let off, but impossible to tighten, and the mechanism clamping the boom onto the mast was loose, meaning the boom had gradually slipped down 6 inches, giving me a very inefficient and uncomfortable sailing position. The airvent plug in my board (Katie) had also not been tightened, meaning water could well have got into Katie's delicate innards. I made some makeshift adjustments, sat across my board with the rig unplugged, and laid across my lap. The RIB came in close, and sheepishly shouted that they had forgotten to load the food and drink containers from Maiden, and wanted to divert into Yarmouth on the Isle of Wight. I was already fuming inside, and after the constant warnings I had from the experts to keep my energy and fluid intake up, this was the final straw. I was almost past the shouting temper-tantrum stage. Anger was somehow replaced by a sad resignation, and my subconscious kept throwing my day's overriding goal back to the surface, i.e. to get out of the Solent. I didn't throw the book at Andy, but made it very clear that we were certainly not stopping to 'go shopping' until I had cleared the Solent. Stokes Bay was now well out of sight, and I was now on my way into the unknown.

My mind cleared as we approached Hurst Castle. I knew the shoreline landmarks well from numerous training runs, and started to really enjoy eating up the miles broad-reaching, across flat friendly water, and carving some nice fluid gybes. The Hurst Castle tidal race was in relatively benign mood, and I came through without any real difficulties. All the way round, I would set myself short-term goals, and this was the first one to be cracked. We had actually cleared the 15 miles from Stokes Bay in not much over an hour. Despite my rumbling temper and frustrations, it felt absolutely wonderful. I then sailed up to the RIB, dropped my sail, and with the aid of some colourful language systematically listed to Andy everything that had gone wrong. He did not make any excuses and we agreed to talk later one to one. We were sitting off Colwell Bay between Hurst Castle and the Needles, but there was only a beach, and no jetty to accommodate our ocean-going RIB. Andy thus volunteered to swim in and pick up some sandwiches, whilst I climbed in the RIB, and had a rest and a chat.

Ever-present Duncan and I had agreed a goal that we would take a short detour south to the Needles, to get some digital photos with his Nikon coolpix which would be e-mailed to the national press that afternoon. The wind was now starting to pick up to a F5, and my 9.4m sail was becoming a serious handful. Duncan thus had one pass to get what he wanted, and then I sailed across, into the lee of Hurst Point, and myself and Andy went for our first sail change at sea. It took about forty-five minutes, and was like a couple of five year olds reading the News at Ten: hilarious to watch, but otherwise clueless and useless. No-one lost their temper, and we were never that bad again, but unfortunately Sarah had it all recorded on the video camera. I eventually sailed away on the 2.77 board (Lady Di) with 7.0m sail, and made progress in the fresh easterly wind down towards Poole via a series of screaming broad reaches. At one stage I came in close towards Christchurch, where I could see twenty or thirty windsurfers reaching back and forth from the beach. I was on a slightly different mission, and going in a very different direction. This was how I used to sail. Out 300 yds, gybe, in 300 yds, gybe again, repeat the process twenty times. Now I was gybing every 5 miles, and on some days, would be on the same tack for 50 miles. I made one gybe close to shore, and a few people saw my sail logos, realised who I was and waved. Then I was gone. I didn't realise it at the time, but this was to be the last time I would be on the water with any other windsurfers for nearly 2,000 miles.

Through a combination of my nervous tension, and the dry tasteless nature of the sandwiches Andy had collected from Colwell, I had not eaten much; I had now been on the water for nearly three hours and was parched and famished. Duncan wanted to be dropped off in Poole so he could e-mail his stuff to the media, so I suggested I could beach my board near Bournemouth pier, and wander along the front to pick up some food and drink. To the families holidaying on the beach, I must have looked like the man from Atlantis, but it got worse. I had to walk some distance back from the beach towards the centre of town, to get what I wanted. It was the closest to an out-of-body experience I had ever had. Three hours earlier I had been surrounded by tearful friends and family on perhaps the biggest day of my life, and now I was like some neoprene-clad alien, time-shifted into a culture of funfairs, amusement arcades, hot dogs, and naughty postcards. I had been transformed from celebrity to oddity by a 25-mile journey down the coast. People looked at me in that careful 'I'm not staring' way we look at badly disabled people. No-one spoke, because clearly they did not expect we would share a common language. Worried about someone borrowing my board, I walked back down to the beach and found a perspex bus shelter (for the beachside tram service) in which to keep an eye on my kit and consume my energy and fluid out of the wind. I struck up a conversation with an elderly lady about the weather. She clearly assumed that aliens talk about the weather as well, so this was pretty safe ground. She then asked me what I was doing here, and I told her the truth. Her earlier look of amazement turned to one of pity. I was obviously one of these people who dress up in ridiculous garb, and make up ridiculous stories to impress strangers. With the benefit of hindsight, me talking about life at home on Mars would have probably been more believable to her.

Anyway, looking out to sea, I saw that the RIB was now back from Poole, and it was time to break some more waves. The wind had now swung a bit more into the south giving me a fantastic high-speed beam reach, some 12 miles SW across to Anvil Point, south of Swanage. Maiden had by now caught up with us, and I thoroughly enjoyed blasting, into and out of her vicinity at 20–25 knots. Around Anvil Point the sea became bigger and more confused, and as we had already decided on Poole for our overnight stop, we called it a day around 5.30 p.m., derigged and motored in. Maiden had secured a perfect town quay berth about 20 yards from the nearest pub. I showered in the back of the pub, had my fifty minutes of stretches and massage supervised by Denise, then sat down on a bunk in Maiden's main (and only) cabin, to eat a huge carbohydrate-based meal with the rest of the team. The feelings around the table were a heady mixture of relief, elation, exhaustion and worry. We then had our first team meeting, the idea being that every night we would review the day's happenings (good, bad and ugly), and based on the weather forecast, plan the next day. I didn't make a big fuss about everything that had gone wrong. We had covered 39 miles, in half a day's downwind sailing with lots of stops. I had actually sailed some 60 miles over the water (taking into account my zig-zag route) and had only spent three hours actually on my board. This was no bad thing, my plan was to build up the hours gradually to avoid damaging my hands and body by trying to do too much too soon. After another radio interview, I went up on deck under the night sky with Andy. He didn't let me start, preferring to admit right at the outset that he had seriously ****** up, and that he was as disappointed as me, and that it would not happen again. This was good enough for me, and we agreed upon some necessary changes in working practices, and to be 100 per cent open with each other going forward. I finished this monumetal day recording my dictaphone diary and doing a video-diary piece to camera for Sarah. I collapsed into my bunk, absolutely exhausted, but slept fitfully. My mind was still racing from the intensity of it all. Despite all the traumas and cock-ups it was a great, great day, memories of which I will treasure for ever.

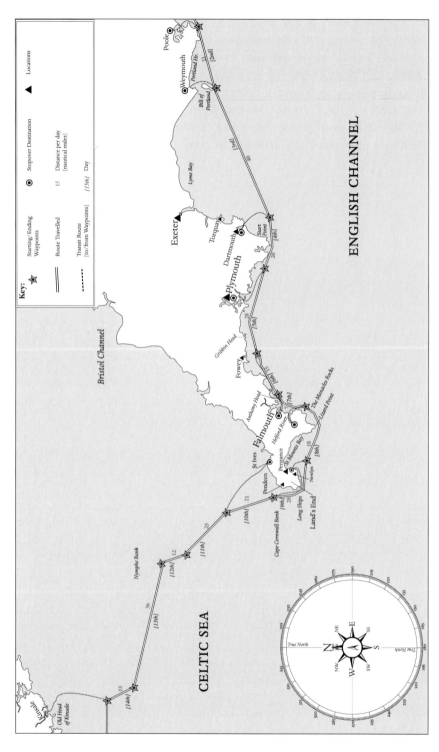

Chapter VII

To Cornwall and the Celtic Sea

Would'st thou – so the helmsman answered
Learn the secrets of the sea
Only those who brave its dangers
Comprehend its mystery.

H.W. Longfellow, 'The Secret of the Sea'

Once out of Poole on the RIB, we started to hit some seriously steep and confused 7–9 ft seas. It was a slow, bone-jarring, 45-minute run down to our waypoint, just south-east of Anvil Point. Back during my earliest fact-finding on this mission, several people had warned me that seasickness could be one of my biggest problems. Tim Batstone had suffered just about every time he did any distance on his support vessel in anything other than flat seas. As we ran past Swanage and approached my starting point for the day, I felt decidedly queasy, as apparently did the rest of the RIB team and John Beecroft, our cameraman for the day. Fortunately this was the last time I would feel even mildly seasick on the whole trip. The anemometer was giving a windspeed of 16–22 knots, which seemed similar to yesterday, so we rigged the same 7.0m sail, and plugged a small 28-cm fin into Lady Di (the 2.77 board). The wind was from the east, meaning more hairy broad reaches. My stomach was churning for different reasons than yesterday, and once on the water I realised that either the wind was stronger than yesterday, or I was weaker, because there was no way I could comfortably handle the 7.0m sail. I climbed back on the RIB and we changed to a 6.0m. Despite the rough seas, we managed to derig one sail and rig the replacement within thirty minutes, a huge improvement on yesterday. Andy was a quick learner, and his strength and agility were massive assets in these demanding conditions.

I was much more comfortable with the smaller sail, and once round the point, staying relatively close in to shore, past St Alban's Head towards Kimmeridge, the seas flattened off somewhat. The sea cliffs along this seemingly uninhabited stretch of coastline have a stark and intricate pattern of sedimentary rock layering. Each lump of this striking cliffscape was different, and I was able to measure my progress downwind quite accurately by using transit points on the shore to measure how broad I was sailing. My gybe angle was, however, still over 110 degrees, meaning I was still only sailing 30–35 degrees broader than a beam reach. We lunched on the

RIB just off Kimmeridge, and had to motor a good half a mile back to our interim waypoint for the restart, due to having drifted west on the tide. My broad-reaching confidence was slowly increasing, and as I powered away from shore on port tack, I was able to use the increasingly large but smooth and well-spaced swells to steer the board even further off the wind. My desired direction down to Portland Bill was roughly south-west, and the wind was still from the east, meaning I needed to sail about 45 degrees off a beam reach. My broad reaching in heavy swells was best when I could let the board accelerate down the swell face, bearing away all the time, and then if necessary head up a little riding up the back of the next swell to maintain speed. The 15-mile broad reach across from Kimmeridge to the Bill was certainly new territory for Richard Cooper, the windsurfer. It was my first-ever long-distance, high-speed broad reach over quite sizeable 7–8 ft swells, and a quite wonderful feeling to be able to efficiently harness the power of the sea to get me where I wanted to go.

The closer we came to Portland Bill, the bigger and steeper the seas became, and the worse the visibility. I now struggled to stay broad, and could not avoid some high-speed crashes, and the board becoming regularly and seriously airborne. The RIB was also struggling to keep up with me, without slamming into the swells, and the RIB team were becoming drenched, cold and tired. John the cameraman looked ill and potentially hypothermic. He had also been unable to get any meaningful footage whilst holding on for dear life. In these horrible conditions, with an increasing risk of me injuring myself, or becoming separated from the RIB, we decided to call it a day early. I had sailed for only two hours, with 21 miles covered, and 45 miles sailed, giving an average speed of 22.5 knots. Riding back towards Weymouth from our end-of-day waypoint 5 miles south of Portland Bill, the seas were bigger and steeper than anything I had ever seen before. I was not afraid and trusted implicitly Steve's RIB driving skills, but I was clinging on very tightly to the guard rails at the side of my seat. On several occasions the RIB would climb up a 10–15 ft wall of dark angry water, seemingly at 45 degrees or more, and then crash violently down into the following trough.

Everyone was seriously relieved when Weymouth harbour came into view. We were obviously not the only ones having trouble with the conditions, as we ended up being moored next to a huge dismasted 80-ft catamaran, which had apparently been towed in earlier. The locals were shocked to discover that we had been out 'Windsurfing?' round the Bill on a day like this. Coming into port soon after lunch gave us time to sit down and rethink our modus operandi on the RIB. We did not need to carry Big Bertha, and 10m sails for conditions like today. The Quiverack boxes were cracked and working loose from their fixings. Andy's proposal was to dispense with these boxes, and split the kit into strong wind (F5+), medium wind (F3/5) and light wind (<F3) sets. Thus we could carry much less on the RIB, thereby speeding up transitions, and reducing risk of damage or loss. This all made lots of sense, and Andy busily went about laying out on the harbourside our 3 boards, 10 sails, 8 masts and 8 booms, and sorting this melee of monofilm and carbon fibre into three clusters. This was also an impressive sight for the locals, and we set up our MCS fundraising stall alongside. The reporter from the *Dorset Evening Echo* who later interviewed me was certainly no Einstein, and he produced a colourful, but ridiculously inaccurate piece.

Waking on the morning of Tuesday, 24 August I could hear a steady wind whistling through Maiden's rigging. It looked to be about F3/4 in the harbour, meaning a possible F5/6 off the Bill. More high adrenaline, high injury risk, downwind sailing in big seas was not top on my agenda of preferences. Today would potentially be our first serious offshore sailing, with an objective to sail SW some 45 miles from Portland Bill to Start Point south of Dartmouth. In the middle of Lyme Bay we would be around 30 miles from the nearest land; and thus if I only made it halfway across, we could be looking at up to two hours transit time into our scheduled stopover in Dartmouth, and of course two hours back again the next morning. Motoring out through a misty haze to the waypoint, it was clear that the easterly wind had dropped. I set off broad reaching in a decent F3, on buxom Katie, and a big 9.4m sail. Within fifteen minutes the wind had dropped further, and I was onto Big Bertha. All day the wind swung between 6 and 11 knots, and all day I alternated between Katie, which in 10–11 knots of wind could reach 15–18 knots board speed, and Bertha which would be faster at the bottom end of the wind range, but slower at the top end. Fortunately the wind also veered towards the south-east, meaning I didn't need to sail so broad. Even when we were 2–3 miles off the Bill, I couldn't see land, due to the mist, so had to trust that the boys in the RIB were pointing me in the right direction. It can be horribly disorientating, sailing on a featureless horizon; and there were times when I was convinced we were going in completely the wrong direction. It was a very frustrating stop-start day, but we managed to cover 40 miles, without too much zig-zagging (55 miles sailed) to finish about 7 miles east of Start Point. I was on the board for five hours, and could have gone on longer, but for another completely unexpected natural obstacle. Apart from all the board changes, I had spent the whole day trying to avoid clumps of floating weed whose sole biological function was clearly to become wrapped around my fin. Most of the time, I could avoid most of the weed, but every few hundred yards my speed would suddenly halve, as 3 kg of stringy green matter enveloped my fin or daggerboard. The less tactile clumps could be released by throwing the board into a tack, and sailing backwards for a couple of yards, but otherwise I had to drop the sail, and grumpily reach down to remove the offending stuff. It was a very effective form of mental torture, like coitus interuptus, but worse; and my language and general demeanour deteriorated from unpleasant to shameful. We never had weed that bad again on the whole trip, and it would be interesting to know whether this is a regular Lyme Bay phenomenon, or just a one-off organised especially for us.

Towards the end of the afternoon, the dank misty conditions, were replaced by very low cloud, similarly awful visibility, and a steady penetrating rain. Motoring into Dartmouth was a beautiful but eerie experience. The rain eased and cloud lifted just as we approached the narrow cliff-lined entrance to the harbour. It seemed that the sombre, dark green sea cliffs had shed their cloaks of mist and cloud for our benefit. Everything was sodden and still, including the four of us in the RIB. Maiden was well behind, and we brought the RIB up alongside the town quay. I had made the mistake of staying in my wetsuit for the journey in, and was uncomfortably cold. I gathered my damp dry-clothes bag, and changed from wet slimy neoprene to damp cold cotton in the nearest public conveniences. We then all gathered to wait for Maiden, in a warm, cosy, quayside café, steam visibly rising from our sodden clothes and bodies. The waitress did not look pleased, but we were in good spirits, and despite the frustrations, we had crossed most of Lyme Bay and achieved a record day of 40 miles. The team spirit was also developing well as we got to know each other, and the piss-taking humour dominated much of the conversation. Sitting out in a RIB all day, watching my attitude to the stringy green matter go from mild irritation to unnatural hatred, must have been highly amusing; and I often caught a cackle of laughter on the wind as I began shouting at the weed the way an out-of-control teacher admonishes a bemused child. Many had thought me 'one banana short of a bunch' to take this challenge on in the first place. Now I had become heated and emotional with a clump of seaweed. Maybe they were right.

We didn't know it at the time, but Wednesday, 25 August (Day 4) was to set the trend of almost two weeks of windless days which nearly destroyed me and the mission. We got out to our waypoint at around 9.30 a.m., and sat in the RIB for two and a half drizzly hours, waiting for some wind to arrive. The banter was lively, predictably base, and unfortunately recorded by John Beecoft's ever-present camera. By midday all the day's rations had been consumed. Steve obviously preferred to consume his sandwiches fresh, as throughout the trip he would rarely have any of his 1 kg allowance left after 11.00 a.m. I started sailing on Bertha, with the 10.0m sail, in less than 3 knots of wind. This was a 'ride the tide day', and at times we were getting 2.5 knots of tide to augment my 2–4 knots board speed. It was mind-blowingly tedious windsurfing, but once the rain cleared, I asked the RIB to drop a mile or so behind, and I started to really enjoy the emptiness and tranquillity, although the visibility was such that land was never in view. It was also quite hard work, and I never once had enough pull in the sail to use the harness. The day also brought my first dolphin sighting, but the flat calm conditions made it painfully easy to observe the all-too-frequent human debris. It was mostly plastic bags, sweet wrappers, and plastic margarine tubs, with the occasional oil drum or discarded fishing net to add to the variety. Surrounded by this unsightly human litter, I remembered a statistic from the Marine Conservation Society that each day 300 million gallons of sewage are discharged into UK waters. I didn't relish the thought of sailing through this floating refuse dump every day, but at least if we could raise awareness and money, we could contribute to the clean-up lobby in some small way. We covered 20 miles that day in four hours sailing, giving a surprising 5 knots average board speed. With tide against we would have been lucky to make 5 miles.

Maiden had given up on the idea of sailing in these ultra light airs, and had motored all the way to Plymouth arriving well before us. We had been kindly invited to stay at the Mountbatten Centre for the night, and various local rag photographers were waiting for us on the pontoon as we motored into view. We then had to rig a sail and plonk around in the windless harbour whilst they got some action(?) shots for tomorrow's readership. We had a lively team meeting that night in the Mountbatten Centre bar, with the conversation dominated by the topic of whether we should risk a direct crossing from Cornwall to the south coast of Ireland across the Celtic Sea, or take the land-hugging route, up the north Cornish coast, across the Bristol channel to St Davids Head in south-west Wales, and then across St George's Channel to Roslare on the south-east tip of Ireland. This would be a big, big decision. The direct route was a minimum 150-mile crossing which would take at least 2 days, meaning we would could be spending nights at sea, 60–70 miles from land, out of radio contact with the coastguard. We had the added logistical problems of potentially having to transfer people and equipment from Maiden to the RIB in big rough seas. Steve also became paranoid about damage to his precious RIB, if we were forced to tie it alongside Maiden for a rough night at sea. Terry was pro the direct route for the simple reason that it was 100 miles shorter, and in prevailing SW winds would be a fast and straight beam reach. The conversation swung this way and that, sometimes heated and emotional, and sometimes calm and reasonable, but all agreed that we had first to get to Land's End and then make a decision based on the 3–5 day weather forecast.

Day 5, looked like a big improvement on Day 4, with 9–11 knot (F3) winds from the south-west. We needed to follow a heading of just south of west towards Fowey and the Lizard, and assuming that the closest I could sail to the wind was 45/50 degrees, I would have something like what we termed a 3 to 1 beat. I would need to sail 3 miles on port tack for every one mile on starboard tack. I set off on port tack on Katie, with a 9.4m sail, and made really good speed parallel to the shoreline passing Stoke Point, the Great Mew Stone, and the entrance to Plymouth. On this kit I was however struggling to sail any closer to the wind than 55 degrees. There is a big lump of rock called Gribbin Head west of Looe, which I had in my sights for hours. After stopping just short of this rock for lunch, the wind dropped to a F2, and I swapped to Big Bertha. Meanwhile something strange was happening with the tide. It should have been in my favour, but we must have been caught up in some sort of tidal eddy pushing us eastwards, because my tack angle even on the big board was awful. I was making very little headway upwind, and after two 5–6 mile beats had still not got past Gribbin Head. Was this thing moving westwards, or was I going mad? In the end I spent nearly seven hours on the board, and sailed more than 60 miles, but only covered 28 miles waypoint to waypoint. A very demoralizing and exhausting day.

It did not get any better. The morning of Day 6 was spent on maintenance and media chores stuck in Falmouth. I even resorted to doing an instructional talk to the rest of the team on windsurfing and kit technicalities. What an anorak! By midday the slightest of breezes had filled in and we motored back to our waypoint south of Fowey. Andy worked hard to improve my upwind technique in light airs, and we made steady progress towards Anthony Head. We had 3–5 knots of wind from the south-west to start with, and I decided that the only way I could keep up my determination and concentration on days such as this was to focus on a 'must be achieved/never give up' target. We had started late, and I was absolutely determined that we cover the 18 miles to round Anthony Head, and bring Falmouth into view. At around 6.00 p.m. I was still 5 miles short of my target. Surely I could make 5 miles in the two hours before nightfall. The wind was easing and the tide starting to turn against us. It felt like I was doing 3–4 knots SOG (speed over the ground) but the radio messages from the RIB suggested I was down to 2.5 knots. But this was still enough. Five miles at this speed would take me two hours. I could not face a second successive day motoring 'backwards' out of Falmouth to our starting way point. I was tired and aching all over after yesterday's exertions, but gave it all I had, to squeeze every last drop of speed out of my huge 10.7m sail. Andy and Steve wanted me to give up at 7.00 p.m. but I refused. We were only 3 miles from Anthony Head and somehow the more difficult my goal became, the more important it was that I got there. At that moment I would have kept going until midnight if that was what it took to achieve my goal. The reality was that my SOG had dropped to 1.5 knots, and was slowing further, but I was blind to reality. The only thing that mattered was to reach that bloody headland. Andy and Steve were by now becoming very irritated with my pig-headed stupidity, and finally at 8.00 p.m., I was metaphorically dragged off the water, two heartbreaking miles short of my target. We motored in in silence. I was a beaten man. I did not want to speak to anyone. Later on during our meeting Andy made it clear that my self-perceived failure and depressed mood was bringing down the morale of the whole team. He was right.

I went to sleep trying to fill my mind with positive calculations. It would take only a couple of 60-mile days to put us ahead of the 40 miles per day target average. The difficulty was that the big high on the weather chart centred over south-west Britain looked ominously static. Day 7 arrived true to the forecast. There was not a breath of wind, but we motored out to the site of my last great defeat, just east of Anthony Head to ride the west-going tide. There was still not a breath of wind, so for most of the time I just sat on my board and drifted at a scintillating 1 knot, and at times even removed the daggerboard and tried to paddle. After clearing the point, it became obvious that the tide was taking me due west in towards the Helford river, which was certainly not where I needed to be. The slightest of breezes of no more than 2 knots gradually arrived, and I set my target to sail south to get round a series of rocks known as The Manacles, just short of Lizard Point. To implement this 4-mile plan in such a pathetic breeze, and a tide sucking me west, my only option was to rhythmically pump my huge 10.7m sail. Pumping is an exhausting method of increasing board speed, by sliding the sail forwards, and then sideways to catch a lump of air, and then pulling backwards against what little resistance there is, to propel the board forwards. Four months before I set out on this crazy mission, I had tried pumping a big sail for thirty minutes non-stop. I couldn't do it, and the attempt left me absolutely shattered. It is a bit like being on a rowing machine without being allowed to use the big leg muscles. On this day with The Manacles in my sights I pumped virtually non-stop for two hours, and slipped between these razor-sharp rocks just before the tide swung dead against us. Over nearly four hours, I had moved 7.2 miles. The average speed would be something like walking at less than half normal speed (i.e. plenty of time to take in the scenery!) Strange as it may seem, I was happier with this end result, than those of the previous two days. I had reached my target, and my fitness was way ahead of expectations. Various muscles in my arms and back were seriously inflamed that evening, but Denise did her physio tricks to ease the discomfort.

Whilst I had been toiling for Britain, the Maiden contingent had entered a team in the Helford village carnival, which seemed to consist of a series of waterborne fiascos (such as the one-oar rowing boat race) and downing copious amounts of the local brew at every available opportunity. They apparently won the 'Best team effort' prize but little else. The RIB team had also had a pleasant day of chat and banter in the sunshine, and this stark contrast in 'fun factor' between me and the rest had me feeling somewhat lonely and left out at times. That night I sat up alone on Maiden's decks with my dictaphone diary, and then laid out on the crumpled foresail to stare at the stars. Looking out into all that space, I tried to come to terms with the enormity of the challenge I had taken on. Its all well and good playing one match at a time, but even that seems a bit pointless if you simply can't see a way to finish the season. I had covered only 166 miles in a week, and for the last three days every mile had seemed like swimming through treacle. This was supposed to have been the easier bit with warm summer breezes and long days. From now on we could look forward to Land's End, the unpredictable expanse of the Celtic sea or Bristol Channel, the Fastnet rock and all that rugged exposed Irish west coast, the equinoxal storms, shortening day length, and falling temperatures. All that before we got anywhere near the North Coast of Scotland. It was more than daunting, and I cursed my ridiculous belief in the possible, which had brought me to this doomed-to-fail situation. I had clearly become carried away with my own hype, and my timing to set off late summer stank. This just-discovered common sense told me that the probability of success was less than 20 per cent. In a way it was the distance rather than the fearsome headlands which I could not grasp. I must have dozed off under the night sky, and when I woke cold and ready for my bunk, somehow things seemed better.

Day 8 (29 August) dawned windless and foggy, as Maiden rocked gently from side to side on its Helford river mooring. Myself and Steve nipped out of the river in the RIB mid-morning to check whether there was any wind further out. There was not much, but maybe 3 knots from the SW, and the tide was due to turn in our direction soon. We dragged Andy and Gaz reluctantly into action, with their lack of urgency really irritating me. After unloading me back onto my waypoint just west of The Manacles I proceeded to impress Andy by tacking through 70 degrees. The favourable tide was enabling me to sail at a ridiculous 35 degrees to the true wind ... impressive stuff. At one stage, rounding the Lizard, I had a 3.5 knot following tide and was managing 7 knots SOG in only 3–4 knots of wind. The wind stayed light all afternoon as we tracked across Mounts Bay. Seeing the shady form of Land's End emerge through the haze was a huge boost to my battered spirits. It had taken us eight gruelling days, but we were now on the verge of turning the first of the six major corners. My earlier air of pragmatic resignation was transformed into a mood of hope and satisfaction, and I celebrated by energetically pumping into a turning tide to cover the last two miles. This juxtaposition of mournful lows and unexpected highs was something I had not experienced much over the last ten years. The highs are logically much higher when sandwiched between the lows; and I, like many others, lived in a comfort zone without the deep peaks and troughs. Maybe it was even impossible to feel true elation without the precursors of struggle, worry, doubt and failure. I was not to know at the time, but the troughs were set to get deeper and the peaks steeper, as the journey progressed.

Our ending waypoint left us some 9 miles east of Land's End, having covered 18 miles in six hours on the water. I had sailed 25 miles giving us another high-speed tide-assisted day averaging 4 knots! Our stopover destination was Newlyn, one of the UK's biggest fishing ports. I had many times wandered around harbour walls fascinated by the sights, sounds and smells of a busy fishing port; but entering from the sea, mingling with the incoming and outgoing traffic, was a new and more fascinating experience altogether. What I remember most vividly was the contrasting condition of the vessels, and faces of their crews. The sparkling, new, multi-million pound trawlers were decked out with sophisticated-looking fishing and navigation gadgetry, and crewed by tidily attired, arrogant looking deckhands. The spartan, oily, smelly rust buckets, chugging in alongside, were crewed by rough, scruffy old-timers, whose eyes looked empty and distant. It was as if their sense of life and purpose had been drained from their bodies over many years of fruitless fishing trips, and livelihood-destroying EU fisheries politics. Maiden was tied up outside a fisheries agency patrol boat. To get to the quayside, we first had to clamber across this well-maintained, battleship-grey centre of officialdom, and then across an old decrepid lump of red iron, which would have looked more at home lying on its side wrecked and battered at the base of some rocky cliffs. Maiden was thus on the outside of this stack of three very different bedfellows, and to the locals we were rich yachties and adventurers who should leave the real world alone and bugger off back to Cowes, to play our silly rich man's games.

I did not feel safe walking along the empty dockside after dark on my way to meet the others in the pub, but they were already bonding with the locals around the pool table. Face-watching in pubs such as this can be dangerous, but the two roughest-looking, hardest-drinking characters we had, Kevin and Duncan, were blending in well, and the ongoing pool game gave me a useful diversion and vantage point. The resident senior drunk was being helped out of the pub by a ruddy-faced 20-stone landlord, and what appeared to be the drunk's son and daughter in-law. A chain-smoking young woman, with red teary-bleary eyes, and tattooed shoulders, was pitifully trying to draw some sort of apology from a dark swarthy young fisherman. Had he beaten her up? Was he her drugs supplier? Had he left her to fend for herself with the three young kids? Or had he taken up with another chain-smoking tattooed young woman? Three rough-looking lads at the end of the bar were flashing cool and aggressive glances towards us poncy yachties. The landlady looked hard and ruthless. I wondered what she did for pleasure. This was a world apart from the trendy marinas we had so far frequented. For a clean-living, well-to-do father of four from twee Marlborough in lovely Wiltshire, it was a welcome dose of perspective. I was phenomenally lucky to have the freedom to even contemplate this wonderful adventure; and needed to snap out of my fear-of-failure driven depressions, and simply enjoy the experience of it all.

My first chore on the morning of Day 9, was an interview with BBC Radio Cornwall at 7.0 a.m. before anyone else had surfaced. We then had an executive meeting with Terry, and Steve, and decided that with a light wind forecast we were unlikely to cover more than 20 miles, and thus should return to Newlyn for a second night. Decision making on the Celtic Sea crossing could thus be deferred another twenty-four hours. Duncan, John and Sarah all wanted to be in the RIB to film the rounding of Lands End, but Steve had made it clear that there was only safe space for two out of the three. I left them to sort it out between themselves, which resulted in John and Duncan getting the berths via drawing of lots. At least poor Sarah would get first call next time. John and Duncan did not always see eye to eye, and the prospect of them clambering all over the RIB getting in each other's way, amused Andy and Gaz. They were also amused by Duncan's irritation when, after 6 miles completed, I announced that we would have to change from the 10.7m Neil Pryde sail (which I had borrowed) to the 10.0m Tushingham (from one of my main sponsors). After giving me some £8k worth of kit, I doubted whether Tushingham would be best pleased to see the front page 'rounding of Land's End' shot featuring a Neil Pryde logo. Duncan felt we could potentially miss the best light of the day by faffing around with sail changes.

The rounding itself was relatively uneventful, in light 3–5 knot breezes, a friendly sea state and clear sunny skies. I really enjoyed the celebratory element and the sailing with Maiden to get both of us in the shots; but the deeper thrill was the sheer aura of the place. So many ships and lives have been lost off this desolate headland. The form of the land was so different from anything witnessed so far. There was not a tree in sight, and the soil looked so thin that even the sheep's fescue was struggling to get a foothold. The wind and sea were 'resting' today, but the feeling of

latent power was omnipresent. The only blot on this infamous landscape
was the bulbous glassy visitor centre on the headland, which I put down
to the price of being famous.

After the paparazzi had got what they wanted, Maiden returned to
Newlyn, and we harnessed what little wind and tide there was to travel
due north past the Longships lighthouse, to finish 6 miles west of Pendeen.
I had sailed 30 miles and covered 20 miles in 6.5 hours, so at least my
average speed had topped 4 knots. Back in Newlyn that night, the shall-
we-shan't-we argument on the proposed Celtic Sea crossing raged again.
This time another pro-factor was brought into the equation. We had now
covered 210 miles in nine days at an average of 23 miles/day. At this rate
the remaining 1,600 miles would take us ten weeks. Terry felt it would be
absolutely ludicrous to add another 100 miles onto this already mammoth
journey, when we had light winds and gentle seas forecast for the short
cut. We now had no choice. To stand any chance of getting round in the
allotted eight weeks we had to take the direct route. Steve eventually
accepted that if we could rig up some sort of sea anchor for the RIB, she
could be strung out down-tide or downwind of Maiden overnight to avoid
damage. So that was it – on Day 10 we took aim for Ireland. Maiden was
to call us on the radio around midday to see what sort of progress we
made. If it was looking like another 20-mile day, Maiden would divert into
St Ives, and we would track back at the end of the day's sailing. If the wind
kicked in and we were looking like being 40 miles offshore, then Maiden
would follow, and we would have a night at sea.

The sea at our starting waypoint was as flat and glassy as the Bristol
Channel has probably ever been. The anemometer was showing less than
1 knot of wind. There was simply no point rigging a sail. Once all the
sandwiches and chocolate biscuits had been consumed, a game was devised
whereby the participants had to try and walk unaided around the wetted
tubes of the RIB from starboard quarter to port quarter via the bow. Pulling
off a carve gybe in 1 knot of wind would have been easier. All contestants
ended up in the Bristol Channel, but Andy took first prize based on the
quality of his dismount. At midday, the faintest stirrings of a breeze teased
the vanes of the anemometer into action, and I went to work. Over the
next seven hours I covered another 21 miles at a blistering pace of 3 knots,
regularly glancing over my shoulder until the north Cornish land mass
eventually disappeared from view. The absolute tedium of the sailing
allowed my mind to divert elsewhere, and I started keeping a mental log
of all the floating garbage I saw. The biggest article was a 50-gallon oil
drum, but I also recorded 3 pallets, 4 discarded lumps of fishing net, a
cathode ray tube, 7 plastic drinks containers, 15 plastic food containers, 12
sweet wrappers, and at least 40 plastic bags. This was a terribly depressing

roll call of human debris which took the gloss off a wonderfully contrasting experience that afternoon, when I sailed within 18 inches of an 8-ft juvenile basking shark. I couldn't help turning over and over in my mind the MCS statistics that 100 million sharks per year are killed as by-catch, or for their fins; and that every year three times as much rubbish is dumped into the world's oceans as the weight of fish caught.

Maiden was happily anchored off St Ives beach when the RIB contingent returned to base. St Ives had been my first ever holiday destination without parents. Yours truly and three other acne-ridden sixteen-year-old lads had hitched down from Lancashire in search of sex, drink and rock and roll. In reality we drank lots of beer, played lots of pool, tried unsuccessfully to chat up the tourist talent, and slept every night in a damp tent, 3 miles from the main drag. I had no great wish to be reminded of these heady times, and so stayed on Maiden whilst the others did the town. John had decided that the documentary would look better with some glamorous female content, and he had managed to coerce a very Cornish blonde bimbette into perching atop a rock mermaid style, and wishing us well for the treacherous crossing of the Celtic Sea.

We went for an early start to Day 11 (1 September), but after motoring 30 miles out to the waypoint, again had to wait until midday before any wind arrived. The light 3–4 knot breeze was from the south-west, giving me a slow but comfortable beam reach north-west towards Cork. Another seven hours on the board gave us a slightly better 25 miles covered. We were now 50 miles from Cornwall, and 100 miles from Cork, and I was ready for my first night at sea. Steve was all huffy and puffy as they strung the RIB out on a line, 50 yds down-tide of Maiden. I had my recovery massage, and we all ate up on deck under a still and tranquil twilight. This to me was something really special – chatting and relaxing on the gently rolling deck of Maiden, miles from land and civilization. I wanted to savour the stillness and emptiness alone and so took myself up to the bow, and lay out on the folded foresail as darkness descended, and a brilliant starscape both filled and accentuated the emptiness. We were apparently well clear of the major shipping lanes, but I could still make out the occasional navigation light on the distant horizon. We were also not the only mammals enjoying the moment. At first all that could be heard were distant intermittent blowing noises. But then over the best part of an hour, the wheezing perpetrators came closer and closer to investigate our mysterious presence. It was difficult to see anything other than an occasional swirl in the inky blackness, and we didn't know whether it was whales or dolphins; but to know that the watchers were also being watched added to the power of this experience. Most of us found it difficult to sleep as Maiden rolled with the swells, and every now and again a rogue swell would slap hard against the hull, and roll us that bit further. In line with maritime law, we needed an overnight watch which was covered by three teams of two. The dawn shift had a good view of our visitors, and identified them as a pod of pilot whales, looking like double-sized dolphins with no beak.

Breakfast on deck soon after dawn was just glorious, watching the sun rise over the eastern horizon, but there was no significant wind and what little there was came from the south-east, giving me a horribly difficult dead downwind run to achieve our necessary north-west heading. The sea was slight but lumpy, and with only 2–3 knots of wind into the unwieldy 10.7m sail, I had nothing to balance against, and needed an unnatural and unsustainable level of concentration just to stay on the board. I fell in regularly and made very slow progress. By 2.00 p.m. I was physically and mentally exhausted, having covered only 12 miles in 4.5 hours. Despite the early hour, I had taken enough punishment and decided to give up for the day. It had been my most difficult day yet in windsurfing terms, and the mood on Maiden reflected the pathetic progress. True to form, something would always seem to happen to spice up an otherwise boring day. Mid-morning, I had been first to spot a strange shape on the horizon some 15 miles away. I had become used to recognising the distant shape of freighters, fishing boats, motor launches and of course yachts; but this was something quite different. Its silhouette was square, like the side of a house, and moving very slowly. Even when the object was 4–5 miles away we couldn't identify it. In the end Maiden diverted to intercept its route, and radioed back to the RIB that it was a leather-skinned, replica, fifth-century Celtic sailing vessel, and that its alternative-looking crew were trying to recreate the voyage of their forbears from Ireland to Cornwall to Brittany. We were worried about getting caught out here in foul weather, but I would not have given this leather-bound oddity much chance in any sort of storm. Anyway the two nutty entourages went their separate ways, and they clearly thought we were the fruitier fruitcakes.

Again that night we were checked out by the pilot whales, and I spent ages on deck peering over the side into the glowing phosphorescence. I don't understand the biological reason for this microscopic algae to give off such a beautiful green-yellow light, but like a child, I could have spent hours pulling an oar through the soup-like brilliance and soaking up this wonder of nature.

The next day dawned just like the last with minimal wind and clear blue skies. The morning's progress was painfully slow, but at least what little wind there was had swung right round to the north-west giving me a beat, rather than the awful downwind run. By midday we had done 10 miles and the wind suddenly died to nothing. I climbed into the RIB convinced that our bad luck was holding firm, and that there would be no more

Right: Kevin cuts free a dead gannet from a discarded fishing net.

Below: The replica fifth-century sailing vessel which we met in the Celtic Sea.

sailing today. After an hour of lunching and contemplating the conse-quences of further windlessness, a 3–4 knot puff arrived, and I was quickly underway. This wayward puff gradually grew into a steady 5–7 knots, which was the most we had experienced for eight days. As a recreational wind-surfer in past years, I would have sneered derisively at this totally inadequate level of wind. Today with the 10.7m sail it felt like paradise. At last I was able to sit back in the harness, and drive the board onto its rail. The sun was still beating down, and the earlier chop had become a long, smooth, east-running swell, of about 6–8 ft, but with 50–60 yds between the soft tops. We sailed for hours alongside Maiden, and even had Sarah and Duncan up the mast taking aerial shots of me. With so many windless hours behind us, I was determined to use every last minute of this heavenly breeze. From 1.30 p.m. until 8.00 p.m., I took only 20 minutes rest, and we ended up sailing due west dead into a spectacular sunset. There was no way I was going to lay down that sail until the lost glob of crimson had disap-peared from view. We had covered 36 miles in nearly ten hours of sailing. I felt weary and drained, but as high as a kite. This had been a really special day, where my addiction to progress had totally overruled my tired and objecting body. Denise's nightly massage was very very welcome, and by now finding Maiden's rolling motion soothing rather than destabilising, I slept like a baby.

The mood the next morning was as upbeat as it had been since the start, and to cap it all the light breeze was still there. We had only 50 miles to go to reach the Old Head of Kinsale, and everyone was drooling at the prospect of hot showers and cold Guinness. I was up and away by 9.00 a.m. In all yesterday's excitement sailing into the setting sun, Andy had not dared tell me to tack, and we had been on too much of a westerly heading. A straight line transit to Newfoundland had not been the game plan. In today's southerly breeze, I thus had to bear away on a north-west heading towards Kinsale, which was particularly uncomfortable and had me regularly falling in. The wind machine was stuck in first gear, and was also spluttering badly. Compared with yesterday's light but steady blow, today was all over the place with highly erratic direction and strength, so that I was broad reaching in 0–5 knots coming from south-east to south-west. No wonder I had the occasional splash.

Even if the seaborne traffic this far out was thin, we still had our early afternoon double-boom airshow from Concorde, and today there seemed to be a surprisingly high Irish Air Force presence. One particular air force reconnaissance plane flew down close enough to read my sail logos, which we assumed was a friendly gesture. Maiden later informed us that they had been on the radio, asking for identification and a detailed description of our mission. Apparently Kinsale had been the site of several recent very large drug busts, and despite the ceasefire in Northern Ireland, gunrunners were still working, and ever more inventive in their camouflage. On reflection afterwards, I came to the conclusion that a windsurfer would probably not have been an ideal hiding place for half a ton of cocaine or semtex.

Despite the military amusement, a huge mid-morning row was brewing between Steve on the RIB and Terry on Maiden. The engine on Maiden was playing up, giving them a maximum speed of 5 knots, which meant that they needed a good eight hours to get into Kinsale. We were making steady progress, and at this rate would get to within 25 miles of Kinsale by late afternoon. The RIB with its 30-knot cruising speed on flat water could easily get into Kinsale from 25 miles out in under an hour. Steve was of the opinion that we were a team out on the Celtic Sea and that if the wind died, and we were stranded out here, we would be far better off to spend another night on Maiden, than to have to run into Kinsale and face a 35-mile return journey the next morning. I sided with Terry, and we let Maiden motor off into the haze as I took a coffee break. One hour later I began to seriously regret my decision. The wind had dropped to 2–3 knots, and I had only covered about 13 miles. The RIB ran on well ahead to give me some peace, but my SOG had dropped to 2 knots meaning the 14th mile took half an hour. Whilst plodding ever onwards, I thought I caught a glimpse of something large and dark breaking the surface 200–300 yds away, and about a minute later, the massive forms of a whale and calf arched in and out of my sight about 150 yards ahead. Being so close to such an immense animal in its natural environment was an amazing experience. I could feel my heart thumping faster and faster against my chest as I sailed into the patch of water where the whales had been. What would they do next? What would happen if the tail slapped next to my board? I was part terrified, part elated, and part inquisitive. What type of whales were they? The mother seemed to be about 25 ft long, with a small black rearward-positioned dorsal fin. I needed to get a second look with my brain in gear. I spent a good five minutes trying to scan the sea all around my board, but either they went on a long dive, or I was facing the wrong way when they did surface. The whole experience was simply fantastic, and all the better for being such a complete surprise. I gabbled my sighting over the VHF to Andy in the RIB, and they motored back to widen the scan, but my majestic visitors had gone.

I was still on a high for the next hour, but the wind died further, and the 15th mile took nearly one hour. This was ridiculous. I had to give up. No-one spoke as I climbed onto the RIB, and we packed away the kit. Steve was at his worst when overruled and then proved right. He was stewing and sulking for Britain. Gaz was showing appropriate military solidarity by stewing and sulking with him. We were still 36 miles from Kinsale, which was OK on today's flat sea, but if it blew up rough tomorrow, the return journey could take 3–4 bone-jarring hours. On the way in we caught up with Maiden, and I tried to get Steve and Terry to air their grievances and diffuse the obvious tension. This was an impossible task with the two of them shouting across a 15-yard airspace, so I gave up and decided to have another go later on dry land. After yesterday's brilliant 36 miler, expectations had been high, and to be forced into submission after only 15 miles, and then have to deal with a squabbling crew, was absolutely the last thing I needed. It was uncanny that yet again a mega high with the whale sighting was followed by a mega low. Was this some sort of celestial job interview, where my emotions were being mercilessly stretched and stressed, and a guardian angel would pass judgement on my strength of character?

Kinsale was another beautiful harbour entry passage, except for some awful, angular, brown flats built on the facing hillside. As soon as we docked the customs officials were on board, but in true Irish tradition, were more interested in our epic adventure than in searching the RIB. I had imagined a triumphant arrival in Ireland after all the trepidation about the Celtic Sea crossing, but we were still 36 miles offshore, and thus hadn't reached Ireland at all. Disregarding this practicality, we went in search of a pint of Guinness, and found a lovely spot on the verandah of the yacht club bar. Kinsale is something like the St Tropez of Ireland, and the view was suitably expensive.

I put the pints down on the table, fostered five minutes of small talk, and then suggested that we all open our hearts and bring our grievances out into the open. Steve had by now pulled out of his sulk, and stressed that a big part of his down mood was caused by the lack of progress, and the sadistic tricks the wind seemed to be playing on us. Andy and Gaz tried to get through to me and Steve that the weather will be what the weather will be, and that we had to be patient, and take our opportunities to cover the miles when we could. I suggested to Steve that there was now a huge tension between the RIB team and the Maiden team which needed to be diffused, and to his credit when Maiden arrived he left his Guinness and went down to quietly sort things out with Terry. That evening, after the first showers in seven days, we decided a night out was called for to celebrate being in Ireland. It was a great night with lots of laughs and togetherness ... maybe we had crossed the Celtic Sea after all!

Chapter VIII

Elation and Desperation off Ireland

Man is made for joy and woe,
And when this we rightly know,
Safely through the world we go.

J.B. Priestley

*A*part from being Sunday Bloody Sunday, 5 September 1999 was Day 15 of our journey. We had so far covered 320 miles averaging under 23 miles per day. At this rate we would not reach the north coast of Scotland until mid-October, when the winter tends to begin in earnest. We had to start pulling this average up over the next fourteen days, or the probability of success would drop into single figures. Today's forecast was for sunshine, and light and variable winds. In Kinsale harbour there was no wind, but 36 miles out could be different, so we motored out to the waypoint across glassy, almost soupy waters, to find that the open sea was just as windless as the harbour. With our newly discovered 'what will be will be' mentality, we were not deterred. We decided to enjoy the wilderness and tranquillity, whilst periodically confirming via the anemometer that there was less than 1 knot of puff, which is not dissimilar to the convection currents that move air around a centrally heated room, and certainly well below anything you can feel on your face. We had a visitation from what was later confirmed to be a sunfish (a 5 ft long 3 ft wide, dinner-plate-shaped fish with no tail and a sharks fin on either edge of its flattened body), and generally bummed around telling jokes, and sorting out the world for five hours. Yes, we sat out on the RIB, 36 miles from land for five hours, and never once had enough wind to even consider rigging the sail. Three days ago this would have driven me mad, and we hypothesized that I had become a born-again fatalist, and somehow felt at peace with my predicament. Maybe religion is simply a clever system of bringing order, reason and codes of behaviour to a potentially 'free for all' human race; and of course accepting the 'will of God or Allah explanation' was a neat way of overcoming the pain of an adverse turn of events. Was I turning into a Muslim? Were religions born because we needed them? It all got a bit heavy, so we fired up the engine and set off for Kinsale.

Halfway in towards Kinsale, Andy spotted a troop of bottle-nosed dolphins 200–300 yds away, and we pulled the engine down to idle. There were about twenty of them of varying sizes, and they quickly realised that

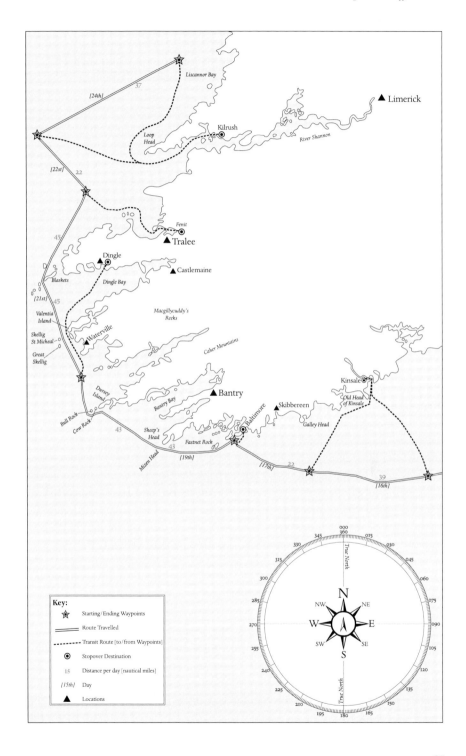

Key:

⭐ Starting / Ending Waypoints

—— Route Travelled

---- Transit Route [to / from Waypoints]

◉ Stopover Destination

15 Distance per day [nautical miles]

[15th] Day

▲ Locations

they had an audience. At first one pair started doing synchronised jumps, and then another held itself vertically inverted, whilst slapping the surface of the sea repeatedly with its tail. This was evidently a troupe speciality as three others followed suit, pretty much in a line. This blatant show of exhibitionism from a group of wild animals for a human audience was just mind blowing. I know nothing about dolphin behaviour, except that they are one of the few mammals to have sex purely for pleasure, and that they have a well-used system of verbal communication. So, as sex-crazed show-offs constantly yattering to each other, they obviously have nothing in common with human beings! I then remembered an MCS (see Appendix II for details) statistic that 1,000 of the world's dolphins are killed every day in drift gill nets. I wondered how the outcry would look if 1,000 human beings perished every day in the same way, and the thought of such wanton murder of such amazing animals completely erased my earlier euphoria.

Back in Kinsale after our first zero miles day, the rest of the team were surprised to see us so relaxed, and apparently suspected that we had hijacked a consignment of wacky baccy. I still had my massage (old habits die hard) and then did a long interview with a lady called Deborah who was writing a piece for the *Cork Examiner*. The Irish media in general got much more excited about our venture than their apathetic British counterparts, and the Cork 103 FM radio station reporter was onto us several times day, for morning and evening news bulletins. We decided to have our evening meeting in the yacht club, and most of the others went on ahead whilst I was still being interrogated by Deborah. Sophie was one of the last to leave, and despite being in full flow to Deborah, I could hear her chuntering angrily that someone had taken her beloved yellow Musto jacket. I was not a witness to what followed, but apparently Sophie stomped up to the yacht club in the rain to find that John Beecroft had used the jacket to drape over his camera to keep it dry on his walk to the yacht club. Sophie went ballistic in front of the bemused yacht club clientele, and John responded even more aggressively. By the time I arrived, the warring factions had been separated to opposite ends of the room, but the atmosphere was cold and brittle like blue ice. This incident hurt Sophie badly, and was to become the first of several clashes between John and others on the team.

Ironically on Day 16 (6 September), the wind finally arrived, but the RIB had been booked in for a service and gearbox oil change, so we didn't leave until midday. The wind was blowing 10–15 knots (F4), and the sea was lumpy with 5–6 ft swells, so the journey out to our start point took the best part of two hours. The wind was coming from somewhere between south and south-west, so I needed to point at around 55 degrees to the wind to give a roughly westerly heading towards the Fastnet. I set off with the 9.4m sail on Katie, and a huge 50-cm fin. After ten days on Big Bertha and the heavy 10.7m sail, this combination felt light and responsive, and I was in seventh heaven driving it upwind and steering up and down the swells to maximise forward momentum. The visibility was awful, and we were less than 2 miles away when I saw a ghostly oil rig emerge out of the mist. I wanted to sail in close to get a feel for the size and solidity of its unsightly but impressive superstructure, but apparently the charts specified that all passing shipping had to stay at least 1,000m distant. It felt good to be classed as Passing Shipping, so I did as I was told. With so little time on the water, I wanted to take the maximum miles out of these favourable conditions, and over the first 20 miles I was averaging 14–15 knots board speed. The wind then picked up to 16–20 knots and the swells increased in size and steepness. I was blatantly overpowered, and needed a smaller board and sail, but we only had sixty minutes of sailing time left, and a board/sail change in these conditions could easily have used thirty of those precious sixty minutes, so I kept going, when necessary killing the speed by screwing into wind. During this phase, I passed within 50 yds of a violently rolling fishing boat, whose crew stared incredulously at this lunatic muscling his way through horrible seas and weather. It gave me a perverse pleasure to shock people this way, and sure enough the word soon spread to other fishermen of the 'eejit' on a windsurfer, on his way around Ireland. My average speed dropped to less than 10 knots whilst in this survival mode of sailing, and I had a couple of big wipe-outs landing from inadvertent take-offs. It was however a very productive 3.5 hours, sailing with 39 miles covered, taking us within 30 miles of the infamous Fastnet rock, which gives its name to the annual yacht race in which sixteen poor souls lost their lives some twenty years ago.

Our nearest stopover was, however, still Kinsale, and we had a great ride in on the RIB, surfing down the north-west running swells; but we were not alone. A bunch of white-bellied common dolphins were also enjoying the surf, and I felt very envious seeing these fantastic animals burst through the blue-green leading edge of these fast-moving walls of water. Steve later explained to me that you can judge the thickness and thus steepness of a wave by its colour. The lighter and more steely blue the colour, the steeper and more dangerous the wave for us humans, but the more fun for our dolphin relations. That evening was our third in Kinsale, and there were more traumas at the meeting that night. The topic of the disagreement was ... sandwich making! The Maiden crew didn't see why they had to do all the cooking and sandwich making, and that the RIB team should take their share. This time I came down in favour of the RIB crew, whose job it was to safely maximise the miles I covered, adding that Maiden's job was to be our travelling base camp, and to service me by servicing the RIB crew. This didn't meet with universal approval, but I had started to lose my patience with what to me seemed like childish 'its not fair' squabbles.

There was wind again the next morning, but first we had to fuel up the RIB, and I did an interview from the local hotel for RTE National Radio. Time in Ireland is not about being on time and we waited forty minutes for the harbour diesel pump attendant to be dragged out of his Guinness-induced oversleep. The upside of this delay was that the pump attendant couldn't work his calculator and we got an 80 per cent discount. We were thus late setting out again, and had to stop at the mouth of the harbour for another critically important (?) interview with Cork 103 FM on the mobile phone. We had just escaped from this diversion when Terry came on the VHF saying that a National TV crew were on their way down, and could we come back into the harbour, rig up a sail and give them some action footage of me 'windsurfing into Kinsale'. This was perfect fodder for the pro- and anti-media factions. Andy was furious, saying we could kiss goodbye to any miles today, if we gave in and stage-managed a ✱✱✱✱✱✱✱ harbour show for the ✱✱✱✱✱✱✱ TV. Terry said we would be ✱✱✱✱✱✱✱ crazy to throw up an opportunity such as this, which could be the ✱✱✱✱✱✱ catalyst for the UK TV companies to start taking an interest. Just the sort of decision I wanted, hours before I could potentially be taking on the Fastnet rock. In the end I weakly compromised, such that no-one was happy; and we sailed back in for a rushed harbourside interview, and gave them some of John Beecroft's footage to use.

By the time we got to our starting waypoint in mid-afternoon the wind had dropped to F2/3 from the south-west, but sailing close hauled with the 10.0m sail on Bertha, I still managed to cover 27 miles in 3.5 hours sailing. We passed some truly amazing scenery, and I recorded in my diary that night that (in the eye of this beholder) our anchorage in the Baltimore sea lagoon was one of the most beautiful places I had been on this earth. The entry into the lagoon was through a narrow gap in the cliffs, between angular black rock formations clamouring with seabirds. On our right we had the mainland, and on our left Sherkin Island. The swells on the outside were still a good size and there was plenty of white water crashing around. The shallower water also caused these swells to steepen and grow in size through the gap, which would have made a low tide exit in bigger breaking seas very interesting. It was about 8.30 p.m. when we entered the lagoon. The sun had already dropped below the horizon, but the remaining surreal red glow further enhanced the experience. The lagoon itself is open at the northern end through shallow channels between smaller Islands, and at its glistening surface seemed to merge seamlessly with the shadowy hills and mountains around its perimeter. There is something about dusk falling over a body of undulating water that is powerfully addictive. The shadows jink and flicker and merge, and the orange hues die slowly into blackness. It's like watching a good film. Most of the value is lost if you can't stay until the end. I also think part of my perception of the beauty of this place was down to it being my 100 per cent perfect holiday destination. It had acres of sheltered water for 'messing around on boards, and in boats'. It had desolate, shear sea cliffs, perfect for sitting atop to watch the heaving hypnotic sea, and to ponder on the meaning of life. It had rolling, stone-walled meadows for dog walks, and frolicking with the kids. It had history and mystery in the ruins of Sherkin Abbey, and the Dun Na Long Castle. And last but not least it had a great pub 200 yards from the Sherkin Island jetty.

With an imminent gale warning in force, Maiden had anchored in the lee of Sherkin Island, about 200 yds off an antiquated jetty leading up to the ruined Abbey. We strung the RIB off a line 30 yds downwind, had our supper and meeting, and could feel the storm brewing as we took to our bunks. Being at anchor on a rocky seabed, with a storm coming, we had a watch system in operation. The storm was worse than expected, and the big seas were rolling in through the gap and wrapping around into what we thought was a sheltered anchorage. It was thus a rough night for everyone, with Maiden rolling violently. The tension on the anchor lines and the rope between Maiden and the RIB was huge at times, as the swells conspired to drive the two vessels apart. In the dark early hours Andy (on watch at the time) heard a loud crack as the anchor line secondary fixing, and safety rail were ripped from the deck, and Maiden and the RIB started dragging towards the nearby rocky shore. All hell then broke loose as Terry and Kevin got Maiden's engine started, and Steve cursed and cussed until he and Gaz had managed to get aboard the RIB, start the engine, and take it to the safety of the nearby jetty. That morning they were nowhere to be seen. After a sleepless night looking after an open boat in a force 9 gale, they had motored across the bay to Baltimore village and checked into a local B&B.

The storm had mostly blown itself out during the night, and winds were down to F5 but Steve had left messages that he was going nowhere today. His argument was that the seas would be big and rough after this storm for at least twelve hours, and not the conditions we needed for the Fastnet rounding. As he was uncontactable and asleep in a B&B across the bay, I resigned myself to another zero miles day. Duncan had an opportunity for me to drive to Dublin, and appear on a national TV chat show, but the arrangements and timing seemed somewhat vague, and I might not have been back for the next morning, so this was aborted. I did a radio interview for Classic FM, and a video diary session for Sarah, and then got a lift ashore to Sherkin Island on Maiden's tiny, and not very seaworthy tender. In my pocket I had a note that Sophie had pushed into my hand a few minutes earlier. I did not need to read the letter. She had 'sorry I'm leaving' written all over her face. The others who had come over in the tender wandered off in a group. I had to be alone. Sophie's news was not unexpected after her row with John, and a subsequent row with Terry over differences of opinion on Maiden's safety protocols. It would be a blow to me, as she was the best organizer we had, and left me without a medical officer or galley manager, or budget manager, but it was not the end of the world. I was also down about missing another day's sailing, and worried that the overall level of commitment around me was eroding. But most of all, I was missing my family really badly. I had spoken to Mandy and all four of the kids from Kinsale. My youngest son had gone off the rails a bit at school, and Mandy was logically somewhat stressed, but they were all going about their lives as normal. Talking to them over the phone made it worse. There was a festering ache inside me somewhere. The cure was unattainable. I needed to touch my children and smell their hair and roll around on the floor with them all, and I needed it now.

I walked south towards Wilson Rock, which overlooks the gap, and sat on the cliff watching the foaming chaos below. Part of me was sulking about being let down by others. Part of me was pining. Part of me was enjoying being alone in this gorgeous place. But after a while my predominant thought was: how the hell I had got myself into this crazy predicament, and why was it so bloody important anyway to be the first person to windsurf around Britain and Ireland? After what seemed like hours, I wandered back down to the jetty to meet the others. Only Sarah was there. I had been so wrapped up in my own maudlin thoughts, I was not ready to speak to anyone. I had somehow lost confidence in my ability to socialise and communicate. Sarah could see I was not right. She also knew (I think) that it would not do me any good to be left on my own any longer, and gently ushered me up to the pub to join the others. After twenty minutes I was fine, and starting to plan how to resolve the various team problems. I later had one-to-one discussions up on Maiden's deck with first Sophie, then John, then Terry, and finally Steve. I persuaded Sophie to stay on for another two weeks (max) until we could get a replacement, told John he had to become a team player, and had Terry reluctantly accept to give everybody the safety drills that they thought were necessary, rather than what he thought was practical. With Steve, I just had to know whether he was still 100 per cent committed to the success of the venture. He told me he was.

Day 19 (9 September) was the day we rounded the Fastnet rock. It was a day indelibly etched on my memory that had everything: great beauty, big rows, huge seas, team triumph, hopeless exhaustion, real danger, broken records, wondrous excitement, sulky silences, and humble apologies. It was a day in my life, but maybe also a life in a day. It started inauspiciously with light winds and beating south-west on Big Bertha with the 10.0m sail. I was sailing well, railing the board nicely into the wind, as the Fastnet rock slowly came into view. It is only 28m high, but its size and sheer presence are exaggerated by its isolation 4 miles south-west of Cape Clear. The sun was shining, and the paparazzi were ecstatic about the light. In the steady F3 winds I felt confident of taking a line quite close (100–150m) to the rock, meaning I could clearly see the large waves smashing into its base. Alongside the lighthouse and helicopter deck, is a black, sinister-looking, windowless, mound-like building, which I can only assume has a military or meteorological function. Adrenaline was coursing through my veins, and I felt like I was on stage in front of thousands of cheering supporters. On the other hand it was quite a deep and private celebration. Maiden had not dared come in so close, so it was just me and the whooping RIB team, and a lonely fulmar that had flown within 20 ft of my mast tip for the last 3 miles. This elegant seabird had obviously realised something special was happening today, and was far from camera shy!

Getting to this landmark had seemed so impossible at times for all of us, and the release and feelings of great achievement were simply huge. Afterwards, I tried to analyze why the high was so high. Partly, it had to be because yesterday's low was so low, and the goal had seemed so impossibly distant; but the beauty of the day, and the aura of the place were inescapable. I also felt privileged and special, and like some insignificant trespasser in the grounds of a mystical forbidden castle. If a rock can have a personality then this rugged, fearsome, unpredictable character would be a Hollywood idol. Although the weather gods were kind to us at the time, it was also difficult to avoid thinking about the massive destructive power the seas here are capable of, and of the faces of the terrified sailors out here twenty years ago.

As we rounded the Fastnet rock, the swells ramped up to 25–30 ft in size. I had never been on the sea (in any vessel, let alone on a windsurfer) in seas of this size before. Maiden was following another yacht with a 45-ft mast which was totally lost from view when both were in a trough. Fortunately the swells had come a long way and were widely spaced with shallow inclines. It was the definitive roller-coaster ride, accelerating down the glassy faces, and up and over the rounded crests. With a heading that no longer needed to be so high, I changed to Katie for extra speed, and cruised effortlessly past the imposing Mizzen Head and Bantry Bay, with the Caher mountains and Dursey Island in my sights. The air was clear and headlands 30 miles away would be born out of the horizon as I gobbled

Rounding the infamous Fastnet Rock with fulmar as escort.

up the miles. After so much underpowered labouring crossing the Celtic Sea, the sheer speed down, up and over these majestic rolling swells took me off somewhere else; and I had no concept of time or distance until the RIB gave me the news that we had covered some 30 miles in the last ninety minutes. My point of sailing about 60 degrees to the wind was taking me between the Cow Rock and Dursey Island, a gap that turned out to be about 1 mile wide. I was moving fast on a tight but comfortable line, and knew that once past Dursey Island I could let it go onto a beam reach north-west. I was thus incredulous when Andy gave me the signal to tack, and head out to sea to round the outer Bull Rock (something like a 4-mile detour). Andy and Steve were adamant that it was not safe to take the inside passage. Their main argument was that if the RIB engine failed at the wrong spot, we could be on the rocks within ten to fifteen minutes, and in a life-threatening situation.

I very reluctantly and silently did as I was told, and had to change back to Bertha to get upwind. The seas in the lee of this line of rocks were still big but had become more confused and difficult. I fell in several times on the tacks, and found uphauling the 10.0m sail in these huge and confused seas very difficult and strength sapping. As I finally tacked to pass south of Bull Rock, I noticed a severe darkening of the sky, and an almost immediate increase in wind strength. The RIB crew were in no mood to give me a board and sail change, so I hung on for dear life, often airborne, desperately trying to keep control of this huge board and sail in what were now very large and steep 20 ft + seas. After 2–3 miles of this purgatory, my arms were like useless lumps of jelly, and I was a helpless slave to the harness, which gave some horrible wipe-outs. But there was no way I could stop. With F5 south-west winds, and such driving seas, we had to be 2–3 miles clear of Bull Rock before even contemplating a kit change. I somehow made another 1–2 miles, and signalled to the RIB that I simply could not go on. Gaz swore aggressively at me to stop ******* around and decouple my board and rig. After what I had just been through, this was the final straw; and I told him with as much force and anger as I have ever raised to **** off, and never ever speak to me again like that. If I had been in the boat there would have been a certain fist-fight. This ridiculous detour had taken us into bigger, steeper seas, cost us at least 20 miles of progress, and totally sapped all my strength, and now they were swearing at me!

After some calming comments from Steve and Andy, Gaz threw me an energy bar as I sat astride my bucking board 10 yds away from the RIB. This was as close as we were going to get to speaking for some time. With Steve trying to hold the RIB nose into the now breaking swells, Gaz and Andy managed to drag the 10.0m sail onto the RIB, and derig it. At one stage the RIB was spun round and a good quarter of a tonne of water crashed over the starboard bow swamping the RIB and its contents. To do a board and sail change in these conditions was an almost superhuman achievement, and would have been impossible without slick routines, Gaz and Andy's substantial strength and agility, and some help from Duncan. I was aware of the panic and fear in the RIB as they tried to get me aboard, with the RIB sometimes 10 ft above my head, and crashing down violently towards me, but they succeeded and I survived. Maybe because of my extreme tiredness, or because I wasn't aware how quickly we were being blown back towards Bull Rock, I was not as afraid as they seemed to be. Gaz commented later that evening that the thing that scares him most is someone who doesn't get scared!

After a mostly silent thirty-minute rest, where we held our position and watched the Atlantic Ocean smashing its way through the arches of Bull Rock, I went back into the battlefield with smaller kit, and managed an absolutely terrifying 10 more miles. The wind stayed around F5, but also backed to the south, meaning I had to broad reach in these huge seas. I had not done too much wave jumping in my life, and normally at the beach you can head up on take-off to control the jump, and you know that the landing will be relatively flat in the space between the waves. I had none of these luxuries, and my broad reach line was directly down the swells. With this wind and these steep seas, I was accelerating to at least 25 knots down the faces, and there was no way I could kill the speed before taking off into the unknown. Apart from heading upwind (away from my desired direction), the only way to kill the speed was to go even broader, which in these conditions, with no strength to sail out of the harness, was a sure-fire recipe for a face-destroying catapult. Steve was still urging me on, worried about the length of our transit journey into Dingle where we had agreed to rendezvous with Maiden, but I was finished. I don't ever remember being so physically and mentally drained in my life. Pushing myself to the limit in a triathlon was a doddle compared to what I'd just been through. Andy knew how close to the edge I had been; but he got his timing spot on by waiting until all the kit was stowed, and I had changed out of my wetsuit and had a hot drink, before delivering the news that we had done 43 miles, a record day. What a day!

Once in warm and welcoming Dingle, the RIB lads disappeared to the pub. Maiden arrived forty minutes later with a very tired and weary looking crew. Apparently all but one of them had thrown up over the side at some stage during a very rough day's sailing. Whilst comparing notes on the day's epic happenings, I had probably the best and most necessary massage I will ever have. I then went to find Steve, Gaz and Andy in the pub and set down three more pints of Guinness as I joined their table. After an opening light-hearted jibe from me, about not spending the rest of the night swearing at each other, we settled down to honest analysis and apologies. Andy stressed that I had appointed Steve as safety officer, and therefore had to abide by his routing decisions. I accepted this logic, but pointed out that maybe we should have done some more research before-hand on the safety of the passage between Cow rock and Dursey Island. We had not even consulted with Terry and Maiden, who had been in these waters before and took the inside route as apparently does most traffic. There were more gale warnings in force for the next day, so knowing I would not be going out to do battle again, I had a few pints as we celebrated a truly monumental day, and the repaired team spirit. I only found out later that Steve and Duncan had also had a big row out on the RIB whilst I was broad reaching myself to exhaustion. This silly conflict over the identity of the Skellig Rocks on the horizon (Steve thought they were not the Skelligs; Duncan was right) created a coldness between the two of them that never really thawed.

The wind howled all night, and most of the next day, so there were no decisions to take on whether or not to go out sailing. I spent the first part of the morning in session with Steve and Terry, working our way through all the charts of the Irish west and north coasts, planning routing and stopovers. I then sat down with a local radio journalist for an Irish interview, meaning forty-five minutes of general chat first over several cups of tea, and then a further thirty minutes of wandering questions with the tape recorder switched on. John Beecroft had asked for a chat over lunch, and proceeded to tell me that the documentary he was making would not sell unless he had better access to me on the water (and didn't have to work to a RIB rota with Duncan and Sarah), and that to do his fly-on-the-wall stuff on Maiden, he could not be tied to rigid cooking and washing-up rotas. I had put a minority share into the costs of making this documentary, and would get 50 per cent of the revenues, so I needed it to be a success. His starting demands were unreasonable but I worked out a compromise shuttling between John, Duncan and Sarah. The compromise ultimately proved to be a big mistake. I also had several heavy chats with Duncan who in turn was going round the bend trying to manage an efficient livethatdream web site with awkward and petty Ben from Ocean Web at the other end. The afternoon was spent shopping, talking weather forecasts to the harbour master, and fundraising for MCS. We all ate onshore that night to celebrate Andy's birthday, and Denise's last night. I would miss her rejuvenating massages, but my body had, I think, started to adapt to its daily stresses, and the risk of injury had thus lessened.

Saturday, 11 September (Day 21) warranted an early start, as we had a two-hour RIB ride back to our waypoint south of Skellig St Michael. This particular 214m high lump of black rock took its name from a legendary appearance there of St Michael; and despite its total exposure to the elements, the island still hosts a 1,400-year-old monastery. I had several times visited this stretch of coastline on holiday, driving round the ring of Kerry, and stopping at places such as Waterville, Ballinskelligs Bay and Valentia Island. The scenery is big, windswept and barren with long sweeping curves or shear cliffs down to the sea. From the land it is truly memorable. From the sea it was better still. The wind was back down to F3/4, and the tide would be pushing us north until mid-afternoon. Unfortunately the wind direction was north-north-west, meaning something like a 3:1 beat, with the bigger part on port tack. My line was outside Puffin Island but inside both the Skellig St Michael, and the smaller but equally spectacular Little Skellig. I set off on Bertha with an 8.0m sail, and angled in towards Puffin Island. The swells off the promontory were a good 8–10 ft, but this seemed like nothing after how it had been two days before. Two or three tacks later I was clear of Valentia Island, and heading across Dingle Bay towards Blasket Island. The wind was varying from 8 knots up to 14 which meant a lot of concentration, and shifting my weight around, to maintain sail and board trim. It was almost like a pulse wind, with a one minute on, one minute off, cycle. The wind strength did not seem to be correlated with whether I was down in a trough or up on a crest; and I can only guess that the recent big storms had messed up the surface of the sea so much that the surface winds had been similarly messed up.

The passage inside Blasket Island was apparently quite difficult, so I had to tack west and look for a line through the narrow gap between Blasket Island and Inishnabro. On this westerly tack I was suddenly joined by about twenty common dolphins, gliding effortlessly under and around my board. They stayed with me for about fifteen minutes, and at times it seemed as if they were playing a game of dare, as to who could flash by the closest to the underside of my board. The tide out in the middle of Dingle Bay had been very light, but with a big volume of water needing to pass through a narrow, shallow gap, the 1 knot tide further out was expected to be some 4–5 knots in and around the gap. The tide was with us, but with a northerly airstream we would get wind-over-tide conditions going through. The water was flat at the start of the race, and two grey seals bobbed into view 20 yds ahead of me, obviously curious as to what on earth I was. Approaching the northern end of the race I could see some 6–8 ft standing waves lining up to greet me. Wind-over-tide driven standing waves are a completely different breed from the wind-only, driven, open-sea variety, the biggest difference being that the standing variety don't like to let any significant space get between them. Six-foot swells on the sea could have anything from 15 to 150 ft between the crests, whereas these Blasket standing models had nothing more than 8 ft. This, added to the fact that they don't seem to come from any particular direction, makes windsurfing through them particularly tricky. The board just gets buffeted around, and normal steering techniques don't always work. Also uphauling or waterstarting can be very difficult, so rule number one is not to fall in. Rule number two is to stay on a comfortable point of sailing (i.e. not a broad reach). Rule number three, is not to be knackered when you take on one of these races. I broke all three rules. I was tired from the 30 miles we had already covered. I had to bear away to get inside Inishtooskert (another lump of rock facing us as we came through the gap), and therefore I fell in repeatedly and became more and more tired. It was never dangerous because of the way the tide was taking us, but it was certainly very hard work. After leaving these obstacles behind I did another 15 miles on a north-east heading, to achieve another day record of 45 miles.

Once out on the northern side of Blasket Island, I guess we were technically into Galway Bay, with our straight-line target Slyne Head, Connemara, 80 miles away across the bay. We motored in very pleased with the day's work. Including all the tacking, I had sailed some 60 miles, in 8.5 hours, an average speed of around 7 knots. Our designated stopover was Fenit, at the eastern end of Tralee Bay, which was a combination of yacht marina and freighter discharge terminal. I couldn't see that sort of thing happening at Lymington! We had a so-called 'Shit or Bust' decision to take that night. The next easy anchorage for Maiden was Clifden, 75 miles from our waypoint. Another option was to find an anchorage in the shelter of the Arran Islands, west of Galway, but there didn't seem to be any refuelling facilities there for the RIB. The wind forecast was F3/4, veering from south to north-west. Not perfect, but not bad, so we decided to go for it, and scheduled an early 7.00 a.m. start for tomorrow. Maiden would take the direct route and we would motor out 25 miles due west to the waypoint, and then head north-north-east towards Slyne Head. However, if the wind was to veer round to north-west, as per the forecast, it would make sense to set off broad reaching north-west in the southerly wind, and then end up on a nice beam reach north-east in the north-west wind. Also with the south-south-west wind, a north-north-east heading was a dead downwind run, which in these lumpy, gusty conditions was nearly impossible. It was a risky strategy as we were effectively heading out to sea (towards Greenland!), banking on a change in wind direction, but we decided to go for it.

The morning was not easy sailing, but we made 22 miles on a north-west heading. The wind was also starting to veer more to the west, so it was looking like our strategy would pay off. Then disaster struck. The RIB engine started spluttering and stuttering, and Steve could only get a maximum 7 knots. I was hauled aboard, and Steve tried in vain to rectify the problem. There was something wrong with the fuel supply or fuel pump, but we did not have the tools or expertise to do anything about it. With a max speed of 7 knots, the RIB was effectively disabled, and we had no choice but to abort the day's sailing, and limp into the nearest port where we could get it repaired. The other very real risk was that the engine would pack up altogether, and we would have to be rescued. To cap it all, our 'veering-wind strategy' had put us a good 30 miles from the nearest land, and we were not able to make VHF radio contact with the coastguard to relay our unfortunate situation. After limping 5–6 miles east, we managed to get through, and after at least ten crackling, virtually unintelligible exchanges, we gleaned that the nearest port where we were likely to find a marine mechanic was Kilrush, 18 miles up the Shannon estuary. This meant virtually a 50-mile run in at max 7 knots. The various coastguard stations were alerted, and we were asked to give regular updates of our position and the state of the engine. Also, we could not reach Maiden on the VHF, and asked the coastguard to relay them a message of our predicament. Maiden could not get into Kilrush because of her draft, so they had no alternative but to carry on to Clifden, and hope that we would catch up with them the next day. Fortunately the seas were not too big, and rolling roughly in the direction we needed to go. The RIB would not have had the power to take on bigger head on seas, and we would have been certain rescue material. The engine had obviously been mistreated in an earlier life, and itself had access to nautical charts. There is no other explanation for the fact that it decided to clog up at the furthest point from port (excepting the middle of the Celtic Sea) we would be on the whole trip.

The journey in took 7.5 cold, slow, miserable hours. We were all absolutely gutted by this latest slice of misfortune, and conversation was kept to an absolute minimum. For a while I lay down and tried to sleep wedged between boards near the bow, but despite all the layers of fleece and Gore-tex, my body temperature started to drop, and I realised that the only way to stay warm was to stay upright, giving my heart something to do. We were finally let in through the Kilrush lock gates at 8.30 p.m., and directed to a nearby B&B, the Kilrush Creek Marina hotel. The staff there were friendly and fascinated by our story, but we were past gassing over a Guinness, and just wanted silent food, hot shower, and warm bed. Steve had naturally to look on the black side and was worried that we would need new parts from the nearest Yamaha dealer, which could take days. I hoped and in fact believed that it would be a minor plumbing job, and that we would be under way the next afternoon. The mechanic duly arrived mid-morning, and diagnosed the problem as shards of fibreglass in the fuel lines and fuel pump, which had probably been kicked into the fuel tank by the bloody shoddy boatbuilders. It was a superb sailing day, with perfect F3/4 winds from the west, but no-one (except me) seemed to have any sense of urgency, and by the time everything was fixed and the RIB reloaded, it was too late to go out. It was almost as though the day had been written off, and we had admitted defeat before anyone had even looked at the engine. Steve and Andy were wingeing that the RIB had done one year's work in three weeks, and my rush-rush mentality never gave us time for proper maintenance. Maybe they had a point.

The Tuesday, 14 September (Day 24) forecast was for F4/6 winds predominantly from the south, with possible gales later that evening. To maximise our chances of reaching Clifden, I asked for a 5.00 a.m. breakfast, and to leave Kilrush at daybreak. True to form, we didn't leave until gone 9, and after a 2.5-hour run back to the waypoint, I set sail broad reaching north-east, on Lady Di, with a 6.0m sail. With winds from the north, the west, and the south over the last three days, the seas were particularly confused, and I struggled to sail very broad. We also wanted to get nearer to the coast for logistical reasons. I actually sailed 37 miles all on starboard tack to come within 10 miles of the Arran Islands, before stopping for a break and navigational chat. Taking this line had meant that I had only moved some 15 miles nearer Clifden. I had only sailed for 2.5 hours, and the wind had by now dropped to a F3. But I could see from the faces on the RIB that they were going to tell me that they wanted to stop for the day. Why, why, why? It was 14.30, the conditions were fine, and I was about to gybe onto port tack and head directly for Clifden 40 miles away. I had waited two days to get out and make progress. Apparently, a gale warning had come over the radio, with gales expected that night. Steve was worried that we would only scramble another 10–15 miles, and then still be on our way in when the gales arrived. He was also worried about the reportedly difficult passage into Clifden, in fading light. I argued that we were just as far from Kilrush as we were from Clifden, and that even ninety minutes more sailing could get us 20 miles nearer Clifden, and still leave us three hours to ride the 20 miles in before nightfall. His safety-driven argument was that the gales could arrive early. I was absolutely gutted, and did not speak at all during the two hour run-in. The gales duly arrived at about 7.00 p.m.

I didn't want to be with the others that night, preferring my own depressed company. I rang Mandy, who seemed similarly depressed, telling her that our progress seemed so slow and ill-fated. I got up early the next morning to ring the weather forecasters, who again were predicting gales later. Later in weather forecasting means approx twelve hours, soon means approx six hours, and imminent means any time now, so in conference over a late breakfast with Steve, we decided to get out there and give it a go. It seemed that the more impatient I became, the slower Andy and Gaz moved, and we didn't get under way until 11.00 a.m. The ride out down the Shannon was particularly rough, with wind over tide producing a short, very steep chop, even though the wind was only F3/4. Gaz turned to me at one stage, and by asking 'did I still want to go out', inferred that it would be much worse further out, and that this was a waste of time. I acidly replied that this was just wind over tide through a patch of shallow water, and it would not be like this out round Loop Head. My prediction was accurate, and the conditions at the waypoint were near perfect, with a south-west F4, and a gentle sea. Just as we started to rig the sail, the VHF radio calmly announced that the gales were now imminent. Steve inevitably concluded that we had no choice but to run back into Kilrush. I agreed with Steve, probably because he was right, but possibly because I simply had no spirit left with which to argue. It surely couldn't get any worse. Our ability to time things to maximise the negative impact was spooky. Andy likened our existence in Kilrush to being in an open prison. We were let out during the day with grand visions of escape, only to be forced back by the weather for yet another morale-destroying evening. The gales duly didn't arrive until 6.30 p.m.! We also found out that night that we could have run into Liscannor only 10 miles from our waypoint, and thus could have been in a better position to take advantage of gaps between gales the next day. With all our downtime in Kilrush, surely one of my two navigators could have got hold of a chart and a phone and worked this out a couple of days earlier?

That afternoon I went for a long walk in the rain, and seriously thought about giving up. We had covered only 527 NM (31 per cent of total distance) in twenty-five days, averaging 21 miles/day. At this rate the whole journey would take around twelve weeks. When I got back to the B&B, I actually got to the stage of writing two lists: reasons to quit, and reasons not to quit, which went something like:

Reasons to quit:

- Running out of time. Better to quit now, than be stranded by winter in Scotland.
- Charter contracts, team availability, and budget all for 8 weeks. At this rate it will take at least 11. I will end up broke; and having to find new charter boats and crew, which if unsuccessful could force me to give up somewhere on the east coast, close to home. To spend 8–10 weeks, 'nearly' becoming the first . . .!!!
- I can get home and see my family again.
- No more days coping with malicious weather and over-cautious team.

- I have booked mega family holiday in Australia from end November. I would face certain dismemberment and divorce if my prolonged expedition caused our holiday of a lifetime to be cancelled.

Reasons not to quit:

- So many friends, family and other supporters rooting for me.
- Don't kill a lifetime's dream, for the sake of a few weeks.
- Can I live with myself as a quitter?
- Failure means no publicity, no documentary, no book, and no chance to recover investments.
- Success could give me the chance to break out of current job rut.
- Our luck could turn, and with 40NM/day we could still make it in less than 8 weeks.

My radio interview with Classic FM that afternoon can't have been the most cheerful of experiences for the interviewer, and I learnt later that my mood and responses were so melancholy that they didn't use it on air for fear of depressing their audiences. I then rang my family, and told my wife of the analysis I had done. She was blunt and to the point. You have invested so much of your life in this venture, and we have all suffered to help you make it happen. To quit now would be such a waste. You cannot quit until there is absolutely no way to continue. I felt better after this ticking off, and was surprised when ten minutes later I was called back to reception to take a call from my daughter. Mandy had relayed her conversation with me to Rosie, my ten-year-old. Rosie is a good runner, and has broken various school records. One day in July before an under-11s 800m race against the best from fifteen similar schools, she had asked me, 'What happens, Dad, if I'm coming last?' I said, 'So long as you give your best, it doesn't matter; and wherever you are in the field remember you are a Cooper, and you never give up.' Rosie threw these words back at me, and I went to bed remembering that Rosie had won the race by 50 yds, and knowing that quitting was no longer an option.

Chapter IX

Never Give Up, Dad

> What is this life, if full of care
> We have no time to stand and stare.
>
> No time to stand beneath the boughs
> And stare as long as sheep or cows,
>
> No time to see, in broad daylight
> Streams full of stars, like skies at night.
>
> No time to turn at beauty's glance,
> And watch her feet, how they can dance.
>
> A poor life this if, full of care
> We have no time to stand and stare.
>
> **William Henry Davies (Leisure)**

*T*hursday, 16 September was the fourth morning I had woken up in the Kilrush Creek Marina Hotel, but this one was different. My daughter Rosie's words were still ringing in my ears, and I told the lads at breakfast of my analysis and my decision to carry on, come what may. I had somehow started believing that they would actually be quite pleased if I gave up, but Andy and Steve seemed relieved, and equally determined to succeed. Steve was later on the phone to base, finding out if the RIB charter could be extended, and Andy went off chasing the weather forecast. I also told them that my target was to get through the Pentland Firth by Friday, 8 October and that if we slipped past this deadline, I would have to have another think about whether or not to carry on. On reflection, I probably fixed this deadline more as a target for the whole team. I didn't really have any intention of calling it a day if we only rounded the Firth on 9 October.

The mood may have changed, but the weather didn't. The wind was still howling outside, and was due to ease off for a while, and then pick up to a gale again later. In the end we decided that as the forecasts (and weather) had so often changed halfway through the day, we would motor out to Loop Head at the end of the Shannon Estuary, and pick up the 1.00 p.m. update there. If it was good, we could steam up to the waypoint and get sailing. If it was bad we would come back up the Shannon again. It

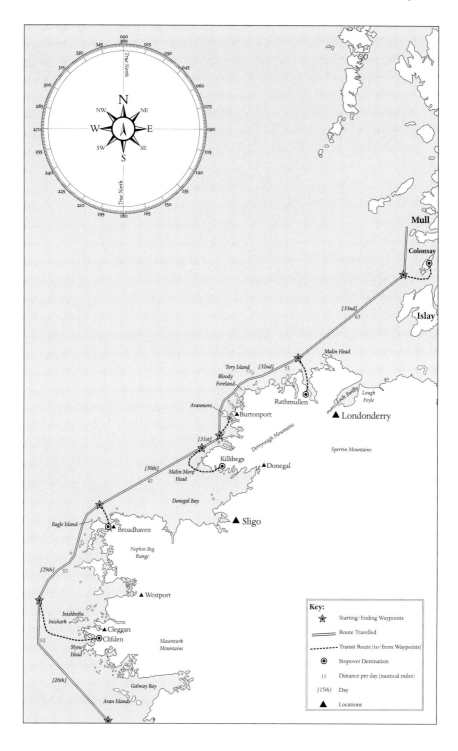

Cresting the swells off Ireland's west coast

was bad, and we returned, disappointed but not downhearted, for another night at the Kilrush Creek open prison.

The south-west F4/6 weather forecast the next morning was the first for four days that did not include some mention of 'gale force winds', and we packed our (very limited) personal possessions for the fifth time. Throughout our enforced sojourn in Kilrush, Maiden had been anchored in Clifden Bay, waiting for us to break free, so they were as pleased as us when we called to say God willing it was today. I set off beam reaching north-west from the waypoint on Katie and an 8.0m sail. The wind started as a F3 , but was quickly up to a F4. I should have gone for a smaller board, but the wind was up and down between F3 and F5, and I was comfortable and fast on this kit, so didn't change. One thing learnt on this trip was that it was far more exhausting to be on a board that was too small 20 per cent of the time, than on something that was too big 20 per cent of the time. After all the recent storms the seas were quite big (10–12 ft) but not as big as we had expected. After less than two hours beam reaching I had covered 30 miles. We then needed to turn more north, so it was over to the dreaded broad reaching in big seas. This time I was up for it, and sailed better, faster and broader than I have ever done before. The area around Slyne Head is quite shallow, and throws up some very big and dangerous seas, so we gave it a 5-mile berth.

Including all the zig-zags, I sailed more than 80 miles that day in 5.5 hours, to cover 52 miles waypoint to waypoint. It was another record day, and for me my best sailing day yet. I had proved for the first time that I could broad reach in big seas, but the day was not without mishaps. I apparently delivered the catapult to beat all catapults. According to Andy, they were following me at speed about 75 yds behind, when all of a sudden, where my head and shoulders should have been were two feet flying through the air at mach 5, followed by an almighty crack and splash. The crack was my boom end, completely destroying Katie's nose. Some 6″ of waterlogged, splintered foam and epoxy had to be rebuilt that night. She was not a pretty sight thereafter. The twilight ride into Clifden, was just spectacular, but also quite hairy. The swells were still 10–12 ft, and there seemed to be sub-surface rocks everywhere, causing these moving walls of water to ramp up and break. Maybe Steve had been right about not attempting to get into Clifden in the fading light.

Running into Clifden Bay we could see the familiar form of Maiden tied up to a mooring buoy about 300 yds from the sailing club slipway. It was a lovely feeling to finally rendezvous with our mother ship again after five days, and despite more gale warnings, the RIB and Maiden crew were quickly into the tender, and on their way to a salsa party in Clifden. Yes, a salsa party in a small town on the western extremes of sparsely populated

Connemara. Ireland was now trendy everywhere … or almost everywhere! Kilrush had somehow missed out. I was happy, but not necessarily in a salsa mood, and a good friend from Marlborough had left me a message that his brother farmed near Clifden, and they would love to have me over for dinner. I had spent nearly four weeks with my motley team, and the idea of a complete change (as much for them as me) was very appealing. I had a superb dinner with my farmer friends discussing my venture, and sheep and beef farming in this part of Ireland. Connemara was very popular with the tourists, but the thin soils and ever-present wind and rain made farming a struggle, so they supplemented their income with cottage lets, and breeding Connemara ponies.

I was offered the chance of a bath and bed for the night, which I gratefully accepted. The wind howled through the night, and I had a phone call at 7.30 a.m., saying that the water in the bay had been too rough to get everyone from the salsa party back to Maiden on the tender and therefore two had ended up sleeping in the van, and one on the floor in the nearby sailing club. Apparently the first tender shuttle nearly ended up with people swimming, so they did not risk another. The two in the van had been Tim and Gaz, who were now on their way to Dublin where Gaz would catch a flight home. I called Gaz to thank him, and wish him well, but it was clear we would not miss each other. I was looking forward to meeting Gaz's replacement, Spider, the one on the yacht club floor! It was still too rough to get out to Maiden, so Spider came back with me to the farm for the day. He was a totally different character, quieter, more reserved, sincere and sensible. I left Spider recovering from his night of discomfort, and the biggest cooked breakfast he had ever seen; and then went into Clifden, to do my regular Saturday morning update for Classic FM, and several other local radio interviews. My minder was a fast-talking, chain-smoking Irishman named Damian, who the others had found in a bar the night before, and immediately hired as replacement crew. Damian had been involved in a serious road accident some years ago, and was not able to walk without crutches. This did not stop him running the local sailing school, and he jumped at the chance to spend five weeks on Maiden, gathering valuable sea miles for his yachtmaster qualification. The rationale for taking on Damian was apparently that … every boat needs an Irishman aboard … perfectly logical.

The wind had now eased to F4/5, but a much bigger storm (Force 10) was on its way, and Steve had no intention of going out, so I relaxed and went for a long walk down a promontory on my farmer friend's land. The farmhouse was set in a protective huddle of wind-angled trees, about 200 yds up from the north-east shore of Cleggan Bay. My perfect place to live had always been a rambling farmhouse with its own fields rolling down to the sea. Ideally my place should be on a relatively sheltered bay or estuary, but with easy access to a rugged west-facing shore where I could go to watch the real weather happen. Some offshore islands to explore would complete the picture. This place had it all, and more. It even had its own lighthouse, and the point of the promontory faced out towards the spectacular Inishbofin and Inishark Islands. What an absolute paradise for adventuring children, artists and writers. I sat up on the crest of the promontory and watched an amazing light show out at sea. I don't know specifically what was happening, but several broad columns of glistening light were moving across the horizon. It seemed like gaps in the cloud were skilfully allowing sunlight through just where there was light rain to illuminate. It made me think how easy it would be to take something like this as a celestial vision or heavenly apparition. It also brought me back to religion again and a recurring thought that the natural world was simply too beautiful and too perfect to have been created by planetary and evolutionary chance. For the rest of that day I pretty much forgot about why I was there, and soaked up the glory of this place, daydreaming about coming back here with my family.

The promised southerly force 10 storm arrived that night, and persisted through the next day. I went exploring again, this time borrowing a car, and driving around to the exposed south-west-facing shores. Up on the cliffs, it was virtually impossible to stand, as the wind gusted up to something like 60–70 knots. My farmer friend told me that gusts of 100 knots are not that unusual there! The seas off the south coast of Ireland must have been awesome after this. Fortunately the storms, and thus seas, were very much from the south, giving us some protection for our destined northerly and then north-easterly route. Back on Maiden most of the team didn't dare to try and get ashore, and spent the best part of two days shipbound, getting over the salsa party hangovers, reading and playing cards. Terry and Duncan had managed to get ashore, and both had decided to fly home and take a break from the livethatdream experience, Duncan for family reasons, and Terry for business. The doing-nothing stress of Kilrush and Clifden had also taken its toll on Andy, who told me that he wanted to take a break to sort out his future life, once we got to Scotland. The team was looking particularly thin, and Maiden evidently no longer had enough crew to raise the sails. I spent some time on the phone looking for new volunteers, but after a while slipped back into the 'what will be will be' mentality.

I finished off my day back in front of the fire at the farm thinking about uncertainty. We all live with it. Most of us try and minimise it; some of us go in search of it. My life before this adventure had been very low on the 'uncertainty scale'. I had a regular income, a stable, enjoyable family life, played golf every Saturday morning, and generally knew who I would be with, and what I would be doing, days and maybe even weeks in advance. This adventure was right at the other end of the scale. I was with eleven people I had hardly known four weeks before. I didn't know where I would be the next day, never mind weeks in advance. The problems I was having to deal with were all new to me. My twenty years of business training was more of a burden than an asset. I habitually wanted to analyze scenarios and make predictions. I suppose I was looking for control, or at least probabilities; and it took several weeks for me to realise that on a mission such as this there is no control – only efficient adaptation to rapidly changing circumstances. Maybe this was chaos theory in action. Chaos theory in a biological context hypothesises that populations adapt much more rapidly when subjected to chaotic stress. The argument goes that if you want your company or your team to adapt and embrace, rather than resist change, it is counterproductive to have rigid organisational structures, the inference being that a degree of chaos and lack of control is good.

I also became somewhat anal about the whole trip, trying to differentiate between enjoyment and achievement. Most of the achievement was simply about making the miles, and generating that collective 'we did it feeling'. There was also the knowledge that my supporters back at home were achieving with me. I suppose I was further achieving by improving my windsurfing in difficult conditions, and sorting out crew problems. The enjoyment came mostly from the journey itself, and the wonderful people, places and environments we experienced. Most of the windsurfing was not enjoyable in the recreational sense of the word; but every now and again, I would be at one with my kit and the conditions, and enjoy effortlessly gliding across the sea. With all the setbacks and conflicts, the team spirit tended to wax and wane, but there was still plenty of humour and wit to enjoy. I wondered whether I, Richard Cooper, had the right balance of achievement vs enjoyment in my life? Was it even useful to try and split the two. Maybe some people enjoy achieving, and some simply enjoy enjoying. I was probably perceived by the Livethatdream team as an obsessive achiever, whereas in Finland, relative to my very serious senior colleagues, I was probably one step beyond Bacchus.

The thought processes went further into categorising people on the team who were primarily there to either achieve or enjoy. Tim, Sarah, Duncan and Kevin to me seemed like 'enjoyers', whereas Terry, John and Steve were 'achievers'. Interestingly, the enjoyers were much easier to manage, and if anything more committed to the success of the venture. The achievers were difficult because they didn't necessarily have my agenda at heart. Andy, I couldn't place, but thinking about Andy took me onto the subject of patience. Why was it that we clashed so much over matters of time. I was always desperate to get out there, as soon as possible, and sail as long as possible to maximise the miles covered. Andy didn't see the point. He felt that the sea and wind would be there tomorrow, and a long there-and-back transit ride for me to cover 10–15 miles was a waste of time. To me, I was 10–15 miles nearer my destination, and had the satisfaction of making progress. Probably the real explanation for our dichotomy was our immediate history. I had spent years running at 100 miles per hour trying to fit a demanding job, expanding family and selfish pleasures into a sixteen-hour day. Andy had lived in Barbados running a windsurf and sailing school ... enough said!

My last pondering topic that day was whether I would get the most satisfaction out of the 'doing' or the 'completion' of this crazy venture. Whilst en route, I felt that the much longed for pleasure of a successful completion would be the climax to beat all climaxes; or maybe not, and once I'd had my finishing climax, maybe the vivid memories of the 'doing' would be that much more important! No sexual parallels here of course!

Clifden had obviously given me too much time to think, but as my function was to windsurf round Britain and Ireland, rather than pontificate on subjects far better addressed by real thinkers, it was time to go sailing. I said goodbye to the idyllic Cleggan farm, and thanked my new-found friends for their wonderful hospitality. Day 29 (Sunday, 19 September) dawned bright and clear, with a F4/6 south-easterly wind forecast. This was a bad direction for the initial run north, but for once the wind gods smiled upon us, and by the time I had started sailing it had backed more to the east. I had a brilliant F4 start on Katie, beam reaching from our waypoint off Inishark, past lovely Inishbofin, and Clare Island towards imposing Achill Head. For the first time in weeks we had an offshore wind which meant I could sail in close enough to the rocks and headlands to get a good view, but not close enough to get in their windshadows. I was averaging a good 17–18 knots, and just as we were about to call Maiden, and suggest a more distant stopover, the wind died down to a F2/3 and I was back on Big Bertha with a 10.0m sail. The rest of the day was a slog, particularly tacking round Eagle Island off Belmullet against the tide. In total I had sailed some 60 miles in just over seven hours, to cover a record-equalling 52 miles. Spider did well on his first day and the atmosphere on the RIB was good. Maiden was struggling to get onto a mooring buoy off Broadhaven when we arrived, and needed assistance from the RIB crew, which they were not allowed to forget.

The next day started with light F2 winds from the east, and I plodded purposefully north-east across Donegal Bay on Big Bertha and a damaged 10.0m sail. I sailed for many hours looking at the panel split getting inexorably wider, expecting a huge crack and tear any moment, but with due credit to Tim and Andy's repairs it held firm. The wind picked up to F4/5 halfway through the day, and I was struggling to hang onto this mammoth sail. For the first time on the whole trip, the RIB team were not paying attention and had run 500m ahead of me. With my VHF radio having long since packed up, I had no way of attracting their attention, and became very frustrated when my frantic one-hand wave had no effect. I then stopped and let the sail fall onto the sea. They might not see my waving hand, but they would hopefully (?) notice if I was no longer following them! My tactic thankfully worked, and they quickly had an irate windsurfer on board. At first we tried to depower the 10.0m sail by putting on some more downhaul, but this only succeeded in opening the old injury near the foot of the sail, rendering it unusable until repaired that night. We had no choice but to go down to the 8.0m sail, which ended up being spot on as the wind levelled out at a steady F5. I was still beating on Big Bertha, but in this wind had the track right forward and the daggerboard inclined at about 30 degrees to vertical to kill some of the lift. For the last three hours I was also sailing into a driving rain, unable to look directly ahead without 40 mph (closing velocity) raindrops taking out my eyes. It was not the most pleasant day's windsurfing I can ever remember, but there was still some magic in the air when the dark and mysterious Malin More Head took shape through the rain 3–4 miles away. I stopped to get some navigational input from the RIB, and there was some talk of packing up for the day as we were now heading away from Killibegs, our stopover destination, but for whatever reason, the lads gave me an extra hour's sailing north, in the driving rain and steepening seas. By the time we packed up, I had sailed for 7.5 hours, and covered 47 miles. The rain lifted for the ride back into Killibegs, and the bright clear evening sky reflected my buoyant mood. Clifden and Kilrush seemed so far away now.

For our last five full days' sailing we had recorded distances of 47, 52, 52, 45, and 43 miles (average 48). These distances had also been achieved in mostly downwind or upwind conditions, meaning the distances sailed were much longer. We now had only about 125 miles to go to Scotland, and a further 200 miles up to Cape Wrath. For the first time Scotland actually felt reachable by the early October deadline I had set. I had no choice but to spend most of the RIB ride into Killibegs doing mental arithmetic, as an essential diversion to override the increasingly urgent requests for an emergency evacuation from the other end of my body. One of my problems on this trip had been the dreaded 'irregular bowl movements syndrome'. My high energy, high sugar, high fat diet had not been accepted by my internal planning department, and I had several times been caught very short out on the ocean. There are of course more pleasant ways to do a #2 than hanging off the back of a RIB, in a force 5 rainstorm, with life-sustaining wetsuit wrapped around one's ankles, so on this particular occasion I was determined to make it to Killibegs. I did make it just, but only because (in the words of Andy) 'never in the field of human conflict, has a neoprene body glove been removed at such speed, and with such evident relief, one thousandth of a millisecond later'.

As a bustling industrial fishing port, Killibegs was the Newlyn of Ireland, and very very different from anywhere else we had been. The accents were closer to Belfast than Baltimore, and the demeanour aggressive and unhelpful. I was charged £3 for a shower in a local health club, which contrasted sharply with the pure Irish arrangement in Fenit, where the showers were free, but if you wanted privacy, then the door lock needed £1! We were again tied up outside various fishing vessels, but the multi-million £ hardware on view across the harbour seemed one step beyond what we had seen in Newlyn. One local claimed that Killybegs was the biggest fishing port in Britain and Ireland. Who was I to argue? We tested out a dockside pub that night, but its clientele were nowhere near as colourful and desparate as those we had encountered in Newlyn. One way or another Killybegs was one of our least memorable stopovers, but maybe my eyes had closed as my mind gloated on the successes of the last few days. All good things of course come to an end, and the gale warnings were back on the evening forecast. There was also another goodbye to handle. Sophie was finally leaving, and Sarah had volunteered to take over running the project budget. We thus had a 'budget handover meeting', where I tried my best to look concerned about the mounting cost overruns. Despite my cost-careful preachings to the team, within myself I was past caring. It was only money. When it's gone it's gone, and there is always a chance to make some more, whereas I only had one chance to make history.

Day 31 (21 September) dawned wet and stormy, so we were going nowhere unless the midday forecast was more favourable. It duly delivered an update, which seemed OK to me but too risky to Steve, with F5/6 southerly winds, occasionally gale force 7/8, and rough seas off exposed headlands. Rough in 'weather forecast speak' means 4m, or 15ft + swells. Steve and Andy were nervous and reluctant, but I cajoled them into grumpily giving it a go on the basis that we would be heading north-east, in hopefully flatter offshore wind conditions. The wind was only F4 when we arrived at the waypoint, but five minutes after I had been turfed into the water, it was up to a good F6, and broad reaching with my 8.0m sail was impossible. We changed to a 5.0m sail, and a small 28 cm fin on Lady Di, but we had got too close to the Malin More cliffs, and the wind was gusty (F4/7) and swirling, meaning I fell in a lot, and struggled to make progress downwind. After so much time with much bigger sails and boards, my small-board-small-sail technique had gone from average to appalling, and I couldn't seem to get the harness lines correctly positioned for high-speed downwind sailing. I didn't get on well with Lady Di that day, which did not bode well for our future relationship. Lots of excuses, but the end result was that after less than two hours, we packed up having sailed more than 20 miles but progressed only 8.5 miles in the appropriate direction. Andy and Steve were almost smirking that their 'waste of time going out' predictions had been proved correct. I didn't see it that way. I had failed to handle the conditions, but we had moved 8.5 miles nearer to our final destination, and those 8.5 miles could end up being critical if we became held up a few miles short of the finish line and missed beating Keith Russell's record by a few hours. Keith Russell had broken the Round Britain record with a time of sixty-two days, and our sudden surge of progress had got me thinking that if we managed to get round Britain *and Ireland* in less that sixty-two days, it would give a big boost to the publicity and respect.

Whilst struggling to complete my epic 8.5-mile success, I had not noticed the squally showers. In true Irish tradition, as soon as I started to get out of my wetsuit and into theoretically dry clothes, the space between raindrops was reduced to insignificant, and their penetrative ability increased to maximum. It was thus a very wet and cold run into our designated anchorage off Stackamore Quay inside Aranmore. The west-facing cliffs of Aranmore were as spectacular as anything we had seen, and I made a mental note to come this way again soon ... without the driving rain! Maiden was well behind us and we were desperately in need of warmth and sustenance. As always, despite the early hour (5.00 p.m.) there was an open, run-down, but friendly pub, populated by a handful of drunken regulars. I was first to arrive, and not sure if it was open, knocked on the door. A happy-looking middle-aged lady beckoned me in, and then nearly collapsed into my arms as she made the tortuous journey back to the bar. We trapezed in clad in sodden Gore-tex oilies, and dripped gallons of pure rain water over their worn-out carpet. The landlord found us somewhere to hang our 50 kgs of breathable (?) apparel, and we settled down to test the Aran Island Guinness. Maiden arrived as the light started to fade, and yet again had great difficulty getting hooked onto a mooring buoy in the strong winds and choppy conditions. This time we used the RIB like a tug to push her into position, and at one stage were inches away from Maiden's bow destroying the RIB's A-frame. Steve's mood was thus black and blue; and Kevin got his timing absolutely wrong, when as soon as Maiden was secured, he asked Steve to take the RIB in darkness through a tricky channel into Burtonport, to pick up his girlfriend Lucy. Needless to say Lucy had to check into a B&B for the night.

Tim joined us on the RIB for Day 32, as he would be taking over from Andy as soon as we reached the Scottish mainland. I was looking forward to Tim's ever-helpful, positive way of working, but was worried about losing Andy's technical input, and strength of character and body. The forecast wind was south-east F3/4 going east F5/7, so a reasonably favourable direction for our north-east route. Once round the aptly named Bloody Foreland Head, we would be turning more east than north, for the third of our six main corners. This was a big day. If we could do another 50 miles or more, we could be in a position to go for a crossing to Scotland the next day.

With the wind from the east, and a falling air temperature, it was time to change from summer to winter steamer (a thicker wetsuit with full length arms) for the first time. My day's sailing started gently with a F2/3 wind broad reaching, and then the wind backed to the east and increased F3/4. I had started on Big Bertha with the repaired 10.0m sail, and once up and running at good speed, had no intention of upsetting her or the wind gods with a change. In the offshore conditions the water was as flat as we had seen since the Celtic Sea, and I was able to retract the daggerboard, slide the mastrack back to its most rearward position, sheet in hard, and settle into the back straps for a glorious sunny beam reach at 17–18 knots past the wonderful sea cliffs of Aranmore. It of course had to be sunny the day I changed to the winter steamer, and the sweat was dripping off the end of my nose. The change to the winter steamer also gave the RIB crew one of their biggest laughs of the week at my expense. At significant cost, this wetsuit had been fitted with a 'pee-zip' which was a horizontal waterproof zip glued into the suit running roughly from groin to groin. A similar zip in my summer steamer had worked perfectly, meaning I could kneel on the board, extract my old boy, and comfortably bladder-empty. This time, I had left it a bit late, and was bursting, but after having ripped the zip across, couldn't seem to get into the airspace where my old boy was waiting. After minutes of desperate struggle, and uncontrolled tittering from the RIB behind, I realised that the people who had glued on the pee-zip had forgotten to cut a hole in the neoprene behind. I had a 'no way out' situation, and the rest (as they say) is history.

As we came past the northern end of Aranmore, I could see Maiden in the distance plodding her way out onto our line. It was the first time we had sailed together for weeks, but the experience was short lived as I blasted past at twice her speed, with the foot of the sail firmly locked onto the deck of the board for maximum aerodynamic efficiency. Showing off is never a good idea and fifteen minutes later the wind dropped to F2/3, and my line had to shift to just north of east, meaning I had to sail on a slower, higher line. The sweeping expanse of Bloody Foreland, and the Derryveah mountains were a superb backdrop to a gorgeous morning's sailing. The track up from Aran Island to Bloody Foreland was about 12–15 miles but felt timeless to me. Cruising at sea, along an enthralling ever-changing coastline, was like a form of meditation. I just became completely wrapped up in the presence and beauty and variety of what was around me. Time slows down, and the mind is gloriously empty of other diversions.

Once past Bloody Foreland the wind dropped further, and we had a west-flowing tide against us. The next two hours were a slow and tedious struggle upwind and uptide in 5–6 knots of wind. We lunched just south-west of the strangely named Tory Island, which apparently has its own King (according to that well-known literary classic, *Round Ireland with a Fridge*). To me it looked a bit like a lump of coastline, that had been cast away to sea, with a splattering of beach huts and holiday chalets. My livethatdream fairy godmother had, however, one more gift to bestow that day, as a steady F3/4 returned, and I cut effortlessly into the wind, with Big Bertha permanently railed up on full daggerboard. After so many hours at sea, in a tempestuous love-hate relationship, I was starting to read its myriad patterns and movement, but its behaviour that day was certainly unusual. Normally I would be able to look at the confused movement under my feet, and pick up the lines of both the distant-born swells and the local wind-blown waves. Today had a neat north-south axis to the swells, but I seemed to be gliding over one line, and then crashing into the next. Then it suddenly dawned on me that the swells were running west to east, and the wind-blown stuff east to west, quite an unusual bakwash-type occurrence which would also be short lived as they cancelled out each other's energy.

We made another 20 miles north-east over the next few hours to end the day just north of Lough Swilly, having covered a brilliant 51 miles, and sailed more than 65. On the way into our rendezvous with Maiden on Rathmullen quay, we stopped in at Buncrana harbour on the eastern side of the lough, to try and find some fuel. The next sea loch along from Lough Swilly, around the other side of Malin Head, is Lough Foyle with Derry at its head. We were thus only a few miles from the border with Northern Ireland, and I somehow expected a Killibegs-like coolness. We asked some blokes messing around in a boat where the nearest marine diesel was. They gave us multiple options, each with copious background information (we were still in Ireland). The easiest option seemed to be a garage 400 yds away, or a similar garage in Rathmullen. They then offered to organise a set of jerry cans, and help us relay 40 gallons of fuel from garage to RIB (not the most pleasant favour to implement!). We were absolutely definitely still in Ireland.

Kevin and girlfriend Lucy had checked into a local B&B for the night.

They had been apart for more than a month, and any form of intimacy was a tad impractical on Maiden, with 18″ wide hammocks, and eight other observers in the same airspace. Whilst Kevin and Lucy were taking a short rest break in the bar between bouts of mad passionate thrashing, I was allowed to use their lovely hot shower. Whilst washing away the foul-smelling layer of body exudate and stale sea water that coated my body every day, I suddenly realised that something was not quite right. The mood and atmosphere among the troops was upbeat and relaxed. Everyone was happy, and it had been several days since the last communal depression or row. I couldn't pin it down at first, but then realised that the permanent tension between Maiden's crew and skipper, and between the Maiden team and the RIB team was no longer there. It then suddenly dawned on me that the kick-point had been when Kevin took over from Terry as skipper of Maiden. Had the extra miles we were achieving distressed the team, or was the distressed team able to cover more miles. Egg-Chicken or Chicken-Egg? All academic but good news anyway.

The meeting that night to decide upon tomorrow's strategy was, however, still tense. It was a big call. We were still 70 miles from Port Ellen on the south-east corner of Islay, our designated next stopover. The forecast was east-south-east F5/6 which would mean beating into some pretty rough seas. The worst possible scenario would be if we only made it halfway, giving long transits in and out again in heavy seas. Once out on the water, the power of our VHF radios was such that we could not communicate directly with Maiden, unless within 10 miles of each other. The RIB could also at times be out of range of any coastguard who could provide a relay to Maiden. We had to stay close, to avoid a situation where the RIB ended up coming back to Ireland whilst Maiden was enjoying Islay's traditional hospitality. Even this was easier said than done. If I happened to get the right conditions, and could power along at twice Maiden's speed, with a 70-mile day in my sights, I was unlikely to be over the moon if asked to sit on my board while we wait for Maiden to get in range so we can have a little chin-wag! The decision taken was no decision. We would wait for the early morning forecast, and take a decision then.

Steve was still nervous, but the forecast came over as east F5/6 dropping south-east F4, with light to moderate seas. This was better than last night's forecast. The second major sea crossing was on. After all the angst, we arrived at the waypoint at 9.00 a.m., to be greeted by a solid F2 from the east (another reliable forecast!). It had to be Big Bertha and the 10.0m sail (again) and I manfully spent the first three hours sailing with around 5 knots board speed, as tight to wind as I could, roughly north-east. The line for Islay was not far off due east, meaning a direct beat into wind, meaning a halving of distance I could expect to cover. The common-sense suggestion, to carry on close hauled north-east towards the island of Colonsay, first came from Kevin over the radio, but was readily accepted by the RIB team and myself. According to the charts there was a suitable ferry pier on the sheltered eastern side of the island. The day was dank, rainy and grey, with only the occasional fishing boat to disturb the visual monotony. Fortunately as the heavy showers passed through, replacing the drizzle, they brought an increase in the wind up to 8–9 knots, which significantly boosted my average speed, and took us well ahead of Maiden.

After eight hours and 55 miles covered (already a new record), the land masses of Islay's and Colonsay's western shores drifted in and out of view through what seemed like sea-level cloud. I had only stopped for fifteen minutes, during eight hours sailing on one starboard tack; but any tiredness I had just evaporated like petrol on a hot summer's day as these dark brooding forms came into view. I had at last conquered Ireland, and would soon be back on British soil. Two weeks before I had still been riddled with self-doubt, and practical worries about getting around Scotland before we became trapped by winter. Now, the self-doubt had gone. If it could be done, I was going to do it. It's amazing how quickly the body tires when the mind has given up, but conversely a soaring spirit brooks no excuses, and I could have sailed for ever that night. I was dragged out of my euphoria by the RIB team at 6.30 p.m., just a few miles east of Colonsay, and 63 miles from our morning start point (another record day). They had spent nearly nine hours following me in the featureless drizzle, and despite sharing my glowing satisfaction, were not totally enthusiastic about tracking north with me towards Mull under cover of rainy darkness!

The ride into Colonsay was flat and easy, but there didn't seem to be anything there apart from an old ferry pier, a telephone box, and a half-road disappearing into the gloom. I part expected the theme tune from the film *Local Hero* to strike up in the background, as we stood looking lost and forlorn on the quayside wondering what to do next. Devoid of other options we set off up the half-road, and a quarter of a mile on turned a corner into a half-village, with a full-sized pub. The pub's clientele were a mixture of locals and out-of-season tourists. We had great difficulty passing as locals or touring yachties. Steve would die if ever taken for a yachtie, and not having the luxury of a cabin in which to change, we would invariably stagger into the pub clad in dripping, foul-weather oilies. Not unsurprisingly our crossing from Ireland (on a windsurfer??), and voyage so far, sparked a great deal of interest and banter. In between bouts of 'mission PR' and 'locality bonding', which roughly translated means buying and taking drinks at will, whilst exaggerating the epicness of our very epic journey, we sat down for one of the most welcome pub dinners I will ever have. The atmosphere between the four of us (Steve, Andy, Spider and myself) was warm and laden with a strong sense of team achievement. It simply felt very very good, and even Steve was in congratulatory mood. This worried me somewhat. Had three days of sailing in the rain leached out his ingrained grumpy demeanour? I was not confident he would be able to drive the RIB and smile at the same time, but comforted myself with the certainty that a good night's sleep would see him staggering out of his bunk as surly and uncommunicative as ever. Maiden arrived at Colonsay just after we had run out of epic stories, and had to leave the pub. They were as chuffed as we were with the day's achievement, and also felt rightly integral to this success with their routing advice. Once in my bunk, my body finally got the message through to my brain that it was shot to bits; but I was still too excited to sleep. There was still one last piece of mental arithmetic to do. We had now completed 799 miles. Estimates for the full distance were very dependent upon our routing. A coast-hugging route could be over 2,000 miles. A straight-line approach could be as little as 1,700 miles. Our plan was obviously the latter, but weather conditions might dictate otherwise. Anyway, the bottom line was that with another 50-mile+ day the next day, we could, in theory, be close to half way after thirty-four days sailing. The old cliché of 'one step at a time' had worked its magic again, and there was something very powerful about the thought of having less distance to do than we had already done. I also thought to myself that I must call Rosie and tell her that her advice seemed to be working.

Chapter X

Harsh Unpredictable Scotland

> The real voyage of discovery consists not
> in seeking new landscapes,
> but in having new eyes.
>
> **Proust**

*M*y watch alarm commenced its horrible morning bleeping at 6.00 a.m. Whilst staggering purposefully towards the heads for my urgent early morning evacuation, I realised that there was a reason for this 6.00 a.m. start. I had stupidly agreed to do a radio interview with Wave FM from Portsmouth at 6.15 a.m. Our mobile phones were useless this far off the beaten track, and I had to use the pier-end phonebox ... more *Local Hero* music ... Wave FM had been following us all the way round, and were one of the stations who wanted weekly soundbites from the man himself. I was half-asleep, but still buoyant from the previous day's crossing. After the normal updates and description of our current location, the interviewer asked me what I thought about during hour after hour of plodding monotony. It was too early to think per se, let alone think about what I was thinking about whilst windsurfing. I gave a waffly, thoughtless answer, and finished the call with a note to myself that this question was something I had to ponder on. Back on Maiden, the rest of the crew were still asleep, so I got my notepad out in the nav station, and started scribbling on the mental aspects of the challenge.

The mental side was probably as challenging if not more so than the physical side, and had several different components. First the daily task of getting my tired achy body out of bed, and into a cold, wet, smelly wetsuit every morning 'hungry for miles', when the conditions were miserable, and the rest of the team far from enthusiastic. Second, the simple challenge of keeping going when the progress was painfully slow, and the easy option would have been to pack in early for the day, and believe the forecast for better conditions tomorrow. Scratching 18 miles out of a day when the wind never exceeds 4 knots is very much a mental rather than physical challenge. Communication with the RIB was an often-used boredom breaker and motivator. I would regularly be asking them for SOG (speed over the ground) heading, and distance covered. I found it much easier to keep going, knowing how far we had come, and being able to do mental predictions of how far we could expect to cover by the end of the day.

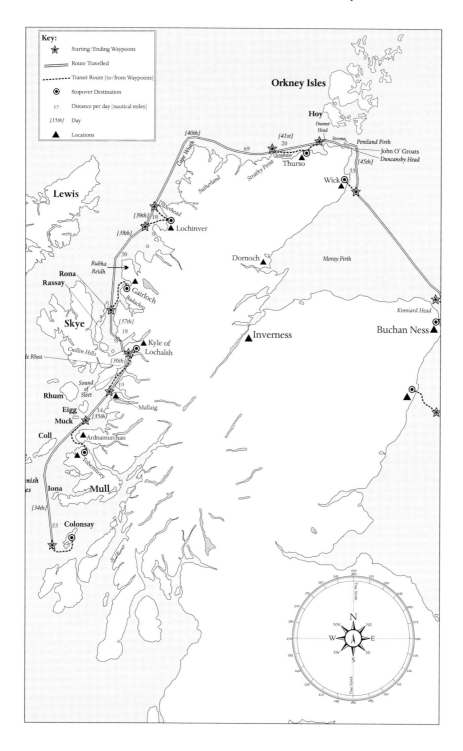

The most direct answer to what I thought about whilst sailing would be that I tended to be absorbed in what was around me. I would be constantly watching the sea, and its myriad patterns of movement, in tandem with monitoring the behaviour of my board on that sea surface. Understanding why the sea was behaving in a certain way would help me enhance board speed, by harnessing rather than being harassed by its rolling lumpiness. Big Bertha was much more complicated to sail than the others, and not having had any serious long-board racing experience, it took me weeks of tinkering to get the right combination of daggerboard angle and mastrack position for a given set of upwind or downwind conditions. I would also be constantly feeling for changes in wind strength and direction, and analysing whether my rig was set up absolutely right for the conditions. My eyes were focused on the sea directly ahead, but also on the horizon, and the all-around seascape and skyscape. I was permanently on the lookout for wildlife, and trying to match headlands and bays with my mental map of the area. It was much easier to stay mentally absorbed with the job in hand when I was physically comfortable. Being too hot, too cold, hungry, thirsty, sleepy, or reluctantly reminded of an irritating sore or aching joint would always slow the passage of time.

At times it seemed like we were very much engaged in a battle of wits and determination against the wind and weather, which consequently took on the personality of a seductive, manipulative, and malicious mistress. Our decision making and thus progress was so dependent upon making the right call on what the wind and weather would do. We got it wrong more often than right, and often it was almost too predictably wrong to be coincidental. It seemed that every time we went for a board or sail change, the wind gods would make us look silly; and at times, I could almost see this demented chuckling face, watching me seething with frustration, after a newly arrived F5 had died back to F3 as soon as the 10.0m sail was packed away, and the 6.0m plugged into the board. It was either going to drive me deeply religious, atheist or insane. After a few weeks we had learnt to be very patient, and that I had to manage with the 'wrong' sail until there was no other option. I had some huge temper tantrums, and also came very close to tears on several occasions when humiliatingly outwitted by the wily weather.

Keeping going, and keeping mentally alive was always easier when there was a goal in sight such as a headland or landmark to pass, and when the sailing was quite technical or fast. The slow tedious days on a grey featureless sea needed different tricks. We would set a mile or time goal, achievement of which would be rewarded with a hot drink stop. I would set my own little targets, such as not allowing myself a pee-stop, until a certain target had been reached. I would also have a series of daydream/

fantasy themes, which I could sometimes switch on to relieve the boredom, when the wind/sea/board/sail dynamics were too steady and predictable to hold my attention. One of the fantasies was of course the triumphal finish down the Solent surrounded by a heaving flotilla of well-wishers. Other fantasies were equally ridiculous, but not for public disclosure. This would have been a long speech for the Wave FM reporter, but at least I had now committed some thoughts to paper.

Colonsay was a lovely stopover in many ways, and for the first time on the whole trip I was actually quite sad to leave the next morning. The big decision for the day was whether we went inside or outside the Isle of Mull. The forecast was for gentle winds from the south-west, and as the outside route was shorter, it was an easy decision. The only downside was that I needed to head due north, meaning a very broad reach. I set off wobbling my way towards the island of Iona, off Mull's south-west tip, on Big Bertha and the 10.0m sail, in F2 winds. We had not been going long when Andy noticed that his repairs done to Big Bertha's damaged port quarter rail had disintegrated, and the sea water was enthusiastically permeating her innards. This was bad bad news. A serious water ingress could cause the whole structure to delaminate. A replacement could take days to arrive, and in light winds we would not be going anywhere without this bulky, durable lady under my feet. Bertha was hauled aboard the RIB and the still localised water drained out. Andy then did another emergency repair using a whole tube of Dr Ding quick-setting hole filler. It might last the day, but we needed either a more permanent specialist repair or a replacement board very soon.

The wind gods were in a good mood, and the forecast south-westerlies veered more west, easing my directional difficulties. We also had a series of squally showers, where the wind picked up to F3/4. Feeling brave, and a bit protective of Big Bertha, I quickly switched to Katie during this squally phase, and on the flat seas we covered around 20 miles in not much over an hour. The rain was like being in a 'top-of-the-range' power-shower; not the densely packed 'more-water-than-air' Irish rain, but the 'big-crashing-droplets' Scottish version. I passed the amazingly shaped Treshnish (or Dutchman's cap) Islands to my right, and despite being pounded by the aforementioned squall, could see the east-facing beaches of Tiree 10 miles away bathed in sunshine. The charm of the weather experienced in the Western Isles is that it all happens at once. The skies are fascinating to watch when a front passes through at speed, with the contrasting warm sector/cold sector skyscape so evident. After the squalls had spent their watery energy, I had to get back onto Bertha and continued the day's sailing in a steady F2, heading north with the islands of low-lying Coll on my left, and mountainous Mull on my right. The cold-sector visibility was now superb, and as we tracked further north round the point of Ardnamurchan; I was simply lost in the splendour of it all.

By 6.00 p.m. I had sailed for seven hours, and covered another invaluable 53 miles, to lie just east of the wonderfully named isle of Muck. There was a gentle 3–5 knots of wind, but I was getting some help from the tide, giving a SOG of around 5–6 knots. I was tired, but felt that I might as well continue for another 45 mins, until the light started to fade. The RIB crew felt otherwise, and I was decidedly grumpy, being ordered to stop, whilst there were still 'miles on the table'. Their reasoning was that we needed to have enough time to get into Tobermory, our stopover rendezvous with Maiden, before nightfall. As it happened we were into Tobermory with at least forty-five minutes to spare, but my grumpy mood was effortlessly banished by the gorgeous vista of this famous island harbour. A big part of the impact is its suddenness. One moment we were cruising past the uninhabited craggy northern shores of Mull, and then rounding greener, tree-covered, east-facing headlands; and then there it was, nestling at the head of a steep-sided inlet. Everything is packed quite close to the water's edge, and the buildings seemed to be Victorian in shape, and Celtic/Nordic in colour with soft pink and blue-painted houses. It was also a lovely clear late September evening, and we had just done our third successive 50-mile+ day. Life was good, and I decided it was time to give the troops a meal out ashore. The team were as relaxed and together as they had ever been. This was maybe also the first time I had relaxed enough to put my all-consuming ambition to the back of my mind for a while. However, I still went off to sleep doing my normal mental arithmetic, working out that with five more days averaging 40 miles we would be through the Pentland Firth on 29 September and that I would only accept that our probability of success was over 50:50 once through this daunting obstacle. While I was fast asleep (no doubt with my subconscious still checking the calculations) the others were celebrating Andy's last night, and bonding effortlessly with the locals during a sustained tequila slammer frenzy.

Andy and John Beecroft left the next morning early, and I wondered whether I would see them back on the project. Andy had honestly left it open, saying that we should speak after 7–8 days. I said I definitely wanted him back, but would understand if he needed to focus on getting a proper job. John had gone to sound out various production companies, as to the saleability of the film he was making. With Andy and John leaving we were getting quite short of bodies. Terry and Duncan had returned from their breaks, but Terry wasn't sure how long he could stay. Even with Terry, Maiden was down to a crew of four, meaning they were motoring everywhere, and more importantly the food preparation rotas came round that bit quicker.

The tide was forecast to be against us all the next morning and the forecast was for light and variable winds. We also needed to do some maintenance on the RIB, so it was an easy decision to declare a morning off. I bought some more robust epoxy filler, and set about doing a more permanent job on Bertha. The RIB team serviced the RIB. Maiden was reprovisioned, and I did my normal series of Saturday morning radio interviews. There was also time for wandering around Tobomoray's quaint harbourside shops ... such luxury ... whatever next? We were out to the waypoint by 1 p.m., but there were only 2–3 knots of wind from the south, and the following tide was less than 1 knot. I dutifully plodded forward, on a dead downwind run, with a SOG of less than 3 knots. After the blinding succession of 50-mile+ days, this return to the Celtic Sea-like stagnation was tough to take. The tidal atlas that we were using indicated very strong tides (up to 6 knots) approaching and going through the Kyle of Rhea, some 20–25 miles ahead. If only I could get to this race whilst the tide was still flowing north (by 6.00 p.m.) we could hitch a ride all the way to Kyle of Lochalsh, 33 miles away, and the non-existent wind would be irrelevant. The tidal atlases can only give a macro picture. Local effects, particularly in an island-strewn passage such as this, can be very different from the predicted macro flows, as we were soon to discover.

After two hours and only 5 miles covered, the wind died completely, and I sat calmly on my board having a coffee and a sandwich. This was something I would always do if we had favourable tide. There are no specified rules for round Britain windsurfers, but after referring to Tim Batsone's book, we decided that as long as I was on my board, whether with sail hoisted or not, any tidally assisted forward progress was valid. Of course, in an adverse tide, we would quickly take an interim waypoint, and I would climb into the RIB to lunch, returning afterwards to our restart position. After a twenty-minute rest, and interaction with a couple of friendly seals, I asked the RIB for my speed and direction of drift. They answered that I was being taken west towards the Isle of Eigg at 1 knot, rather than north-east as predicted by the tide tables. This was not what I needed. For a while, I removed the daggerboard and started to paddle north (also something Batstone had done), but this was very hard work and gave me less than 2 knots SOG. I was still, however, convinced that once away from the Isle of Eigg, and into the narrowing Sound of Sleet, the tide would pick me up and whisk me northwards. In the end the slightest of breezes returned, and I was able to pump another 5–6 miles up the sound. The tide had no interest in whisking me anywhere, and the bottom line for the day was a pathetic 13.5 miles covered in five hours, to now sit some 2 miles north-west of Mallaig. I still felt that I should have been allowed to pump for another 3–4 miles, but gave in again to the edict of our safety officer.

I could not disguise my gnawing frustration. If we had kept going for another 5–6 miles last night, we could have caught today's tidal bus, and been 15 miles further on. Every decision taken has its cascade of implications which become evident over time. The only thing we could do was to think carefully about the 'what ifs' and based on the forecast and some assessment of probabilities, make our decisions. If this had been a race, we would have been much more focused on this way of working. Maybe it was a race to me, but not to the others.

We motored in up the magical Sound of Sleet between 3,000-ft peaks (Monroes) to our left on Skye (the Black Cuillins), and to our right on the mainland. Our stopover for the night was Kyle of Lochalsh, which boasts a modest marina and harbour just before the bridge over to Skye. This was a particularly poignant place for Spider. The last time he had been here was in 1996 on HMS *Fearless*, which in turn was the last ship of its size to visit the waters south of the controversial new bridge. HMS *Fearless* had in fact 'escaped' only days before the central span of the bridge was put in place.

The next day (27 September) was as windless as the last, and after waiting at the waypoint for forty-five minutes, it was clear that the wind gods were otherwise engaged, and nothing was imminent. We decided to pig out on bacon rolls in nearby Mallaig, and I went shopping for prezzies for my kids. I actually got moving at 1.30 p.m., but it was a long hard slog in less than 3 knots of wind. I became obsessed with reaching the Kyle of Rhea tidal race and either pumped or paddled for hour after hour, inching slowly closer, burning huge amounts of energy for minuscule reward. The famed tidal bus didn't materialise until we were 100 yards away from the Kyle of Rhea tidal narrows in the fading light at 7.00 p.m. Steve had, I think, regretted pulling me off the water too early the previous two nights, and possibly felt I would be suicidal if he did the same again. We reached the narrows in fading light with only about twenty minutes of favourable tide left (so maybe the paddling was worthwhile!). One minute I was running downwind on the slightest of southerly breezes, and the next moment I was beating into what felt like a northerly draft. In reality the tide had picked me up and was pushing me into still air, creating some 3–4 knots of apparent wind. A weird experience, made more memorable by the bubbling, swirling mini whirlpools all around me, and vicious eddies, which at times seemed to be trying to spit me back the way I had come. I also had an audience of inquisitive seals who always seemed to be present when we took on a tidal race. I completed the last few miles feeling like an athlete on the last mile of an all-uphill marathon, and managed to sail to within 100m of Maiden's berth for a virtually non-stop six-hour slog of 19.4 miles. It was 7.45 p.m., and almost dark, the first time I had sailed past nightfall on the whole trip. I had a couple of pints of heavy in the pub that night whilst watching our golfers lose the Ryder Cup from what looked like an unassailable position. Hopefully not an omen for us!

After our latest-ever finish on Day 36, we had our earliest-ever start on Day 37. The 100m run out to the waypoint helped, and we needed to make the most of a predicted north-running tide which would be with us until 9.00 a.m. At 7.47, I took to the water, and paddle-drifted on the tide under Spider's bridge. A gentle F2 arrived for thirty minutes and then disappeared again – the wind gods having their laugh. At one stage, where we had no tide and no wind, I actually lay out on my board, closed my eyes, and cat-napped. The RIB team woke me, not because the wind had arrived, but to enjoy a pod of harbour porpoises who had obviously come to investigate this seemingly dead marine mammal. Some wind finally arrived, but it had swung through 180 degrees to the north, meaning a painfully slow beat back and forth across the inner sound with spectacular Raasay, Rona and Skye over my left shoulder. I remember sailing for what seemed like an eternity towards a distant lonely white cottage on the mainland shore, wondering about the highs and lows of life in such a beautiful but isolated location. For a while I considered beaching my board, knocking on their door, and having a good natter about our respective existences. Then I drifted back into reality and realised that as a reserved Englishman, such an act of wanton spontaneity would be considered tantamount to insanity.

Although zig-zagging much further that day, I only covered 18 miles in nearly 10.5 hours on the water, but we had now done just over 900 miles, and I felt safe in declaring that we were past halfway. The Maiden crew didn't need an excuse to celebrate, and by the time we made it into Badachro, they had been in the pub several hours, and were happily sloshing back the beer and slurring epic stories of our venture to the similarly sloshed locals in the Badachro Inn. Badachro itself was a tiny little fishing and pleasure boat quay at the head of a sheltered inlet halfway up Loch Gairloch, with the brooding red-round North West Highlands as a backdrop. As often seems to be the case in these isolated pubs, the landlord and landlady were from Bingley. Damian had talked up our venture to such an extent that I was reluctantly cajoled into signing autographs, and having my picture taken with some 35-stone couple from Bradford. After two or three hours in the pub, I had had enough of drunken congratulations, and wandered outside to try and get through to Mandy on the mobile. There was of course no line, so I reclined on a bench outside the pub, and gazed aimlessly into the star-filled emptiness above me. People leaving the pub obviously thought I had taken one dram too many. My final memory of that day was lying in bed listening to Kevin's girlfriend Lucy spouting forth an alcohol-induced diatribe of semi-conscious lewd wanderings.

There was more wind forecast for Day 38, but it had swung back to the south, meaning virtually dead downwind sailing. It was a horrible day's windsurfing, where I fell in a lot trying to broad reach and run in small but confused seas on Bertha and the 10.0m sail, with F2/3 winds. The scenery was again wonderful, but it didn't stop me gesturing to Steve, that I would rather have a six-inch rusty nail hammered through my scrotum into the kitchen table, than do any more of this awful downwind sailing. We passed craggy Rudha Reidh, and as the late afternoon visibility improved could see the Isle of Lewis in the Outer Hebrides 25 miles to the west. It was another long arduous day to cover 36 miles, but we were now only 50 miles from Cape Wrath, and corner number 4. The ride into Lochinver that night gave us a scenic vision which would, I think, feature in anybody's top ten. The sugarloaf-mountain-shaped form of Suilven was bathed in that typically Scottish purple-red light, and the southerly winds had partially dislodged a wispy halo of iridescent cloud from its summit. No words (certainly not mine) could do justice to this glorious picture. Its beauty was also enhanced by the moment. We had been out on the water for nine hours. I was physically and mentally drained from the day's exertions, and I couldn't help thinking that the same force that dispensed character-building setbacks also had a soft spot, and knew precisely when to deliver such uplifting wonder.

With the only inevitability being change, surprises and new challenges, we had two more incidents that day to complete the picture. First the VHF radio on the RIB decided to pack up on our way in, sending Steve into his trademark grump. This was bad news. We couldn't safely go out without a fully functioning VHF radio, and up here miles from anywhere wasn't probably the easiest spot get it repaired or replaced. Secondly Sarah whilst climbing from Maiden onto the pontoon in Lochinver, managed to drop our only set of van keys into the inky black harbour depths. It didn't look like we would be going anywhere the next day until these two little setbacks had been overcome. Damian, in his inimitably forward Irish way, had decided that I needed a massage to placate my aching limbs; so I temporarily forgot about these minor problems and went to see a lovely lady called Rosemary, who as a retired nurse and vicar's wife had decided to take up aromatherapy and massage. She was fascinated by our exploits, but I particularly enjoyed chatting about family life in this rugged and isolated area of Britain. She had that slow, contented, and 'nothing's too much trouble' demeanour, that seems so rare in the fast-moving south, and the chat did me as much, if not more good than the massage. In bed that night, I was confident we would somehow recover the keys from 30 ft under the sea, and Steve et al would fix the radio somehow. Worry is, anyway, a pointless emotion, once the facts and appropriate actions have been sorted.

Above: Sarah and Frogman in Lochinver.

Below: Absolutely wonderful Suilven in north-west Scotland.

If only I could capture and bottle this 'no worries' formula. Maybe we all need a regular visit to one of the Rosemary's of this world to put life in perspective?

Maiden was a hive of activity the next morning, with mobile phones buzzing left, right and centre. In this town of 350 souls, Sarah had managed to find a local scuba diver, and persuade him to drop whatever else he was doing, and come over to Maiden in search of the missing keys. We were not sure we could get any replacement keys off Fiat, and despite the surface humour and banter on the pontoon as our saviour donned his kit, there was an underlying worry that all he would find would be black mud. He did in fact find plenty of black mud, but sticking out of that mud 30 ft below the surface, he also found our beloved keys. He emerged from the inky depths to great cheers, and Sarah was then ceremoniously presented with a bright orange 12″ marker buoy, to be attached to the keys at all times. Steve and Spider returned around lunchtime and spent the next few hours fitting the new radio. It did not go unnoticed that the day when the radio packed up, and the keys went sightseeing under the waves, was also the day when the wind returned. We had a solid but cold F4/5 northerly wind all day. Not a good direction, but a full day's beating could have realised 30–40 miles of progress. I was actually not too concerned, as my body had averaged 7.5 hours sailing per day over the last week, and the rest was probably necessary before taking on Cape Wrath. We did, however, go out for two hours late afternoon to cover 10 miles. For the first time since Donegal Bay, we were back into 10–12 ft swells, and for the first time on the trip, I needed to wear gloves and a neoprene helmet. Despite my head-to-toe covering, it still felt bitterly cold in this northerly wind, which was a worrying portent for our trip round the top, and down the east coast, where water temperatures would be 3–4 degrees lower. The upside of these northerly winds was that we were in typical cold-sector weather, with fantastic visibility and clear blue skies. Duncan got some of his best shots of the trip that day, and we still had magical Suilven in the background.

Day 40 (30 September) was Cape Wrath day. I woke jittery and appre-hensive. The forecast was for F3/5 winds from the south-west, which yet again would be dead downwind sailing until round the Cape, and then a starboard tack broad reach along the top. It seemed that the whole of Scotland's west coast had been either downwind in southerly winds or upwind into northerlies. Whatever happened to the prevailing westerlies? There is an eerie feeling about this Sutherland coastline. The shoreline is craggy and dark, and the sea also felt darker and more mysterious than its southerly equivalent. The land was all peaty soil barely covering the ancient rocks of this skeletal landscape.

I set off on Big Bertha, with the 10.0m sail in a lumpy F2/3 wind on a lumpy sea. The rhythm of the sea was more radical jazz than rock and roll, and I struggled desperately to synchronise my board management with the jumpy, unpredictable motion beneath. After two hours of struggle and falling in, I was ready to accept defeat. In these conditions 25 miles would be a good day, and Cape Wrath would have to wait. My arms were like useless lumps of jelly. My lower back was aching for Britain, and I was unable to get comfortably into the harness for more than a few hundred yards before the board was forced off line by the awkward seas, and I would be pulled inexorably over the front. At one stage after yet another fall off Stoerhead, I punched the base of the sail, and came very close to dissolving into floods of tears. This was just impossible. I swore to the skies at the top of my voice, with the most foul abusive language I knew, and sat motionless on the board for several minutes trying to find some inner calm. It sounds corny, but I also kept repeating Rosie's 'never give up dad' instructions quietly to myself.

When they judged it was safe to approach, the RIB came over, and cautiously suggested that despite the light winds, I should change to an 8.0m sail, which would be slower but easier to handle. They were right and I made the change. As if by order, the wind then picked up to a good F4, and we replaced Bertha with Katie. Bertha was not happy about being discarded, and obviously made some connections with the forces above. Within twenty minutes I had effected a high-speed catapult fall, and Katie's makeshift nose was once more smashed to pieces. Back on Bertha, the stronger wind meant I could pull the track right back, and sail well powered up in the back straps. The sea also seemed to flatten off for a while as I pushed my dancing lady further and further off the wind, in a series of blistering broad reaches. Knowing of its awesome reputation, and permanent west-running tide close in, I was keeping well clear of the Cape. My mind was focused on one thing and one thing only – I had to get past this dreaded obstacle, and had no intention of stopping until it was many miles behind. I was apparently gybing through 80 degrees, meaning I was sailing 50 degrees off a beam reach. As the wind increased further to a F5, I also knew my speed was a good 20 knots, which was faster than I'd been since the west coast of Ireland. Maybe I was intoxicated by the speed itself, but I was certainly oblivious to time, and didn't see with any great interest the steep mossy cliffs of the Cape itself which were coming into view. It was like one of those dreams where you can run and run and run, without feeling tired, but completely unable to stop. I rounded the Cape on a powerful gust, which I was informed later had taken my speed up to 24–27 knots, over 4–5 ft seas. This was the fastest, hairiest sailing I had ever done on a board of this size, and at times I couldn't stop it doing 10-ft long jumps off the swell lines. From time to time I looked back to check the RIB was still with me. It was a good 500m behind, and throwing up massive spray trying to keep up.

After what seemed like twenty or thirty minutes (but was actually more than three hours) I had turned corner number 4, and could no longer see the Cape over my right shoulder. The wind had by then dropped back to a F3/4, and the RIB pulled alongside with Tim waving his arms frantically for me to stop and lay down my sail. My system had obviously forgotten how to stop, because in the process of acknowledging Tim's request, I lost concentration and pulled off another big catapult fall, leaving a 1″ deep dent in Bertha's foredeck. Despite the ignominious dismount, I climbed back on the board, and punched the air in triumph. What a brilliant brilliant feeling. Cheers from the RIB team seemed to be somewhat inhibited and short-lived, which had me thinking, 'Do they realise what this means to me?' They apparently had another more biologically pressing priority. I had sailed non-stop for 3.5 hours, which was five hours since they had been able to bladder empty over the side. They had been waving frantically at me for the last hour, but were unable to catch up and get close enough for me to notice. With bladders joyously emptied, food and drink consumed to refuel my system, and Bertha's new dent filled with Dr Ding, I was back in the harness, and reaching eastwards on a weakening wind. Steve was keen for us to get as close as possible to Scrabster (our designated stopover) and the Pentland Firth, so I kept going until the light started to die at 7.00 p.m. for an ending waypoint just off Strathy Point. Although most of the miles were covered during that phenomenal 3.5-hour blast, I had sailed for ten hours and nineteen minutes to cover a total of 69 miles (a new record distance). I had actually sailed nearer 90 miles on a point of sail that is as hard as it gets on the arms, back and legs. It was another day when the soaring spirit (possibly helped by endorphins, adrenaline etc.) totally over-ruled the exhausted body.

With all the excitement and speed, I had not had time to take in the dark and sinister scenery of this far-north wilderness. I remembered passing two incredulous fishing boats (they don't see many windsurfers in this part of the world), and also seeing some remarkable white sanded beaches, nestling between the grey-green cliffs. I also remembered thinking about the reasons I had given people for wanting to take on this challenge. I had often spoken of 'pushing myself to the limit ... going to places where physically and mentally I had never been before ... and of it being some sort of test (to myself) as to whether or not I could hack it'. In my own world, I had passed my self-imposed 'can I hack it' test with flying colours today.

It was pitch black when we rolled into the big busy fishing and ferry port of Scrabster, and Maiden was well behind, not due in for a good three hours. There was only one place to be. We found the smartest-looking quayside pub, which in Marlborough, Wilts, would have been too rough to get a licence, and settled down with a very special pint, and an order for four haggis specials despatched to the kitchen. Everybody including Steve was smiling, and we renamed Cape Wrath as 'Cape Big Girl's Blouse', a dangerously disrespectful action. In fact the word wrath in Gaelic apparently means 'turning point', so its angry Anglo-Saxon language image was misplaced. It was almost unreal that we had started so badly, and finished so elated. I have never been so low and so high within the space of five hours. Such a range of feelings and emotions represents a massive dose of intense living. The last time I felt this alive was at the birth of my first child. We were on top of the world both metaphorically and physically (providing one's world stops on the north coast of Scotland). Sarah, who had been with us trying to film the day's events, had an ear-to-ear grin that was there for the night, and I even got a compliment from Steve. He said I was the fittest 40-year-old he'd ever met. Wow, I was now up to one well done (after the crossing from Ireland) and one compliment. I felt confident it was only a matter of time before he went the whole hog and brought me a smiley breakfast in bed! The physical tiredness hit me when, after our two-pound haggis special, I tried to lift my useless body out of the bar chair. Maiden arrived around 11.00 p.m., with Terry immediately and annoyingly declaring that we had to be up at 5.00 a.m., on the water by 7.00 a.m., and back at Dunnet Head by 9.30 a.m., to have any chance of getting through the Pentland Firth before the tide turned.

Following Terry's orders, we left at 6.15 a.m., and were immediately head into an awful steep 8–10 ft wind over tide sea. The F4 wind was still blowing from west-south-west, and the tide was still running west. In these conditions the RIB could only manage 8–10 knots, and it took us over two hours to slam and plunge our way 17 miles back to Strathy Point. I had never felt less like windsurfing in my life. It was bitterly cold. I was still aching from yesterday, and the conditions looked very tricky. I was on the water by 8.45 a.m., by which time the wind had dropped to F2/3. The swells were still big and confused coming mostly from a north-west angle. On Bertha with the 8.0m sail, I was in and out of the harness surfing down the swell lines, and then losing forward momentum on the uphill backsides. It was exhausting sailing again, and I had regular crashes and strength sapping restarts. After three hours and 20 miles, we were within sight of Scrabster, and Dunnet Head (the most northerly point of the British mainland), but I needed a serious rest before taking on the Pentland Firth.

Maiden was waiting for us off Scrabster, and Terry was all in a hurry for us to get going. It was around midday, and we apparently had another two or three hours of favourable tide. This didn't tie in with his earlier assertion that we had to be at Dunnet Head by 9.30 a.m. at the latest. After calling up another forecast which was F4/6, they gave me a twenty-minute rest whilst we discussed options with Maiden. After a lot of soul-searching and dithering, we decided to give it a go. One of the main drivers was that the weather was forecast to get worse, suggesting that if we didn't get through today, we could be holed up here for three or four days waiting for a window of calm weather. The seas approaching Dunnet Head were particularly rough, and despite the F4 winds (which I had broad reached in quite comfortably all the day before), I struggled desperately to make significant progress downwind. After thirty minutes of stubborn effort it was clear that my strength had gone, and no amount of determination or adrenaline was going to bring it back. Steve rightly pointed out that it was nonsensical to take on one of the most dangerous passages of the whole trip when I was weak and exhausted. We called Maiden, and told Terry of our decision to call it a day. He was critical, complaining that we had just thrown away possibly our best chance for a week to get through the Firth. This made me very angry. I was not superhuman. Did he think that the 80 miles I sailed yesterday, and the 20 miles of torment this morning were just light workouts? In Terry's defence he wanted us to get through the Firth today because he was as desperate for us to succeed as the rest, but just had an impatient, irritating way of showing it.

Back in Scrabster the atmosphere was hung with disappointment, and I settled down to an afternoon off, catching up with my video diary, and talking through the technicalities of the Pentland Firth with the resident coastguard. He was an English exile in Scrabster, but still full of tales of terror for ships caught in the Firth when 12-knot tides came up against 40-knot winds. It was patently clear that we could only go through on an east-flowing tide, with as little wind as possible, preferably from south-west through to north-west. Steve and Spider had meanwhile gone looking for a night of comfort ashore, and reported back that the pub we were in the previous evening had rooms available for an extortionate (?) £12 per night. I decided I could live without Maiden's palatial luxury and checked in. The hot bath was simply wonderful, but the room fearfully cold. I had three blankets on the bed, but still had to get up in the night to put on a sweatshirt, and this was only the end of September. Evidently the hardy souls up here don't bother with central heating until November when it gets properly cold, or maybe you have to pay more than £12 per night to get central heating as well as a bed!

The forecast for Day 42 (2 October) was marginal, starting north-west F3/4 in the morning and then increasing F5/6. I did not at all fancy downwind sailing through the Firth in a F6, but the weather was due to get worse, so we decided to give it a try. The tide would turn in our favour around midday, so we could only start at 11.00 a.m. giving us an hour to make progress on the weakening west-flowing tide before it turned. I started with a 7.0m sail, in a good F4, but within minutes the wind was up to F6, and we made a change to a 5.0m sail. The seas approaching Dunnet Head were getting bigger and nastier, and after forty-five minutes of manful struggle and little progress, I came up to the RIB for a tactics chat. I laid my sail in the water, and the RIB slid in downwind of me, near enough for us to hear each other speak in the howling wind. Suddenly a steep swell lifted the tip of my sail a few inches out of the water, which was enough for a powerful gust of wind to rip it out of the water, and send it sything across the deck of the RIB at great velocity. The solid carbon fibre mast was inches away from doing some serious damage to Spider's skull, and during it's high-speed cartwheel it completely destroyed our VHF aerial, and badly damaged the GPS aerial. Steve was furious, but not blaming anyone. With the benefit of hindsight, I should have noticed that after laying my sail in the water downwind, the swells had spun me round such that the sail was now upwind of the board. Also, in these conditions, the RIB should not have come in downwind of me. A lesson learned, but also the day's efforts brought to a premature end. We could not take on the Pentland Firth without a properly functioning radio. By this stage Maiden was 5 miles ahead and the tide was on the turn. They could not realistically turn around and hope to make progress against the strengthening east-flowing tide, so we agreed that they would continue to Wick around the corner and 15 miles south. We went back into Scrabster, and waited for the van to come and collect us. Meanwhile Maiden continued round in the growing gale and horizontal hail, navigating her way between the ship-eating rocks by dead reckoning, their radar having decided to pack up at a particularly inopportune moment.

No-one spoke much on the ride across to Wick. I had tried twice to get through the Firth and had been beaten both times. There were now gale warnings in force for the next two to three days. It was bitterly cold in the north-west winds, and my nightmare scenario of being trapped by worsening winter weather seemed to be unfolding around me. I was not in a mixing mood that afternoon, and after a quick look around the shops in Wick, I found myself a pub, and to take my mind elsewhere watched England thrash Italy in the Rugby World Cup. I also had a good long mobile phone chat with Mandy and the four kids that evening before joining the others on Maiden to eat. My family seemed happy, and contented, which put me in a better mood, and I went to bed resigned to the fact that we could be here for several days; but that once round corner number 5, we would be on the downhill section, which both previous round Britain windsurfers had found much easier and quicker.

I awoke on Sunday, 3 October to the noise of Maiden's fenders grinding against the Wick harbour wall, and a good healthy gale whistling through the rigging. I moped around doing diaries and updates for the web site, and then made a few phone calls looking for extra crew for Maiden. I then did my laundry, read half a travel book on Chile, and generally tried to take my mind off the bloody Pentland Firth. The atmosphere among the others was good, and Duncan, Kevin and Sarah were becoming a close-knit, fun-loving triumvirate. In the end we had three days marooned in Wick with no miles covered. It would never be top of my list of holiday destinations, but it had a hard and honest character. In the memories of all the crew with us in Wick, the salient recollection will always be the pubs and the drunks. It was a **fundamentally rough run-down place**, with a now negligible fishing industry, and no obvious way back to prosperity. After three days playing pool, watching Rugby during the afternoons, and nights 'local bonding', we (meaning primarily Duncan, Kevin and Sarah) got to know the regulars in one particular pub pretty well. On the second night one drunk remained comatose under the pool table for seven consecutive rounds of winner-stays-on. When he did come round and stagger to the bar shouting incoherently for a drink, the landlady had decided he was no longer welcome. She was this side of the bar deep in conversation with another middle-aged lady (probably discussing the priestly merits of their respective spouses) when suddenly she broke off the conversation, grabbed the drunk by the lapels, propelled him violently towards the door and sent him crashing out of the pub with an effortlessly powerful right hook. She then returned to the conversation with her friend as if the interruption had been to tidy up an errant beer mat that had fallen to the floor. The same drunk was back the next day looking bruised, sober, but eager, and exchanging pleasantries with the landlady as if nothing had happened. To add to the absurdity of the situation Duncan also used the telephone socket in the same pub to connect to the Internet, and would often be found mid-afternoon, surrounded by drunken mayhem, quietly pinging away on his keyboard in a corner, downloading weather forecasts, and composing press releases.

After a while we came to the conclusion that as these people did most of their talking when they were drunk, their completely incomprehensible loud, slurring, repetitive speech had become the rule rather than the exception. They didn't need to understand each other, as the conversations were the same each night, and they couldn't remember anything anyway. They asked us many times to explain why we were here, but as with the lady in the bus shelter in Bournemouth, the truth was simply too out of their world to be true. Another drunk took a regular fancy to Sarah, and would wander over to us, sit down beside her, and plonk his awful-smelling armpit onto Sarah's delicate shoulder. His minder at the bar would comfort us with the guidance that he was a 'harmless wee bastard'. Sarah to her credit did not reel in disgust at this approach, but would humour the drunk for a couple of minutes, and then if he didn't move on at her or Duncan's request, the minder would do the job for us somewhat more forcefully. Kevin's view was that over three heavy drinking nights in this colourful establishment the only time they felt remotely threatened was when demure, fifteen-year-old Linda, complete with violent tattoos down both arms, took a shine to Duncan, and struggled to accept that her very direct and 'here and now' approach to a relationship was not quite what Duncan had in mind. Linda was the intellectual of the group, and had deduced that as Duncan was the only one standing, he was probably the only one capable of giving her satisfaction.

Duncan and Kevin did, however, come close to being on the receiving end of some grievous bodily harm at the hands of the local nightclub bouncers. However, being Wick, the cause of the altercation was somewhat unusual. Duncan and Kevin were propped up at a night club bar, virtually the last to leave, when they noticed the two resident gorillas starting to carry various large children's cuddly toys onto the dance-floor. Their sniggers and fun-poking comments did not go down well. What they didn't realise at the time was that the night club doubled up as a creche, and the bouncers had to get everything ready for the next morning's influx of somewhat younger, but probably equally wild clientele. In a way Wick was a sad desparate place but at least it was honest and real. There was always someone there looking after those in the worst shape, and even the landlady's right hook was only used as a last resort to stress the point that another drink was maybe just one too many. I would never have gone near a pub like this in my other life, but the experience of Wick's hopeless alcohol abuse was a good life-tutorial which will not be forgotten.

Tuesday, 5 October (Day 45) was the day we made it through the Pentland Firth. I was up at 4.30 a.m., and doing a pre-dawn radio interview at 6.15 a.m. on the dock wall of Scrabster harbour. The day before we had spent hours looking down at the maelstrom of turbulent water forcing its way past Duncansby Head against a north-westerly gale, and chatting to the Scrabster coastguard who had told me that the wind and seas were forecast to ease by tomorrow. Despite these comforting words my stomach was still as churned as the seas of this famous tidal race, as we motored out to the waypoint in light westerly winds with a sombre black sky above us and undulating inky black sea below. The same coastguard had also told us that if we set sail at dawn we would have maximum three hours to sail the 12 miles west, and out past Duncansby Head. This was the first realistic chance of getting through the Race we had for three days, and with a forecast of more strong winds to come, could also be our last chance for another three or four days. This was it. Another now or never situation.

Steve made one final call to the coastguard and asked for confirmation that we had three hours of favourable tide. It was a different coastguard on duty, and his reading of tide tables told us that we had no more than fifty minutes of east-running tide. If his information was correct, then we didn't have a hope in hell of getting through. I had a blazing row with Steve, whose pessimistic nature automatically assumed that today's coastguard was right. He wanted to pack up there and then, motor back to Scarabster and sit on it until the tide turned again. This made no sense to me. The winds were light and favourable, and my optimistic nature had me firmly aligned with yesterday's coastguard. We had to give it a try, even if we only managed to move three or four miles nearer the target. The others in the RIB, and particularly Tim, seemed to support my position, without actually saying so, and thus wound Steve up even further. I was turfed over the side onto Bertha with the 9.4m sail and wobbled dead downwind over the small but lumpy seas. Conversation during the rigging process on the RIB had been slashed to the absolute minimum, and the atmosphere between myself and Steve was as black and razor sharp as the famous Manacles rocks we had passed some five weeks earlier.

With only 3–4 knots of wind and 3 knots of tide, going in the same direction there was almost no discernable pull from the sail, and thus nothing for me to balance against as the board was buffeted by the short and confused chop. It was exhausting, very difficult sailing, but I was absolutely determined not to fall in and thereby waste a few seconds of priceless time. I put everything I had into maximising my forward momentum, and drifted past Dunnet Head, and towards the Merry Men of Mey, expecting the tide to go slack and then turn against me at any moment. It didn't, and after a good hour I gestured to the RIB that the bubbling water flow around a nearby lobster pot suggested we still had a good 2 knots of fair tide. Yesterday's coastguard was right, bless him, and thus we had about ninety minutes left of the weakening east-running tide.

I drifted slowly but surely through the Merry Men of Mey race, and through the Inner Sound between the Isle of Stroma and the mainland, and just managed to get past the imposing Duncansby Head before the tide turned. My emotions were more of relief than achievement, but also some deep, quiet satisfaction that my impatience and optimism had in this case paid off. The Pentland Firth had been in and out of my mind for much of the last few days. Now at last the tick was in the box, and with a triumphal clenched fist and a heartfelt cheer from the RIB, I turned south for the first and last time. Now there was definitely no turning back. We simply had to finish.

My celebrations were however short lived, and within minutes the tide had truly turned and I was being swept backwards from whence I came at a good 5 knots. There was no point trying to sail against a 6–8 knot tide, in 3 knots of wind, so we motored back into Wick, and most of us had an afternoon kip. The four hours of downwind balancing, often with less than 2 knots of apparent wind in my sail had been hot hard work, and once I stopped moving, I became very cold very quickly. Even in my sleeping bag with woolly socks on it took over an hour to get my feet warm. The colony of grey seals we had encountered just off Duncansby Head had no such problem. It was their mating season, and the thirty or so females, and five or six males were busy sorting out who was going with who. My presence was an additional complication for the stressed males, whose machismo over the next few days would sort out whether they had weeks of endless sex and fighting, or just quiet isolation. They had clearly been given advanced warning that I had been away from home for six weeks, and saw me as a competitive threat. As I sailed through the colony, every few hundred yards, an angry bull would pop out of the water 10–15 ft behind me, and violently slap the water with his hind flippers, before disappearing in a swirl of angry bubbles. This was all witnessed by those on the RIB, but by the time I'd turned round, all I caught was the bubbles.

The day's sailing was completed with another three-hour session late afternoon, giving us a 36.5-mile day, and a very big feeling that maybe we could make it after all. The only incident of note that afternoon which caused great hilarity in the RIB was when I 'fell asleep at the wheel'. According to Sarah, I just fell slowly and inexorably backwards into the sea. There was no other explanation, other than the fact that I had fallen asleep. Falling asleep in a nice comfy seat, in a warm windless car is one thing, but on a windsurfer during a bitterly cold October day off the coldest corner of Scotland. This was something else!

Despite starting the day with a huge row, Steve was as chuffed as everyone else that we had at last made it round the top. It was also his last night before being replaced by Philippe, and we had a warm and relieved session in the pub that night, and openly discussed what made us tick in such completely different ways. He had privately set himself a goal of getting us through the Pentland Firth before leaving; and felt good that he had delivered. We had come through hell and high water together over the last forty-six days, and when we said our farewells there was an unspoken current of mutual respect and friendship between us.

Chapter XI

The Easy East Coast

With sloping masts and dipping prow,
As who pursued with yell and blow
Still treads the shadow of his foe,
And forward bends his head,
The ship drove fast, loud roared the blast,
And southward aye we fled.

Samuel Taylor Coleridge
(**from** *The Rime of the Ancient Mariner*)

I awoke around 6.30 a.m., and went about my cold and unpleasant morning routine of urgent #2, breakfast in the nav station ahead of the rush, and then the ceremonial donning of the cold, wet, smelly wetsuit. With an air temperature of 4 degrees C, and a brisk F4 wind, it was time to go for extra layers. I used a thin neoprene rash vest under my winter steamer, and made sure the hat and gloves were on the RIB. Once into my neoprene prison, I would drag on a couple of fleeces, and my full heavy weather oilskins, before climbing onto the Wick quayside, to loosen and warm my resisting body. Running any distance in size 11 wellies, and five layers of neoprene, fleece and Gore-tex, was a challenge in itself. Thus I normally only managed a few high-stepping laps of the quayside, and then the obligatory stretches.

The atmosphere on Maiden that morning (Day 46, 5 October) was a heady mixture of sad farewells, new optimism, and old frustrations. Kevin was back as skipper, Terry away again on business. Steve was leaving, which was sad for most, and a relief for some. I and some of the others had briefly met his replacement Philippe, but it was clear from the outset that he was here to enjoy himself, and contribute to a successful mission, rather than take himself too seriously. Enthusiastic Peter Head had arrived as replacement crew for Maiden, on the day we were scheduled to berth for the night at Peterhead, north of Aberdeen. Peter, as a student of Euan McGrath (my fitness coach), and keen windsurfer-cum-sailor, was just thrilled to be on the team. John Beecroft had decided to rejoin the project, which was a negative development for the majority, with the bad chemistry evident immediately. John had done his research into the saleability of the documentary he was making, and came back assuring me that it looked good. I still needed this documentary to be a **financial success, and**

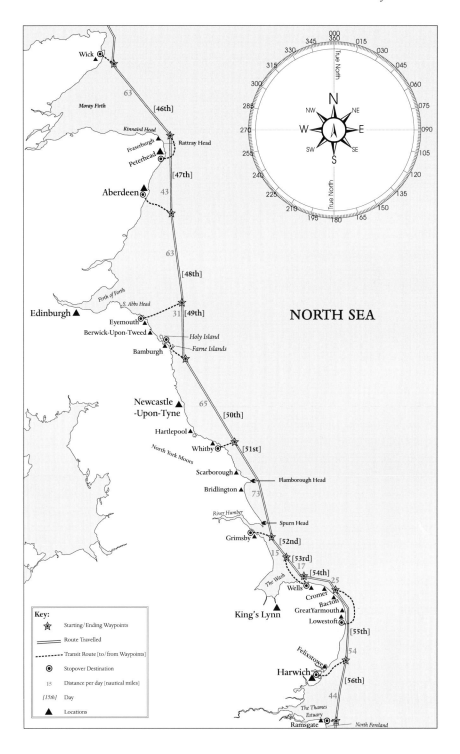

thus overrode the resistance of John's 'Fan Club' to have him back on board.

The RIB team leaving Maiden from the Wick quayside that morning, comprised; Philippe, Spider, Tim, John Beecroft and myself. The forecast of south/south-west F3/4 was favourable, and gave us a fighting chance of making the 65-mile crossing of the Moray Firth to Aberdeenshire. My private mood was buoyant and optimistic. After nearly seven weeks of slog we had turned south, and were heading for home. It was a highly comforting thought to know that each mile sailed would take me closer to rather than further away from Stokes Bay. I also had time during our three-day sojourn in Wick to play with the nautical charts and dividers; and for the first time had a reasonably accurate estimate of the distance still to cover. On the ride out to the waypoint, I once more revisited my therapeutic calculations. Assuming we could take the straight line route across the Moray Firth, the Firth of Forth, The Wash, and the Thames Estuary, I had only some 560 miles to go. At best, averaging fifty miles per day, we could thus finish in eleven more days, giving a time for the full circumnavigation of fifty-seven days, or just over eight weeks. An eight-week finish would be nothing short of miraculous, considering the awful start we had. At worst, averaging 25 miles per day, I could finish in sixty-eight days (just under ten weeks). We all knew as a team that the fat lady was far from bursting into song, but we also knew that beating the 62-day round Britain record was a definite possibility. Of course the real 'at worst' scenario would be if I didn't finish at all. My general optimistic nature didn't give much time to the nightmare scenario of sustaining a serious injury close to home, although the others reminded me of a John o'Groats to Land's End cyclist, recently in the news, who had done just that. If my mind tended to avoid nightmare scenario worries, it positively embraced the probabilities game. For the first time on the whole journey I mentally accepted that the probability of success was now greater than 50:50.

My spirits were further boosted by the perfect F4 beam-reaching conditions at the waypoint. With an early start and wind like this all day, at least 70 miles should be do-able, and even 100 possible. However, in true Livethatdream (or as it had sometimes been renamed Livethatnightmare) tradition, there had to be a spanner in the works from somewhere. For the second time in Scotland the van keys halted our progress. Kevin came on the VHF saying that the van keys could not be found anywhere and that John was the last person to have them to unload his camera kit early that morning. Without the van keys, Steve couldn't be taken to the station, and our land support system was disabled. I was just furious, but outwardly kept control. Was this yet another continuation of my celestial job interview, with some greater force lining up the cumulative positives, and then throwing in a blood-boiling negative to test my mental stability? John stridently declared where he had left the keys, and checked his pockets 'just in case'. John's low standing with the rest of the team had just gone subterranean. Despite this being his first day filming for two weeks, I decided that as he was the last one to have the keys, we would have to run back into Wick and leave him on Maiden to make sure they were bloody well found. We then tracked back to the waypoint minus John, and eventually got underway around 9.00 a.m., by which time the wind had dropped to a F3, and veered to south, giving me a day of close-hauled sailing on Bertha and the 9.4m sail. The keys were of course found on a ledge somewhere inside the van, and John made the best of his day in deepest Coventry by volunteering to do van-driving duties.

I sailed for a good nine hours that day, all on starboard tack, and covered 63 miles to lie 5-miles north-east of Rattray Head. We had successfully crossed the Moray Firth under a high but grey and murky sky. The hills of northern Aberdeenshire appeared as islands out of the horizon, until my southwards progress gradually diminished the disrupting influence of the curvature of the Earth on my line of sight. The evolution from virtual islands, to bona fide mainland was an imperceptibly slow process; but in some ways this break on the normal speed of time, constantly looking for minute changes to my vista, helped take my mind off the sailing tedium and the biting cold, which for the first time forced me to wear gloves all day. To take my mind off my numb fingers, I pontificated for ages on how human beings use various mediums to both slow their own mental pace, and deepen their consciousness. Some use prayer and worship, and some meditation. For some it is simply three timeless hours in the garden, or a long walk with the dog. Music, literature or art are the chosen medium for others. For me it was that fresh air thing again, and preferably in an environment that was slowly but inexorably changing around me. A cynic would have added that I didn't need to windsurf around Britain and Ireland to slow down my hyperactive mind and 'deepen my consciousness'.

Our designated stopover for the night was Peterhead marina. The port of Fraserburgh was nearer, but apparently yachts are not welcome there, so we took the hint. The RIB arrived well ahead of Maiden, and we found ourselves a pontoon tie-up, before asking a resident boat owner named John about showers and the like. John turned out to be a maverick ex-TV journalist/presenter, who lived with his young son on an old wooden brig, tied up to an adjacent pontoon. He soon had us out of the biting cold and into the homely warmth of his mobile, water-borne equivalent of a thirteenth-century thatched cottage. He then dispensed strong filter coffee liberally laced with Laphroig whisky, to make sure the inside warmed at the same speed as the outside. We openly discussed our epic journey and his unusual lifestyle, and John allowed us to use his boat for a series of radio interviews. He was also quickly on the phone to his ex-employer, Grampian TV, to fix up a TV news interview for the next morning. People like John made the journey that much more meaningful. The warmth, hospitality and humanity of the many varied souls we came upon added great depth to the colourful canvas of the journey itself.

After battling against strong north-running tides, Maiden finally arrived at around 9.30 p.m., and found a town quay berth in the fishing dock. I had my obligatory carbohydrate binge, and after a series of visitors looking over Maiden we settled down to the first nightly meeting with Philippe and Peter on board. Peter had that day showed himself tough and competent as Maiden crew, and Philippe's positive light-hearted demeanour had already revitalised life on the RIB. As an ex-Round-the-World sailor he also seemed to be an excellent reader of the weather, both from synoptic charts and the sky. Life was good again, and there was somehow a hidden warmth in the fearful cold of this part of the world.

On Day 47 (7 October) myself, Tim and Peter were first up at 6.00 a.m. I got myself breakfasted and fully kitted out for the day's sailing before doing the Grampian TV interview on the pontoon. This diversion, together with the customary faff, meant that we didn't start the day's sailing until 9.15 a.m. The wind was roughly F3 from the south/south-west, so I set off on Bertha with the 9.4m sail on starboard tack (why break the habit of a lifetime?). After a good first hour averaging 10 knots boardspeed with some help from the tide, the wind picked up to a F4, and I called for a change to Katie. Neither the wind gods nor Bertha liked the idea of me flitting along eating up the miles on Katie at 18–20 knots, and within ten minutes the wind was back down to F2/3, and I was back on Bertha. I considered whether I was being taught a lesson on the merits of monogamy over polygamy, and vowed to try and become a more faithful windsurfer in future! Back on Bertha I covered another 30 miles before Philippe called a premature halt to proceedings at 3.30 p.m., in order to get into Aberdeen in time to lift the RIB out of the water for a gearbox oil change. Five hours sailing to cover 43 miles was still an excellent result; but I couldn't help feeling that we had left a further 20 miles 'on the table', and why the hell hadn't Steve sorted out the gearbox oil change whilst we were stranded in Wick? As events transpired, the lifting gear we had pre-booked wasn't suitable and the oil change was deferred to another day.

Motoring into Aberdeen was a fascinating experience, and so totally different from anything so far. The vessels in residence were primarily oil industry supply and service ships. Everything was 'heavy duty'. I had never seen chains, cables and steelwork of such magnitude at close quarters before. Maybe it's a male hormonal thing, but big powerful, indestructible gear has a similar aura as the growling engine of a super-powerful car, or the intimidating momentum of a high-stepping 18-stone back row rugby forward. Size and power do seem to matter. Perhaps its only conditioning, but there again, size and power (and of course guile) have until recent times been reasonably reliable markers of evolutionary success for the male of the species.

That afternoon I did two radio phone-ins and a TV interview for Aberdeen's Channel 10. Having bombed out with a photographer from the *Daily Telegraph* on Day 1, I now hit the pinnacle of fame as a photographer retained by the local prison newspaper turned up to capture the moment! After such a media blitz, I needed to relax and refresh; first borrowing the harbour master's private shower to cleanse the grimy North Sea residue off my body, and second retiring to a city centre pub to talk next-day tactics. The pub we found was also a first, in that it closed early when we were the only customers remaining. Were we really in Scotland?

I was awake and out of bed by 5.45 a.m. on Day 48 (8 October), ready for our scheduled 6.45 a.m. departure. Our very ambitious straight-line target was the Farne Islands, 85 miles to the south. We duly left at 7.15 (only a mini faff), but then had to wait thirty minutes whilst the a.m. Aberdeen harbour rush hour cleared. The wind was again F3 from the south/south-west, and again I set off on Bertha with the 9.4m sail close-hauled on starboard tack. I had now covered 99 per cent of the last 200 miles on starboard tack, and started to consider removing the port side footstraps and harness lines to save weight! Yet again the wind picked up to a F4, and flaunting the risk of being exposed as a philandering polygamist, I again called for Katie. This time my high-speed adventure was allowed, and over the next ninety minutes close-hauled on Katie, I averaged 18 knots, giving a record 40 miles covered by lunchtime. It was another bitterly cold day, as the Angus coastline disappeared from view, and a grey featureless horizon became my target. The air might have been cold, but my spirit was glowing warm and strong, as thoughts of even reaching Newcastle another 40 miles beyond Lindisfarne started to permeate my consciousness. The maths were simple: 40 miles covered in three hours, could be easily extrapolated to become 120 miles in 9 hrs. I could see the record-breaking headlines, and began to prepare my triumphant speeches to Newcastle TV and radio interviewers, colourfully illustrating how we had re-entered English waters in a blaze of glory. Extrapolations are easy, but keeping a favourable wind was not, and within ten minutes of my lunch break the wind was back down to F2/3, and backing to the south, so I had to make do with a laborious beat on Bertha down towards the Borders coastline north of Berwick-upon-Tweed. My record daydreams had been dashed, but

I was still upbeat. The GPS log showed a waypoint to waypoint distance of 63 miles, meaning that in three days' sailing we had virtually seen off the east coast of Scotland averaging 56 miles/day. Maybe an eight-week finish was possible after all.

We ended up still 22 miles short of the Farne Islands anchorage, but the RIB still needed to get into a fishing port to refuel and be lifted for the gearbox oil change. A quick VHF conference with Maiden concluded that the small fishing port of Eyemouth was our best choice. We approached between rocks following navigation lights towards what looked like a beach with a sea wall at one end and a few scattered holiday cottages on the hillside. 'This can't be right' was Spider's comment. Once round inside the sea wall we entered a miniature version of the Panama Canal, which 200 yds further on opened out to reveal a busy fishing harbour surrounded by pubs.

That night in Eyemouth, after showering at the Seamen's Mission, I sat down with my diary and thought long and hard about why our average daily mileage seemed to be improving week by week. It did not take a genius to work out that the wind and weather was still the primary driver, but attitudes, systems and abilities had also changed. The RIB team were quicker to get going in the morning, and more willing to let me sail closer to nightfall at the end of the day. As a team we seemed to be making better tactical decisions on routing and board/sail selection. Philippe and Tim were certainly less paranoid about being caught out in bad weather than Steve and Andy, and probably more ambitious on target distances. Since leaving Clifden, Connemara on Day 29, I had averaged eight hours on the board for each full day's sailing, compared with only six hours per day pre-Clifden. This had also been achieved despite the shortening daylength. Not only were we starting earlier and finishing later, but I was spending less time on the RIB on food and rest breaks. My body was 100 per cent tuned to the job in hand, and I had finally become 'match fit'. My windsurfing ability and confidence had also steadily improved, and particularly on Bertha with big sails, in marginal planing conditions, by optimising daggerboard and mastrack positions for a given set of conditions I was able to coax another 5–10 per cent board speed out of my big fat lady. Disregarding this clever analysis of teamwork and abilities, our east coast success was also very much driven by the fact that we had fairly gentle and consistent offshore winds, meaning relatively flat seas, and steady, physically easy progress (so far!)

It had been over two weeks since I had treated the team to a pub meal ashore, so a suitable-looking Eyemouth hostelry had the pleasure of our raucous company for the night. At around 11.00 p.m. I left the serious drinkers to their sport, and climbed back down onto Maiden. Despite the relatively easy sailing, these long cold days on the water were still very draining, and I felt virtually asleep on my feet as I stripped off three of my four layers, and climbed into my trusty sleeping bag. Something was wrong. Despite my semi-conscious, terminally-exhausted state, I could smell diesel, and my right side was decidedly damp. I wrenched my furious but reluctant frame out of the sodden bag, switched on the lights, and realised that my welcoming nightly haven been liberally doused with diesel-ridden oily bilge water. Somehow, Maiden must have been heeling particularly hard that day, and my bag on the lower bunk had soaked up the spillage. This was absolutely the last thing I needed. I had to have access to nice warm sleep right now. I was simply desperate. In a Second World War interrogation I would have been ready to spill the beans to betray King and Country for the promise of my warm, dry, horizontal fix. Fortunately the KGB were not visiting Maiden that night, and I was able to borrow Sarah's sleeping bag as she was away seeing mates in Edinburgh.

The next morning was designated (again) for RIB maintenance/oil changes. The outgoing gearbox oil looked as tired and worn out as I had felt the previous evening. Apparently the RIB had already done two year's work in seven weeks, which was also not dissimilar to how I felt. I did my customary Saturday morning radio link-up with Classic FM, and then wandered lazily around the harbour fascinated by the ultra-short, tall, bulbous fishing boats prevalent in this part of the world. I would love to have understood why certain fishing boats are built the way they are, and how their design fits to the type of fishing done, and predominant sea state. Both out at sea and in port, these multifarious vessels had been our most dominant companions, but I knew less about what they were doing than they probably did about me. Next time (?) I would take the time to talk to the fishermen and better understand their world. One of the negatives of this all-consuming quest was that being always hungry for miles was often incompatible with a journey of discovery and local interaction.

I started sailing at midday, with very light F1/2 winds 'on the nose' from the south-east. I was on Bertha with the colossal 10.7m sail, and our run of big-distance days looked like coming to an abrupt end. During the morning session, slowly inching towards the Farne Islands, I passed the time meticulously composing an article for the windsurfing press on the pros and cons of the equipment I had used. I then drifted into daydreams about my triumphant arrival on Stokes Bay beach, arms aloft, but tearful and speechless amidst the family embraces. This tearful and triumphal return fantasy took many different forms, and inventing a new angle was always an easy way to pass half an hour's tedium in what seemed like five minutes. By mid-afternoon, the wind had veered to a more favourable south-westerly direction, and increased to an inconsistent F2/4, meaning a good deal of sail and board trim changes, and no time for further daydreams. At the top end of this wind range handling the 10.7m sail was like wrestling with an angry gorilla, but a clearing sky and the emerging shapes of Lindisfarne and outer Farne Islands on the horizon kept me going. After such a slow late start, I was well pleased with the 31 miles logged. We had sailed some 10 miles south of the Longstone lighthouse, which sits atop the outer Farne Island, and in all the earlier daydreaming and then fighting with an oversized sail, I had completely forgotten that we were now off English soil for the first time since 31 August. It was both sobering and intoxicating to review the traumas, triumphs, and emotional depths I had experienced over the last forty days. What an incredible venture, and I still had 420 miles to go.

Motoring in through the inner sound past imposing Bamburgh Castle towards low-lying Lindisfarne (Holy Island), with its famous priory, was a magical experience. The sun had just left us for the day, but its short-term legacy was a flimsy red-orange sky which exaggerated the mystery and majesty of these famous ruins, and the dark shadowy rocks offshore. It was one of those moments that takes a sacrosanct, ring-fenced space in the memory banks. Maiden was already anchored off the southern shore of Holy Island when we approached gingerly against a 4-knot tide and increasingly strong westerly wind. The day's progress, and the magnificent beauty of our stopover location had everyone on a communal high. After eating and discussing the next day's heavy weather forecast, a scouting party of four were swept quickly to shore in the tender downwind and across the tide. The beach they headed for was already occupied by what looked like a chain of ghostly druids carrying lighted torches down to the shoreline. I did not envy them their return journey, but Philippe, Sarah and Kevin were on their way to the pub, so they were not thinking so many bridges ahead. Apart from finding out about the druids' light show, they also had to meet up with John who had been van driver for the day.

I was in my bag and asleep by 11.00 p.m., but the 30-knot winds and slapping swells had me tossing and turning half awake at 1.00 a.m. I suddenly realised that the pub party were still not back. How the hell did they expect to get our pathetic leaky tender back to Maiden against near gale force winds, and across strong tides. I got up and talked to Damian who was on anchor watch. He had not given it much thought, but I started to worry uncontrollably. Maybe they had tried to make it back but had been swept away to sea by the wind and tide. They had life jackets, but we could not be sure they had any other survival or rescue equipment with them. I considered calling the coastguard, but then rationalised that on the basis of prior form, they could well still be in the pub. We then tried getting telephone numbers for the police station and pubs on Holy

Island. The existence of a police station was a brave call anyway, and I only succeeded in raising one irate landlord who knew nothing of our four wayward souls. Damian and Peter calmed me down, and convinced me that they had many years of seamanship between them, and that if the conditions were too rough, they could always crash out in the van (or the pub) until morning. I got back into the bag, and lay awake trying to put the various nightmare scenarios out of my mind. They (Philippe, Kevin and Sarah) eventually made it back at 2.00 a.m. (when coincidentally the wind and tide had eased) very drunk, very loud and not at all understanding our concern. I was mad, glad and tired. Sarah and Philippe were in the two bunks above me and I lost my fragile cool when various bits of Sarah's bunk-end wardrobe started falling on my head as Philippe tried to dislodge her from her bunk. I used very bad language, and sent the first hard heavy article I could lay my hands on fizzing in their general direction. After that, I received humble apologies, and it all went quiet ... at last.

'Sheepish' was probably the best word to describe the general atmosphere the next morning. Fortunately for me, but not for those with huge hangovers, we had to leave the anchorage by 7.00 a.m., to ensure enough water for Maiden to clear a sandbar between Burrows Hole and Castle Point. John Beecroft had not fancied the return tender trip in the windy darkness, and had thus slept in the van, with an arrangement for Sarah to call him on his mobile at 7.00 a.m., whereupon the RIB could collect him from the jetty, and deposit a replacement van driver. Sarah apparently tried to call, but could not get through, and there was no sign of him on the jetty. We did not know where the van was parked and did not have time to find him before being trapped by the sandbar, so he was again left to fend for himself for the day. I was still very grumpy with Philippe and Sarah, but sober apologies were enough. I felt a bit sorry for John, but also felt that as a professional film-maker, he could maybe have avoided the 2.00 a.m. lock-in, and thus been in a position to get himself up and ready to be collected for the day's filming. Ironically, the morning sunrise and the day's sailing were more spectacular than anything John had captured on film so far, which was bad for both him and me. The ruined abbey and outlying rocks were wonderfully silhouetted against the rising sun, as we navigated our way out over the sandbar and round the rock-indicating cardinal markers. The morning was desperately cold, but just as memorable as the previous evening. We never did find out what the torch-bearing druids were up to, but if it was anything to do with stunning sunsets and sunrises, then I need to know how to book them for future events.

On the way down to the waypoint, the inshore shipping forecast confirmed the previous night's prediction of F4/6, occasionally F7, southwesterlies. It was going to be a big day, but forecasts are of course more often wrong than right, and we were not surprised to be met by a flat-water F2 at the waypoint. I set off on Bertha with the trusty 9.4m sail, and made very slow progress against the tide for the first hour. The wind suddenly came up to a solid F4, and Bertha was replaced by Katie. Within fifteen minutes it was back down to F2/3, and I was back on Bertha. After plonking along slowly for another thirty minutes, the wind suddenly picked up to F5, and no amount of brute strength and determination was going to enable me to handle a 9.4m sail and 3.80m long raceboard in these increasingly rough conditions. So far we had been out for nearly three hours, but with one sail change and three board changes, and seemingly most of my time on the wrong kit for the conditions, I had only covered 12 miles. The demented chuckling face, watching me seething with frustration, was up there again.

Frustration and anger eventually gave way to rational analysis on the RIB. If we were to believe the forecast, then the predicted F4/7 conditions had now arrived (after a few false starts); and my beam/broad reach course realistically needed a 6.0m sail, and Lady Di. We decided to compromise with a 7.0m sail on Katie. Over the next four hours the squally wind oscillated between F2 and F7, normally staying at these extremes for thirty to forty minutes. At times I was in pure survival mode, screwing airborne into the wind to kill the life-threatening speed generated by 35-knot gusts, and at others I was drifting backwards on the tide, trying to keep Katie moving forwards in 4–5 knots of wind. In between the periods of too much and too little wind I also had some wonderful high-speed F4/5 broad reaches. Our strategy was to stick with the 7.0m sail, regardless, swapping between Katie (F4+) and Bertha (F3-). A board change took around five minutes, whereas a sail change could be anything up to thirty minutes. I estimate that I was either seriously overpowered or underpowered for 70 per cent of the day, and altogether we made eleven board changes. With all this decision making and frantic activity, we progressed unknowingly down the English north-east coastline, passing out of sight of the Tyneside and Teeside conurbations. Towards the end of this topsy-turvy, physically gruelling day, the high ground of the North York Moors came into view, and having lived in this part of the world in the early 1980s I knew that the fishing port over my right shoulder was Whitby, and that we had come a bloody long way from Holy Island in Northumberland. The RIB log showed a distance covered of 66 miles, our second-best day yet. There is no way I could have handled, mentally or physically, a day such as this even three or four weeks before, which made the success all the more satisfying. I felt that I had now reached the realistic peak of my windsurfing ability, and windsurfing fitness. I had set sail as a very fit, but very average windsurfer. I now felt that I had moved into a relatively small fraternity of sailors who could handle the mental, physical and technical demands of a day such as this. My confidence in completing the course inched another notch upwards.

Towards the end of the day I had been forced to sail broader and broader off the wind to keep my south-south-east course, meaning that the wind was veering from south-west towards north-west, but in all the frenzied single-minded activity, I had not noticed that the seas had actually become quite rough. Maiden could not get into Whitby due to her draft, and was waiting for us in Hartlepool 28 miles back up the coast. Thus after packing up the kit, we were faced with a run back up to Hartlepool, into a F6 north-westerly, and steep 6–8 ft wind-over-tide seas. It was immediately evident that the RIB could only manage about 8–9 knots average SOG, without trashing the stored boards through the very heavy slamming. Both the Windsurfer and the RIB team had been through a particularly demanding, gruelling day; and the thought of three to four hours more of this bone-jarring, cold-shower purgatory was too much to bear. Spider suggested we divert into Whitby, and get the van to come and ferry us back to Hartlepool. There was no argument, and within twenty minutes we were climbing up the quayside and quizzing the harbour master on where to find a secure berth for the RIB. He directed us to an appropriate marina pontoon, and we directed ourselves to the nearest pub, to wait for Duncan the taxi service to arrive. The team spirit and communal sense of achievement were strong and tangible. We were again very wet, very cold and very tired, sat amidst a pile of steaming all-weather clothing, and explaining our story to the bemused locals. Our general appearance told half the story anyway. In addition to the permanently wet apparel, our faces were wind-tanned, unshaven and weatherbeaten, and my palms had grown thick horny callouses where I gripped the boom. I decided I preferred this tough, sea-smelling, extreme-adventurer image, to my former well-washed, smart, grey-suited lifestyle. Whether my wife felt the same would be an entirely different question! The van ride back to Hartlepool took much longer than expected. A 28-nautical-mile seaborne route seemed to be a meandering 60-land-mile journey by road, so we were very late and tired when finally reunited with the Maiden contingent. There was thus neither the time nor the energy for anything other than food, and then bed.

My watch alarm reliably started its familiar bleeping at 5.45 a.m. the next morning (Day 51, 11 October). Ear plugs out, three layers of clothing on and the usual rush to the heads for my morning constitutional. Also as usual I was first one up, and able to eat my breakfast in peace in the nav station. We had decided the night before to get away by 6.30 a.m., for the one-hour drive down to Whitby. Mornings were always a frustrating time for me, and this was no exception. To my simple mind, if we had agreed a 6.30 departure, then this is when we should leave. No-one else seemed to share this mode of operation, and despite my grumblings, we still only left at 7.00 a.m. Sarah was driving, with myself and Tim in the front seats, and the rest (RIB crew Philippe and Spider and John) crammed into steerage in the back, with all the spare boat parts and windsurf kit. It was a stunning morning, with a bright-red sunrise over the North York Moors. I remembered a day fifteen to sixteen years earlier when I lived in Wetherby and used to come to these moors taking photographs. I thought I recognised the row of terraced houses, seemingly alone on a hillside, which had been the subject matter for one of my favourite photos, now framed on our dining-room wall.

Roadworks on the Whitby one-way system made it absolutely impossible to get the van to the side of the river where the RIB was berthed (or at least that was our story!). We ended up parking on the north side of the marina, with the RIB a tantalizing 100-yard swim, but 1-mile walk, away on the south side. To complicate life further we needed to find the marina manager to give us keys to get into the south side of the marina, and of course he was nowhere to be found. True to the normal routine, I gave up any hope of the scheduled 9.00 a.m. 'on the water' goal, and sat around drinking coffee, and doing a 'piece to camera' for John in the morning sunshine. Eventually we motored out of the marina up to the main harbour to refuel. John had been bedevilled with camera and other problems over the last three days, and twice had been back to his supplier for a replacement. He was now excitedly twitching the controls on a brand-new digital machine, and clearly very keen to fill up several cassettes with 'life on the RIB' footage. Whilst refuelling, myself and Philippe were discussing navigational tactics for the day. John climbed out of the RIB and onto some greasy-looking steps to try and get an aerial shot of this discourse, promptly lost his footing, and disappeared camera and all, into the dirty murky harbour waters. It was a comical sight, and John also saw the funny side. I laughed at first, but inside was decidedly angry. As an investor in the documentary based on John's footage, I was starting to become increasingly irritated with the series of problems which meant that we had collected very little footage over the last week, missing some of our best and most spectacular windsurfing days. The seaweed-covered, diesel-splattered steps would have been an excellent obstacle for an 'It's a Knockout' type farce, and were odds-on favourite to win against our intrepid cameraman.

Whitby would for various reasons be an easy place to remember! It was a lovely harbour to enter from the sea, and a surprisingly pretty town, tightly packed into the valley. However, in line with its reputation, there were numerous fish and chip shops and amusement arcades overlooking the harbour, which will probably predominate in the memory.

After recalling Sarah to collect our dripping cameraman with the van, we eventually motored out of Whitby and reached the previous night's waypoint at around 11.00 a.m. So much for the scheduled 9.00 a.m. start! Philippe rationally pointed out that my hunger for miles could also be counterproductive. If we had decided to stop sailing the day before whilst still within reach of Hartlepool, we could have been out on the water by 8.30, and well past our start point by 11.00 a.m. It was an interesting alternative view, but I was still happier trying to squeeze the maximum out of each day. The forecast was for strong F5/6, occasionally gale force 7 west/north-west winds. The tides would be against us until midday, but crucially we should have wind with tide conditions for the passage around Flamborough Head mid-afternoon. A strong tide against a force 6 over shallow water would have thrown up some horrendous standing waves. I needed to sail in a south-easterly direction until we rounded Flamborough Head, meaning a fast but unstable broad reach for the first 25 miles. Broad reaching in a force 4/5 I could do, but when the winds reached force 6/7, and my speeds increased to over 25 knots on rough seas, I started to fear for my safety and the prospect of a neck-breaking catapult fall. We rigged a 6.0m sail to go on Lady Di, which for the first fifteen minutes was a perfect combination in a solid force 5 wind. Could this be the dream day when the wind behaved just as required? No, of course not. The wind suddenly dropped to a force 4, and I was forced to change to Katie. Predictably the wind died further to a F2/3, and we had no alternative but to make another change of board to Bertha. In anticipation of the met office forecast actually coming true, and remembering yesterday's successful 'one sail strategy', I persevered with the 6.0m sail for over an hour in conditions which needed a much bigger engine. At one stage the wind suddenly picked up, so we quickly changed back to Lady Di. It was of course only a tease. Being forced to again change back to the bigger board, I swore violently at the empty sky, feeling like punching my fist through the sail.

Our stop-start underpowered progress during the first two hours meant that we had only covered around 10 miles Apart from the odd teasing surge, the wind had been F2/3 now for over an hour. Maybe this was all we were going to get for the day. I hauled myself onto the RIB, and made it very clear that I needed a bigger sail. The current conditions would suggest the 9.4m sail. The latest met office forecast was still F5/6. The cloud pattern suggested a front was on its way with stronger winds. We compromised with the 8.0m sail, and within minutes of climbing back onto Bertha the wind picked up to a solid F5. My signals to the RIB were ignored. The faces of Philippe and Tim told me firmly where I stood. Providing I could handle this board/sail combination without significant risk of injury or

Fully powered up broad reaching off Flamborough Head

damage, there would be no more changes. Second-guessing the wind had proved to be an absolutely futile exercise.

Our late start, and multiple board/sail changes meant that Maiden was some 12 miles ahead of us by early afternoon, and I could just make out her mast on the horizon approaching Flamborough Head. I was fully powered up blasting about 15 degrees off the wind at 20–23 knots, and had the target in my sights. The next three hours proved to be by far the best distance-eating run of the whole trip. I went into that timeless, featureless 'goal must be achieved' mode, and simply channelled all my mental and physical energies into sailing as fast as possible for as long as possible. Philippe called Maiden on the radio, suggesting they wake Duncan the photographer from his afternoon siesta, to capture a high-speed pass with sunlit chalk cliffs in the background. Rather than the promised high-speed pass, I very nearly gave him a high-speed crash; trying to sail very close to Maiden and looking at the camera rather than the water, I failed to notice her 3-ft wake, and suddenly had a very large board completely airborne, nose pointing skywards. I somehow landed the jump and sailed away into the distance trying to give the impression that it was just a bit of showing off in front of the camera ...

Over the three hours after changing to the 8.0m sail, I covered around 60 miles, in 15–25 knot winds. It was brilliant, truly exhilarating sailing, broad reaching, and then beam reaching, blasting past the spectacular chalk headlands of Flamborough Head into Bridlington Bay and south to finish 10 miles east of Spurn Head. The windsurfing purists would quickly point out that I was on absolutely the wrong kit for these conditions. It would have been a much faster and more comfortable sail on a smaller board with 6.5m sail. I agree, but once in the back straps of the big board, cranking along at more than 20 knots, neither I nor the RIB team dared risk upsetting the wind gods by going for a change.

Our fantastic afternoon run meant that we were easily on course for a record day, and I was given the Big T sign to stop at 5 p.m. with the GPS log showing a record waypoint to waypoint distance of 73 miles. I was thrilled but also frustrated. Another hour's sailing could give us another 20 miles, and maybe even a chance to break the 100-mile barrier. Spider in particular was adamant that we could not contemplate the tricky run into Grimsby, our designated stopover destination, in the dark. Philippe and Tim seemed to be siding with Spider, so I gave in. The day had also ended with a navigational disagreement. With these near-perfect conditions, I had wanted to stay on a broad reach sailing in a south-easterly direction on a rhumb line across to Cromer on the North Norfolk coast. The villains on the RIB team wanted me to head up into wind on a southerly course to avoid us having an overlong run into Grimsby. My nightmare scenario was that the wind would turn NW leaving me with a dead-run sail tomorrow.

The run into Grimsby was very different from any other experienced so far. Two nights before we had anchored off the mysterious and beautiful Lindisfarne Island. Last night it was round the breakwater and into compact Whitby harbour. For starters, this was the first time since the Shannon that we were motoring up a narrow estuarine shipping channel into yellow silt-ridden water. It was also the first time we had encountered heavy freight traffic, and offshore refuelling/offloading stations. The tone of the harbour master and coastguard was becoming more brusque and businesslike. Grimsby marina was hidden behind a series of sprawling fishing and freight quays, and fronted by disused, dilapidated fish warehouses. It was, however, full of expensive-looking yachts and powercraft, and the nearest we had ever moored to a yacht club bar (50 yds). Despite the navigational disagreement, the atmosphere in the yacht club bar was buzzing. It had been a record day; I had managed to blast past Maiden at close range for the first time on the whole trip; we were only 280 miles from home, and the bar was full of local press wanting to do interviews and take photos. Again the prospect of an eight-week finish, smashing Keith Russell's record, was a big topic of conversation. For that night I truly felt like a hero and lay in my bunk glowing with pride. The day's success also brought home to me how easy the whole trip could have been with a F4/5 wind, flattish seas and a beam reaching point of sail. That afternoon's 60-mile, three-hour blast, had been the first time on the whole trip we had been exposed to such conditions for more than the odd hour, but wondering what might have been is another pointless train of thought alongside bitter regrets and obsessive worry. The reality was that we had made the best of what we were given and that 84 per cent of the journey was now complete.

This time I was not woken by the reveller's return to Maiden, but got the full story of the previous night's Grimsby yacht club bar events over breakfast on Day 52 (12 October). The large portly barman-cum-vice-commodore was apparently an ex-naval commander. Apart from talking loudly and authoritatively on his chosen subject of battleships and their high-speed handling properties, he also demonstrated an uncanny ability to drink a pint of bitter stood on his head. I had tried this once at university and found that breathing becomes somewhat problematic when one's mouth and nasal passages are brim full of cold fizzy beer. Kevin had no such inhibitions, and with his face going from beetroot purple to sunset red and back again, he upheld the honour of Maiden and all who sail in her. Our friendly barman was however not yet finished with his surprises. In one of the more sensible periods of the evening Philippe had told him that we were missing 2–3 charts for our remaining course. The barman kindly offered to lend Philippe his, and as the evening drew to a close, Philippe and his big friend wandered off towards a swish-looking yacht at the other end of the marina. Philippe blundered back onto Maiden some ten minutes later looking decidedly flustered. The big friend was apparently more interested in boys than girls, and Philippe was just his type. Despite the slightly unusual end to the evening, our big friend also left his legacy by christening the unkempt, bedraggled Philippe as Wurzle Gummidge. In fact his first comment as Philippe walked into the bar was 'Hey-Up, Scarecrow's arrived'. The name Wurzle stuck and has been the favoured means of addressing Philippe ever since.

I was up at 5.30 a.m., for our scheduled 6.00 a.m. departure, which had been declared to give ourselves a fighting chance of getting within striking distance of Lowestoft 78 miles away, apparently the next port on our route capable of taking Maiden's 3.4m draft. Amazingly everyone else was up and ready on time. It would have been silly to expect nothing to go wrong, but on this occasion it was 'circumstances beyond our control'. Without any prior warning the harbour master had closed the gates at the entrance to the dock and marina we were in. We apparently had to wait for ninety minutes until the tide was right again. I didn't get into the technicalities. We just gave up and sloped off to the greasiest breakfast café in the Western world, and then I sat patiently on the dockside writing up my diary. I was frustrated rather than angry.

When we did get away, and out to the waypoint, my dark mood really set in with a vengeance. Despite the F5/6 forecast there was no decent wind (F1/2) and my nightmare scenario of having to run dead downwind on a gently rolling sea was upon me. All I could think about was how easy the extra miles would have been yesterday, and how incredibly uncomfortable today's snail-like progress was becoming. Over the first hour I covered only 3 miles compared with 23 miles in the previous day's last hour, a statistic I gleefully pointed out to the RIB team. After a morning of gesticulating tantrums, and soundless sulks from me, the RIB team (and even Tim) were starting to lose their patience. 'Either you get your mind focused on making the best of what we have, or we might as well pack up for the day right now, and motor back into Grimsby.' I could not face going back to Grimsby. We had to move on, and therefore I had to grow up and forget my grievances. Providing the weather stayed light, there was apparently a reasonable anchorage for Maiden 30 miles away, off Wells-next-the Sea in North Norfolk. I thus plodded manfully forward sweating profusely in my winter steamer under a clear blue October sky. The contrast with four days ago was just unreal. The air temperature was up around 16 degrees, and the water temperature at least 5 degrees higher than off Scotland. By 3.00 p.m., the wind had died further, and I climbed onto the

RIB for a rest. Philippe decided it was time to have his first windsurfing lesson. He showed little interest in borrowing my wetsuit, and spent a good 20 minutes practising his uphauling and steering, clad only in a pair of paisley boxer shorts. I had to pinch myself, to convince Richard Cooper, the pragmatic predictable realist, that all this was really happening. Over the last week or so we had come across a 56-year-old Landlady with Mike Tyson's right hook, a brig dwelling TV presenter, a bunch of torch-carrying weirdos who seemed to be in control of the sunsets, a homosexual naval commander who liked to take his evening pint inverted, and now a nutty photographer windsurfing in the middle of The Wash in mid-October in his boxer shorts.

I had to get back to reality, so I decided to call it a day after 15.4 miles, achieved at a blistering average speed of 2.5 knots. My parents were supposed to be driving down from Lancashire to meet me that evening, so it made sense to get through to them on the mobile phone and tell them where we intended to be. The run down to Wells was easy enough, but getting up the tidal river to Wells harbour was not. The harbour master assured us that by 7 p.m., on the rising tide, there would be plenty enough water for the RIB. The fact that the red and green channel marker buoys were still high and dry on the sand when we arrived at 6.30 p.m., told us that his timings were a tad optimistic. We eventually made it to land by 8.30 p.m., and I was met by my emotional parents. It was the first time I had seen any friends or family since Stokes Bay on 22 August, and the night's chinwag was both necessary and fulfilling. My mum and dad had gone from being dismissive of the whole venture when I first told them it was happening, to now living my triumphs and traumas day by day. They, together with most of their home village, were all diligently tuning into Classic FM's lunchtime updates, hungry for news on the local lad who (although obviously a bit barmy) had gone off doing something special.

It meant a lot to me to have their support, and to be giving them something to be proud about over drinks at the golf club. For them, it was special to see me climb off my second home, the RIB, and to meet again members of the support team. They treated me to a night in a B&B, and after a timeless soak in the bath, we sat down to a fish and chip supper, with Dad telling me in great detail how all the charity fundraising for MCS was going. Before setting off there had been great plans to meet up with friends and family at various stages of the trip. Impracticalities had, however, always seemed to override intent. It was very difficult for people to plan when not knowing where we would be and when. Also even if we got the destination right, I could well be in late off the water, obligated to do media stuff, and away early the next morning. A two-hour window in the pub was not really good enough justification to drive the length of the country. Mum and Dad had earmarked this day to meet us in Yorkshire, but had to travel a little further due to our exceptional progress. I was very glad they made the effort.

Back on Maiden, it was apparently time for a quiet night, the only newsworthy event being the return of Andy, along with a quiet blonde girl called Lindsay who had been taken on as galley manager/Maiden crew (Sophie's very late replacement). Spider was coming to the end of his allotted time, and had to leave in two days' time to get organised for his new job in the Fire Brigade. Andy happened to also be a fully qualified RIB driver, so he went from being my voluntary caddy-cum-equipment-manager, to being an IRS paid RIB coxswain. Tim had a break from caddy duties the next day, and Andy, Spider and Philippe were my treasured company. We arrived at the waypoint at 10.00 a.m., but didn't have enough wind to justify rigging a sail until 1.00 p.m. Andy's comment was 'Celtic Sea, here we go again'. Surely the wind gods couldn't be so cruel as to sit me under a big, stationary, windless high in October, completely erasing the fantastic east coast progress of the preceding week. Today was Wednesday 13 October (Day 53). The forecasters were saying that the wind would be back the next day or Friday, but I knew in my heart that these two windless days had destroyed any chance we had of making the eight-week target. I later picked up some light south-westerly breezes and a helpful tide to cover 17 miles in five hours, sailing within sight of Maiden just off Wells. That evening, sitting on Maiden's deck eating supper, we witnessed another wonderful natural happening. The North Norfolk coast was more scenic than I had expected, with deserted beaches, and well-grazed pastures rolling down to the sea. The clear anticyclonic conditions gave rise to a powerful blood-red sunset, and just as the sun started to hide below the horizon, a massive flock of seabirds crossed the sky to the west. It perceptibly darkened as this oscillating blanket of life journeyed onwards. No-one spoke on Maiden until this avian eclipse was over, but it was certainly another moment to go into the 'protected' section of the memory banks.

Day 54 (14 October) started badly as I discovered that John had put a huge dent in the side of the van whilst leaving Grimsby marina two days before. It was the fact that he had not bothered to tell me rather than the dent itself, which really made my blood boil. We arrived at the waypoint at 8.00 a.m., but with only 1–2 knots of wind there was no rush to hoist a sail. A big part of the first two hours was spent simply sat astride my board drifting eastwards on the 1.5 knot tide. There was simply too little wind to hold the 10.7m sail vertical. By mid-morning at least I had 2–4 knots of wind, and could gently pump my way forwards. I was sailing quite close into the shore, and would line up a foreground and more distant landmark to measure forward progress. The foreground marker was effectively the axis of my rotating straight line. Thinking about the geometry of what I was doing, I realised that to increase the perception of forward movement I needed to be as near as possible to the foreground marker, and as far away as possible from the distant landmark. It was about 18 miles to Cromer from our starting point, and for the final 10 miles (and four hours) I had Cromer Pier in my sights. Because I was moving so slowly, it almost seemed to recede into the distance at times. When we were 5 miles short, Andy on the RIB informed me that I only had about ninety minutes of favourable tide left. With a west-running tide in these pathetic winds, I would be going nowhere. I thus decided that I had to give it everything I had to get past the pier before the tide turned; and began to pump aggressively as though my life depended upon it. Pumping my 10.7m sail was like being on one of my dreaded OBLA gym tests, except it lasted longer. Everything was aching, and I was sweating profusely, as we inched to within 200 yards of the pier. The tide was now starting to run against us, and I was pumping to stand still. There was no choice but to take an interim waypoint, lunch and then take stock of our options.

The wind gods clearly appreciated my gargantuan efforts, and by 3 p.m., the wind had increased to 5–6 knots. We decided to give it another go, with a tactic to stay in close to the shore in shallow water wherever possible to get out of the worst of the 2–3 knots of unfavourable tide. I enjoyed sailing close to the cliff-top lighthouse east of Cromer, located at the end of Royal Cromer golf course, which I had played some ten years before. I also enjoyed returning to beach hut country. The last beach I had sailed along within sight of these glorified but colourful and very British 'garden-sheds-on-the-shore' was on day 1, east of Bournemouth ... another welcoming indicator that I was on the way home. Sailing within 100m of the shore, in 3 ft of water, navigating my way around sunken groynes was also a whole new experience; but it worked, and I made another 8 miles by 5.00 p.m., and my spirits were definitely on the up as the tide against weakened, and my SOG increased to 5 knots. I was thus gobsmacked when I got the Big T (time's up) sign from Andy in the RIB. I had spent three days labouring painfully forwards at less than a two-year-old's walking speed, and now at last I was making some decent speed. Andy was at his officious worst stressing that we had a 35-mile run down to Lowestoft (where 'Maiden was waiting') through a particularly tricky sandbank-strewn channel. Philippe looked confused. On the one hand he seemed to sympathise with me, but he probably felt he had to show sympathy with his fellow RIB crew and started talking about rogue containers reported in this area which float just below the surface, and could on collision destroy a fast-moving RIB and its occupants. My mental map told me that it was more like 25 miles to Lowestoft, so either someone had got their chart reading seriously wrong, or they were bullshitting to persuade me to accept an early finish. I didn't argue at the time, preferring to stay silent but I knew that my mental map was right when it took us less than an hour to get in, travelling at 25–30 knots.

It was Spider's last night, and Andy's second day back on the RIB, so I consigned the issue to my diary, and got on with the evening. We were made very welcome by Lowestoft Yacht Club, which eased the underlying tension between me and the RIB crew, and apparently BBC East had used some of Sarah's footage to run a piece on us on the 6.00 p.m. news, which got the locals properly enthused. True to type, I went to bed early and the hard core took on the yacht club's best over a four-hour pool marathon. Despite the end-of-day frustrations, I still felt upbeat about the 25 miles I had covered over some seven hours on the board. We were most of the way round what seemed like a never-ending corner of north-east Norfolk, and the next day's forecast was for F3/4 south-westerlies. I had been going fifty-four days. We had only 220 miles to go, and in my mind only two more serious hazards to negotiate. The crossing from the south-east corner of East Anglia (east of Felixtowe) to Ramsgate in Kent would be a whole new challenge getting me through Britain's busiest shipping lanes. I was also nervous about the journey through the Dover Straights, where ferry traffic could potentially combine with very rough wind-over-tide conditions to give me a major challenge. The rational part of my brain was urging caution and restraint, but my emotional spirit was telling me that once across to Ramsgate, surely we were virtually home and dry. An accident now which kiboshed the mission would break my heart, and almost certainly scar me for life. I had to be careful, but I also had to cover the miles. The charters on Maiden and the RIB had been extended to sixty-three days, but after that I was in trouble. The race against time, which we had ostensibly won, when rounding northern Scotland in early October, was still on.

Day 55 (15 October) started embarrassingly. Once back at the waypoint, I realised that my earlier morning constitutional had not completed the job. I had to go, and it had to be now. We were sitting some 200m off a beach, and the village of Bacton. Philippe asked if we had time to motor further offshore to avoid upsetting the sea view of breakfasting locals. I was already half out of my wetsuit, and within seconds suspended over the back of the RIB, so the answer was clearly no! Feeling a lot more comfortable, I set sail at 8.30 a.m. on Bertha with the 9.4m sail, in a F2/3. After several steady miles, I began to worry about my little incident off Bacton. What if someone had been watching with a camera? What if an angry old lady decided to call the RYA, MCS, Classic FM and the BBC? The headlines would be highly humorous, but deeply destructive of our credibility. After another hour beating up the groyne and pipeline-laden Norfolk coastline, I plucked up the courage to convince my worrying right brain that I was unnecessarily paranoid, and concentrated on being hungry for miles. Andy clearly felt that reaching Lowestoft would be a good result beating into these relatively light winds. I had much more distant targets in mind, and had to remind the RIB crew to call Maiden, and warn them that they would hopefully need to move down the coast to Harwich. The wind picked up to F3 by midday, and I cruised past Great Yarmouth and Lowestoft at a good 8–10 knots nicely assisted by a south-flowing tide. Maiden duly broke her berth and followed us southwards. I did not expect to enjoy this coastline anything like as much as the west coast, but there was something special about the arrow-straight beaches, and vividly coloured seaside houses. It helped that I was mostly sailing within half a mile of the shore, and that the conditions were not too taxing. I also sailed very close to the Sizewell B nuclear power station. I did not notice any obvious warming of the water, or orange-glowing sealife, but the sheer size of the reactor structures, gave a good indication of the consequences if it all went horribly wrong. The day's sailing was brought to an end at 5.30 p.m. after nearly nine hours on the board, and 54 very satisfying miles covered. Our ending waypoint was only 13 miles north-east of Felixtowe, and a great springboard for tomorrow's crossing to Ramsgate.

The run into Shotley marina (Harwich) was both spectacular and frightening. Our 8m RIB was treated the same as the 50,000-tonne container ships. We had to be in the narrow shipping lanes, and we had to follow the rules of the road. What amazed me was the speed of these colossal vessels. They do not look like they are moving at all until you try and overtake, and notice that 20 knots is not enough. We arrived well before Maiden due to her late start, and enjoyed a lovely hot shower and hot meal in the yacht club. Maiden had great difficulty finding her designated mooring buoy in the dark, but I was too tired to get involved, and crashed into my bunk exhausted but happy.

We always seemed to arrange RIB maintenance for Saturday mornings, and Day 56 (16 October) was no different. The usual oil changes were supposed to take forty-five minutes, but we still didn't leave until 11.30 a.m. Nevertheless I had a productive, enjoyable morning sat outside the yacht club, on a warm and breezy morning. I first had to talk to various media, and to Mentorn who were making the National Geographic documentary, and then to friends and family. Everybody was desperate to know when we were planning to finish. My answer of any time over the next five to seven days, depending upon the wind, was not good enough. Friends and family had to travel from all over the country. The media had to organise camera crews. We needed an official RYA presence to witness the finish. A celebratory party had to be organised and booked. After an hour of denial, I realised that I had to give in, and that we should give a reasonably safe 'estimate', stressing that it could be subject to change. We had 170 miles to go, and a reasonable 3–5 day forecast of strengthening easterly winds. I rationalised that at 42 miles/day, we would be home late Tuesday. Adding a margin of error, I told everyone Wednesday, late afternoon. This also worked well for my wife who, taking my eight-week pre-event time-frame for granted (I was always on time!), had accepted an invitation to go on a girl's weekend away from Friday onwards.

My heavily stressed warnings that this was still very weather dependent were of course ignored and everyone started to make their plans. My last chat of the morning was to Jane Jones at Classic FM. After some of the suicidal-sounding earlier interviews, this chat was as bright and bubbly as an expensive champagne. I was in a good mood, and Jane seemed as excited as if she were on the trip with us. I never got to hear any of these interviews, but this was one I definitely should have had recorded.

With a quite bumpy ride out through the churned-up shipping lanes, I didn't get underway until 1.00 p.m., which left us very tight to make the 45-mile crossing to Ramsgate. The wind was F2 from the east, so we rigged the humungous 10.7m sail, and plugged it into Bertha's battered hull. From a navigational standpoint, it was a highly technical day. Andy, Philppe and Tim had to position me absolutely right to slip between rather than into the massive freighters and container ships, taking into account the ubiquitous sandbanks in this area. With a light wind and massive sail, my speed and manoeuvrability were seriously constrained. The seawash and windwash behind these giant ships added a further complication. At one stage I could see eight or nine vessels steaming down the shipping lane that I needed to cross. The RIB team (and in particular Andy) gave me confidence and clear instructions. I had to go as close as possible to the stern of the passing ship (suffering horrible wind shadows) to avoid being too close to the bow of the next and thus not giving the RIB enough time to get me out of trouble if anything went wrong. The wind picked up to a F4 by the end of the day, and stayed firmly in the east, but I did an awful lot of tacking, beating and downwind sailing considering my due south target. The last ninety minutes were spent sailing as broad as possible, which in a good F4 with a 10.7m sail, was another virginal experience, not to be repeated (ever) whilst I am in control of my own mind. I managed to sail within 4 miles of Ramsgate harbour, where Maiden was waiting patiently. I had sailed for five hours non-stop, with a huge heavy sail, and an awful lot of tacking and gybing. Not for the first time I was absolutely shattered, but glowing warm inside from the 45 miles covered, and one more major obstacle ticked off. Tomorrow we would turn corner #6, and head westwards down the English Channel with only 125 miles to go. What a feeling.

Chapter 12

The Twist in the Tail

> To see a world in a grain of sand
> And heaven in a wild flower
>
> Hold infinity in the palm of your hand
> And eternity in an hour.

William Blake

*R*amsgate was a strange, relatively unwelcoming place. We were tied up against an outer harbour wall giving a half-mile walk to the main drag, and the Royal Temple Yacht Club. The bitingly cold easterly wind didn't help, but I somehow felt more threatened walking the streets here amongst the posturing, aggressive-looking youth, than in desperate drunken Wick. To me it was a characterless place, completely overshadowed by Dover as a ferryport, and Eastbourne as the pensioners' choice. As an uneducated one-time visitor, I may have got it completely wrong, but aren't first impressions what branding and marketing are all about? Towns are no different from products. To flourish, they need committed and wealth-creating businesses and consumers. As Gaz said during week one of the venture, parodying his radical image and behaviour, 'Image is everything, performance is nothing.' Not necessarily my philosophy on life, but Ramsgate's image to me meant that I was not interested in its performance.

The evening meeting in the yacht club was not one of my most enjoyable. Damian had been drinking since mid-afternoon, and did not make our important discussion on how to handle the Dover shipping channels any easier. I snapped at him for the second time in a week. The last occasion was also during an evening meeting, when he insisted on using the 'f' word five or six times per sentence. My heavy castigation in front of everyone else obviously did the trick that time, as he was later heard muttering in his sleep about 'not saying ✱✱✱✱✱✱✱ any more'. This caused considerable mirth the next morning, but the bottom line for me was that Damian found it difficult 'living rough' on Maiden, and had been disappointed by the predominance of sandwich making and van driving over glamorous helming of Maiden. Perhaps we had not been straight with him at the outset, but his enthusiasm waned over time, as logically did his contribution ... The alternative view would be that he was a volunteer who had joined us when we were desperate for replacement crew, and

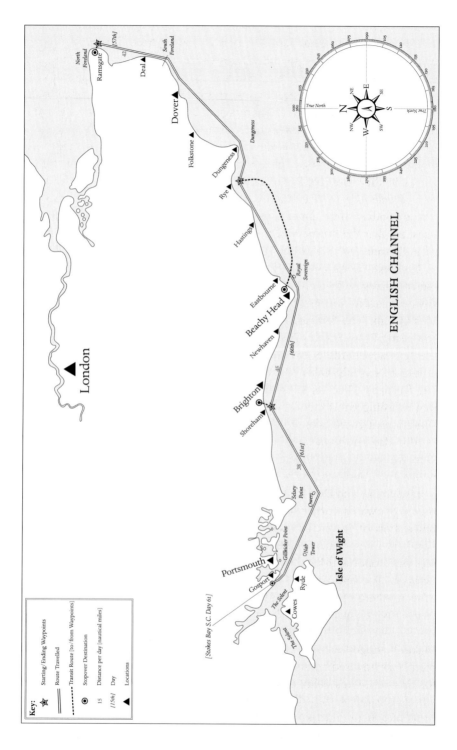

that without him we would have been further constrained. The big argument that particular night was who would drive the van. Everyone wanted to be on Maiden or the RIB for the final corner and the white cliffs of Dover. Not for the first time Sarah came to my rescue, suggesting that she could use the time ashore to work on her edit suite, preparing video news releases for regional TV coverage. I finished off the evening alone in the yacht club's plush conference room, doing a video diary session for Sarah. There was also a wedding reception in the building that night and several times I was most pleasantly interrupted by busty young female guests in their tiny black cocktail frocks. They thought I might be some sort of celebrity (a celebrity doing his own video diary?). Evidently my 'extreme-adventurer' appearance didn't work with these pouting bimbettes. I suspect that the prospect of my 'eau de north sea' cologne contaminating their Channel No 9 was enough to make the visits very short.

The next morning was Day 57 (17 October), and Kevin had to get Maiden out of Ramsgate by 7.00 a.m., to avoid being trapped by the tide. This was always a helpful incentive, and we were miraculously ready to start sailing by 7.55 a.m. The forecast was for easterly winds, starting F3/4, and later increasing F5/6. Southerlies or northerlies would have been my order for the trip westwards down the English Channel. The worst-case scenario would be easterly gales 'up my bum', followed closely by westerly gales 'on the nose'. The three- to five-day forecast given over the VHF earlier that morning was exactly that. This was very bad news. In these weather conditions it could take me at least a week to get back to Stokes Bay. The Wednesday finish was looking increasingly ambitious, but I decided to put it to the back of my mind, and concentrate on the day's big challenge, whilst the conditions were relatively friendly. I cruised southwards past Sandwich Bay and Deal on Bertha with the 8.0m sail in easy F2/3 conditions, moving towards corner #6 which was effectively South Foreland, a few miles short of Dover. I stopped for ten minutes under the imposing South Foreland Cliffs, whilst Maiden and Duncan got into position to take some pics of Cooper and RIB cruising past the white cliffs of Dover. I was very nervous. We had already been on the radio to the Dover Port Control advising them of our route. They had immediately come back and offered to give us a high-speed pilot boat as escort, and to manage the traffic around us! The wind had by now picked up to a good F4, and I was petrified of making a huge fool of myself, falling in, and being unable to restart, as our pilot boat hovered behind, and one of the immense Sea Cat ferries waited for this ridiculous delay to pass. I could just see the quizzical face of the launch coxwain saying, 'This can't possibly be the guy who has gone round most of Britain and Ireland ... it must be some sort of joke', followed by the front-page headlines of 'Round Britain Windsurfer Causes Cross

The white cliffs of Dover, and its big concrete ferry port

Channel Chaos'. It didn't help when I restarted and picked up the dulcet tones of the RIB team choir giving their version of 'There will be bluebirds over ... etc.'

My heart was pumping furiously as we safely tracked towards the glorious white cliffs, and the massive concrete ramparts of Dover port. I was on a reasonably comfortable broad reach, and managed to get clear of the maritime equivalent of Hyde Park Corner without serious embarrassment or delay for the waiting ferries. It was a fantastic feeling to be past hopefully my last major obstacle, but the wind was still increasing, and the sea starting to rough up. I could just about see the sinister-looking form of Dungeness Nuclear Power Station some 20 miles to the south-west. In the strengthening wind I changed to Katie, put some more downhaul on the 8.0m sail, and went forth to do battle sailing as broad as possible. It was high-speed, high-risk sailing. The swells were short and steep, making it that bit more terrifying, handling an often airborne board at 25 knots.

By midday, Katie and the 8.0m sail were simply too big, and my arms simply too worn out. I had made it to a position some 1 mile south of Dungeness mostly on port tack. The wind was up to F5/6, and we decided to risk a session on the fickle Lady Di, with a 6.0m sail. Disregarding the warnings about straying into the military exclusion zone west of Dungeness, I changed to starboard tack, and headed westwards towards Rye. Broad reaching in rough seas puts an inordinate strain on the shock-absorbing, board-trimming back leg. I imagined it to be something like skiing fast through moguls on one leg for hours on end. After the port tack marathon down to Dungeness, my right leg was burning for Britain and could not take any more. Some starboard tack sailing would give my left leg the same pounding whilst the right leg recovered. The next broad reach on Lady Di towards Rye and Winchelsea was the fastest and most frightening I have ever done, or over hope to do. If I had wanted to put myself within a permanent whisker of serious injury, this would have been Plan A, and to me similar in risk profile to Evil Kneevil's motorbike jump across the Grand Canyon. According to the RIB, which had great difficulty keeping up, I was travelling at speeds of 25–30 knots over a steep 4–5 ft chop. Miraculously, I avoided a neck-breaking catapult fall, but over time my bottle started to wane, and I found myself more often than made sense heading up into wind to kill the speed, meaning I was moving more sideways than forward. My mind and body simply couldn't cope any more, and although it was only 2.00 p.m., it was time to pack up. My determined nature would have had me resting for thirty minutes and then giving it another go. Andy and Tim were not interested. The risk of injury would increase exponentially as my mind and body tired further. On this occasion they were absolutely right, and quite possibly saved me from a disastrous final lap injury. We had covered 42 miles, although I had sailed closer to 60. More importantly we were now a few miles short of Hastings, and only 83 miles from Stokes Bay.

Unfortunately the stopover options which could accommodate Maiden's draft were few and far between on the South Coast, and we had to make for Eastbourne, some 20 miles further west. In keeping with the extreme sailing, the RIB ride into Eastbourne was also pretty extreme. The seas were still increasing in size, but stayed steep and confused. At one stage Philippe misjudged his run down the face of one swell and into the back of another, and half a tonne of water came crashing over the A-frame of the RIB. One moment I was holding myself onto my seat as we bridged a crest, and the next moment I was up to my waist in Rye Bay sea water. We laughed afterwards, but a few changes in the dynamics of the moment could have seen one or several of us overboard, and/or some serious damage sustained by the RIB. Maiden was also having a crashing time, running down these seas under very little sail, and the RIB contingent were thus first to arrive into Eastbourne's swish new Sovereign Harbour marina.

The team atmosphere in Eastborne should have been buoyant. It was Sunday evening, meaning we had three full days to cover 83 miles to make the promised Wednesday finish. Any optimistic spirit was, however, killed by the harbour master's forecast, which reiterated the morning's prognosis, stating three days of F5–7 easterly winds. Downwind sailing in F5 I could handle (just about), but in F7 I had no chance. Also with four days of strong easterly winds, the seas would become bigger and rougher, and the air temperature would drop close to zero as the weather system sucked air out of Siberia. After the easterly gales had subsided, a deep Atlantic depression was forecast to move in bringing south-westerly storms. If this all came true, I could easily be spending a week in Eastbourne. For a time I was back down to Kilrush levels of depression. We were so near and yet so far, so tantalizingly close, and yet so impossibly distant. Over several comforting beers with Duncan and Philippe that night I decided to make a decision the next morning, on postponing the scheduled finish until Saturday, or Sunday, or Christmas! Maybe the cynic from *Windsurf* magazine who said I'd be lucky to make it back by Christmas was right after all. Keith Russell's record seemed unassailable right now.

We spent hours the next morning pouring over the synoptic weather charts. Philippe's view was that the forecast could well prove to be over cautious, and by later in the week, the strong easterly flow should subside. However it looked very grim for Monday/Tuesday, backed up by the fact that Maiden's mast top anemometer was right now reading 30 knots, even here in a sheltered marina. I decided to take a risk and specify a Saturday finish. We simply had to make it by this day, even if I had to sit astride my board drifting overnight on the tide. I couldn't possibly cancel my homecoming twice. My wife was far from pleased. She now had no choice but to cancel her girl's weekend away, letting others down. I called everyone else and gave them the news. Some were pleased it was the weekend. Others were irritated, now having to cancel arrangements they had already put in place. It would be 2.30 p.m., Stokes Bay Sailing Club on Saturday, 23 October. Hotels were booked, the party organised and a press release went out to the media. For the rest of the day, I worried and worried about what I had done. What if Philippe was wrong, and the over-cautious met office right? How the hell would I explain a second change of plan? Fortunately Duncan's PR machine was at hand to take my mind off the trap I had set myself. Together with Classic FM, he had arranged an 'exclusive' with the *Daily Mail*. They were sending a photographer and reporter down to get the story later. They wanted shots 'on the water', but as it was totally impossible to take an ill-prepared *Daily Mail* hack out into 10-ft seas, and a F7 wind, we commandeered a partly constructed extension to the Marina, and yours truly did 75-yard blasts back and forth across this gusty pond .. not exactly representative of my venture, but he got the spray-ridden close-ups he needed, and also agreed to use some of Duncan's shots. The reporter spent a good hour quizzing me on my motives and emotional ups and downs, and the end result was one of the most accurate and perceptive pieces written on my little adventure.

I went to bed that night trying to think through why I was so down about our current predicament. Of course it was frustrating knowing that there was a significant risk I could miss my own Cup Final appearance, but there was something else. I had spoken regularly to my family over the whole trip, but my kids had been the most disappointed of all when told of the postponed finish. The closer I came to holding them in my arms, the more painful the longing became. I had tentatively suggested to my wife that I could hire a car and drive home tomorrow, assuming these gales persisted. She would have none of it. This might satisfy my painful longing, but it would be a huge anticlimax for the kids who were expecting to see me for the first time in nine weeks, staggering triumphantly up Stokes Bay beach. I then realised that my reservoir of enthusiasm for this amazing journey was just about empty. I simply wanted to get it over with and be a normal husband and father again, and this last-minute twist in the tail felt more like a stake through the heart to me.

The wind was again howling through Maiden's rigging at 25–30 knots on Tuesday morning (Day 59, 19 October), and the sea beyond the harbour wall was boiling violently. Unless something changed we were going nowhere. I had a bits-and-pieces day, shopping for presents, and trying to sort out film footage rights between Sarah, John and Mentorn. I also started calling various publishers to test the interest level in a book. None were interested, of course. The meeting that night was long and difficult. The forecast was much the same, but I was pressing strongly that we should at least get back down to the waypoint and give it a go. Even if I couldn't sail, I could sit on my board and be moved slowly westwards by the gales and the tide. Andy thought this was a ludicrous suggestion, and more likely to result in hypothermia than any significant progress. Andy also reiterated Steve's hard and fast policy of not going out when gales were forecast. He had taken over from Steve as safety officer, and could not sanction a course of action which he felt to be too dangerous. I stressed that the local conditions off Hastings could be different, particularly if the wind swung to the north-east, and we could sail on relatively flat water close to the shore. We simply wouldn't know unless we got out there. Philippe and Tim were closer to me than Andy, but what swung it was a telephone input from Russ Kerslake (the co-owner of IRS, and Andy's boss). Russ independently suggested that we should get out there and have a look at the conditions at the waypoint before writing off another day.

Wednesday, 20 October (Day 60) dawned just like the last two, except colder. The air from Siberia had duly arrived, and the effective temperature for me, wet and exposed, would be well below zero. I could not think of any worse possible conditions in which to go windsurfing. It was far too cold, far too windy, far too rough, and I had to broad reach all day. We left the marina silent and apprehensive at 7.45 a.m. My private goal was simply to make forward progress, and even 10 miles would be enough. It took two hard slamming hours on the RIB to make it 20 miles back to our waypoint, but my eyes brought some cheer to the battered spirit. We were running dead into wind, which made it very breezy in the back of the RIB, but my reading of the sea surface was that there was not much more than a F4. This observation was in direct conflict with the updated forecast over the VHF, which specified imminent gales. For a second it crossed my mind that I should ask Philippe to turn the RIB around, and run for shelter, but something told me to hold fire. Perhaps because of the forecast and the fact that every time we had ventured outside for the last three days we had been battered by F6/7 winds, our decision making on board/sail selection seemed to ignore the reality of what was blowing right now. We rigged for F6 conditions, namely a 5.4m sail on Lady Di, with a tiny fin, and I struggled for the best part of an hour in F3/4 winds to get it going. Again fearful of a sudden increase in wind strength, we even plugged the 5.4m sail into Bertha for a while, a patently unsuitable combination.

Eventually, after two hours of awkward progress, and only 10 miles covered, our communal intelligence returned, and the 8.0m sail was rigged and plugged into Bertha. For a while the winds stayed at F3/4, and I was in and out of the back straps, averaging 12 knots. At least the tide was running in our favour until mid-afternoon, so we didn't have the dreaded wind-over-tide conditions to contend with. Out in the Channel to my left was the strikingly different Royal Sovereign light vessel. Even from a distance it looked like a massive steel monolith. To me it was shaped more like an alien spacecraft than a channel navigation aid. Beachy Head some 8 miles ahead was my next target, but I knew that going beyond this target would give us some logistical problems, and thus dropped my sail, and called the RIB over to talk. Maiden could not get into Brighton, the logical next stopover, and Philippe did not want to be bringing the RIB back round Beachy Head in the fading light, with heavy wind-over-tide conditions. The agreed solution was to head for Brighton, where the RIB could be berthed, and collect the RIB team by van. As I approached this austere headland, the wind picked up to a solid F5, and I was back into sailing on the edge. According to Philippe (who had sailed the Southern Ocean, and was remarkably resistant to the cold), it was by far the coldest day on the RIB yet; but I was working so hard, and so focused on devouring the miles without dangerous catapult falls, that I didn't notice what had to be around minus 10 windchill. I had extra neoprene layers under and over my winter steamer, and a full neoprene balaclava. Remarkably, after the first twenty minutes, my hard-working ungloved hands stayed warm all day.

Rounding Beachy Head itself and the Seven Sisters was another memorable milestone. I was on starboard tack, sailing some 40–50 degrees off the wind at 20–25 knots, with my back leg burning with fatigue. As on many other occasions, I would have been better off on a smaller board, but I was going well, and in no mood to tempt fate. The sea was flatter closer in towards the cliffs, but the wind also much gustier, so I tried to find the least uncomfortable compromise. I had one big catapult, but managed to avoid injury, and actually started to enjoy the symmetrical clean shapes of the famous chalk cliffs over my right shoulder, despite the high-speed, high-risk point of sailing. Once round Beachy Head, the sprawling Victorian frontages of Newhaven and Brighton were in my sights, and I knew that the day was going much better than expected. I stopped very briefly mid-afternoon, for energy replenishment, and noticed how cold particularly Tim and Sarah looked despite their multi-layer extreme-weather protection. Andy wanted me to give it another hour. I wanted to sail until nightfall, or until I dropped off the board with exhaustion, whichever came sooner. To avoid a decision, I jumped over the side, and set off on a series of broad reaches towards Brighton. The wind was still F4/5, but the sea had become noticeably less lumpy than at any time over the last three days, and the 10 miles down to Brighton seemed to take no time at all. By now I was flying, and thoroughly enjoying the prospect of a 45–50-mile day, leaving less than

40 to go. Philippe was waving frantically at me from the RIB as I blasted along the front at Brighton towards Shoreham. He was seriously worried about Tim and Sarah becoming hypothermic; they said they were OK, but they didn't look it. I reluctantly accepted to finish in 20 minutes' time at 4.45 p.m., by which stage I was just off Shoreham beach with 45 miles in the bag, and thus only 38 to go to dearest Stokes Bay.

My overriding thought on the way in was that whatever the weather I could surely make 38 miles in three days. Brighton marina was a cold, ugly, concrete convenience, but to me it felt as pretty as a Lindisfarne anchorage. My target for the day had been 10 miles. Andy admitted that he had not expected me to get beyond Beachy Head. The easterly gales had relented for long enough for us to get within half a day's good sailing of home. Perhaps this was a final act of kindness from the wind gods. Perhaps they were feeling guilty over earlier mistreatments. But what the hell, we were so nearly there. I might just treat myself to a third or fourth pint tonight. Once into Brighton marina, I went off to see the harbour master about where we should berth, and the others went to refuel. After quickly sorting out the formalities, he asked what we were doing there. I told him we were on the final leg of a record-breaking windsurf journey around Britain and Ireland. He didn't seem particularly impressed, and added that 'There was one of them windsurfers, going like a bat out of hell along the front earlier today, he must have froze to death.' I didn't have the heart to tell him that the only windsurfer out on the water across the whole of Britain today was probably me. Anyone sailing for pleasure in those conditions was more certifiable than the author himself.

Waiting in the pub for Kevin to collect us Andy suddenly chirped up that if we finished tomorrow (Thursday) we would post a time of 61 days, and beat Keith Russell's record by one day. Despite the earlier euphoria, this had not crossed my mind. In all the angst over changing our scheduled finish from Wednesday to Saturday, I had written off any possibility of breaking Keith's record. But then all the horrible practicalities came flooding through. Saturday was fixed. It could not be brought forward now. How could we have two finishes? It was too short notice to get much media presence tomorrow, and would they bother to turn up at all if they knew that Saturday's finish was purely cosmetic? The party was already booked for Saturday. How could we finish quietly, and then come back three days later? I needed time to think it all through, and time to talk to people like Simon Bornhoft and Jon White. I also needed to know tomorrow's weather forecast before getting too carried away.

Back in Eastbourne on Maiden, the air was buzzing with 'will he-won't he' banter. Andy had picked up the forecast which was a favourable south-east F4/5. I called Simon, and asked his advice. He was crystal clear.

If you have a chance to break the record, then you have to go for it, and manage a cosmetic finish two days later as best you can. He added that the media and public interest will die within days, but the record could stand for decades. Jon White was similarly categorical, and agreed to change his schedule the next day, to be on standby as our official RYA finish-line witness. I then went to the yacht club bar and canvassed team opinion. The consensus was clearly in favour, although there were several serious concerns about handling the practicalities. So that was that. After spending two days worrying that I might not make the Saturday finish, we were now planning a 61-day Thursday finish, weather permitting of course. To avoid Saturday being a major anticlimax, we agreed to keep the Thursday finish quiet, except to close friends and followers. We would send out a press release on Friday, telling of the scheduled Saturday finish on Stokes Bay beach, but that Richard Cooper actually completed the circumnavigation on Thursday in a record time of 61 days etc. etc. If only this dinky little adventure had just been about windsurfing! I had my extra pint or two that night, but was too excited to go any further than a half sleep. The excitement was also tempered by a huge sense of relief, driven of course by the receding fear of failure, and the prospect of returning to normal life.

Day 61 (21 October) dawned windless, dank and drizzly. The weather had certainly changed, and Philippe knowingly pointed out that we were 'in between weather systems' as per his earlier prognosis. The RIB team for the day was Philippe, Andy, Tim and John to record the hoped-for finish. Our target was Stokes Bay beach, and thereafter an overnight rendezvous (and crew-only party) in Ocean Village, Southampton. I set off with the trusty 9.4m sail on my soulmate Bertha. There was no way I could contemplate using any other combination of kit for this final leg. As befits a period of meteorological house moving, the light F2 wind was all over the place. I had only about 2 miles visibility, and once away from the shore, had no visible landmarks with which to judge my direction. The wind swung from north-east to south, and I simply followed instructions from the RIB, going from a dead downwind run, to a beat. Without their help, I would probably have sailed round in a big circle. On a flat featureless sea, with no compass, no landmarks and no sun, it was impossible to feel gradual but major windshifts such as this. My target was the Outer Owers south cardinal marker off Selsey Bill. At midday we called Jon White, and optimistically told him to be at the beach from 4.30 p.m. onwards, but progress was painfully slow, and it became evident that at this 4–5 knot board speed, I would not be landing on Stokes Bay beach until after nightfall. What had happened to the F4/5 forecast? Just before rounding the cardinal marker, we noticed a darkening of the sky to the south, and right on cue fifteen minutes later, the wind picked up to a F4 under the squall. I was immediately into the back straps, and away broad reaching towards the Isle of Wight at 15 knots. The strangely shaped and named Nab Tower, off the eastern end of the Isle of Wight, kept appearing and disappearing from view, as the showers abated and resumed. At times I could also just about make out the south-facing shores of Hayling Island, and the Witterings, where I had really begun this amazing journey on my first training session with Simon Bornhoft. The squally F4 only lasted forty-five minutes, but it was enough to get me within 10 miles of my target by 3 p.m. I was now entering the Solent proper, with both the traffic and the tide coming against me, and tricky dead downwind sailing in a lumpy F2 wind, over a small but confused chop. This infernal balancing act was my pet hate. Instead of turning the air blue, after another frustrating plop into the water, which had been my normal recourse in such a situation, I apparently burst into a fit of giggles. Tim asked whether I was ready for the proverbial rusty nail, and I just giggled some more like an out-of-control eight-year-old girl. Perhaps I had finally lost my marbles, nearly nine weeks at sea having leached my brain of all its residual normality.

The last day's sailing was almost a microcosm of the whole journey. We had ever-changing wind and weather, magical landmarks appearing out of the horizon, effortless speed, gruelling tedium, shipping and tidal complications, and of course laughs and arguments. I climbed on the RIB 7 miles short of Stokes Bay just in time to witness the climax of a simmering row between Philippe and John. They had almost come to blows earlier on the journey, and neither wasted an opportunity to put the knife in. This was something I did not need today, and I told them forcefully to stop squabbling like a pair of big kids and grow up. My reason for climbing on the RIB was to find out where Maiden was. Ideally we all wanted to cross the line together, but they had come from Eastbourne in lighter than expected winds, and were a good hour behind us. I simply couldn't bear to sit on the RIB for ninety minutes, with the end so close, and we were also worried that the declining wind would disappear altogether leaving us at the mercy of the east-flowing tide.

Back on the water, and putting the irritation of John and Philippe's bickering behind me, I started to wallow in the familiarity of the shorelines around me. Scale and distance had somehow undergone a step change whilst I had been away. The Solent was surely much narrower, and the town of Ryde that much nearer. At the start of my training period I would not dare venture more than a mile off the shore unsupported. The Solent had seemed so wide and dangerous, and now it was like an overgrown river. I had become used to the mindset that a headland 20 miles away was a near-term target. For a while I felt decidedly claustrophobic. By 5.00 p.m. I was within a mile of Stokes Bay, and could see Jon White and Duncan waiting on the beach. I decided that now was the time to climb back on the RIB, and thank and congratulate Andy, Tim, Philippe and John, before I hit the beach and the champagne. We had not been short of disagreements, but without the energy, skill and determination of my support team, I would have failed long ago. Philippe was a recent recruit who had certainly made a difference down the East Coast. Tim was simply a rock who was as dependable as day turns to night. Andy was simply Andy. He could infuriate me, but was also the person I would want by my side in the heat of a life-threatening moment out at sea. He was too the most outwardly emotional and elated of all the team when we finally succeeded.

The last mile was painfully slow, but I could almost smell the pebbly beach running from Gilkicker Point down to Stokes Bay sailing club, and my smile was apparently visible from 2 miles away. With Andy leading the cheers from the RIB, I crossed the finish line, and ran through the shallows onto the beach, to shake Jon White's hand, and spray a bottle of champagne seawards. With my life-supporting RIB and the symbolic Solent in the background, and yours truly hoisting the champagne in the foreground Duncan got the shots I would treasure for a lifetime, and the papers would use for a day. A seething beachside crowd of two was far from how I had imagined the finish to be. (Where was the massed flotilla of well-wishers anyway?) But it was still a great great feeling to have completed what many (including me most of the time) thought was an impossible task. My time of 61 days, 6 hours and 41 minutes was duly recorded and witnessed in the log book. I then waded out to the RIB with the champagne, and we toasted each other with the warmth, affection and respect that comes from having lived and triumphed together through hell and high water; or in our case through having lived both the nightmare and the dream together.

Like a child needs the toilet, I had a sudden urge to share the moment with the other equally important team members on Maiden. I quickly got out of my wetsuit on the RIB, whilst Andy and Tim stowed the kit, and we motored back to meet them. I jumped across onto her port quarter to be met by a hugging, handshaking sea of faces. They were all wonderful people but Sarah was more wonderful than the rest. She had been permanently cheerful, resourceful, accommodating, determined, and very effective. Philippe said to me later in the bar that if he were selecting a team for any such future expedition, Tim, Duncan and Sarah would be the first names on his list. He was preaching to the converted.

We opened another bottle of champagne and toasted each other on Maiden's very familiar decks, oblivious to the deepening drizzle. The wind had now dropped to nothing, and the crew had to take down the sails as we motored towards Ocean Village. I took this opportunity to slope off to the nav station and be 'alone and quiet with myself' for a while. I wanted to let it sink in slowly and pleasurably, and wanted to commit my emotions to paper, before they became blurred by time and alcohol. It was certainly the deepest strongest feeling of satisfaction and achievement I have ever had. But there was also a troubling worry as to how easily I could now get back into normal life. I wanted to be a homely father again, and wanted a period of stability and predictability; but I also wanted to keep this feeling of being so totally alive. Had the sea now snared me for life with its mystery, challenge and eternity? Had I now irreversibly succumbed to the seductive goddess of adventure? On a more mundane level, how would I cope with not needing to move on every day? My whole reason for being for nearly nine weeks was to inch or leap my way round a predetermined course. In one respect this was one of the purest forms of sporting challenge – Man with all his physical and mental fragility against the unpredictable elements. From an opposite perspective, my venture could be perceived by some as chequebook adventuring. I had the time and money to take a time out from normal life, and to put together a top-class support team. I guess the bottom line would be what it meant for me, and how it had changed me, rather than what others thought. These were questions that needed more time, and right now as we berthed in Ocean Village, I was done with self-analysis and more than ready for a big night out.

It had to be a good night because I woke with a fearful hangover, but also tell-tale bruises on the inside of my knees. I don't know where we were or what we were doing, but the bruises indicated that I had at some stage demonstrated my trademark breakdancing montage on a concrete floor. This ugly misguided routine normally happens in a venue with loud rock music, after pint 8 (when all semblance of self-respect has gone), and before pint 10 (when my motor functions have also gone). It was thus a fairly accurate marker of how much I had drunk. The other reliable marker was of course the severity of the hangover which I was now experiencing. Friday (Day 62, 22 October) was thus a write-off. I bummed around reading newspapers, packing my meagre possessions, writing my thank you speech, and worrying about the horrendous forecast of south-westerly gales for my grand finale. The plan was to motor round to Gosport's Haslar Marina. Haslar was only a couple of miles from Stokes Bay, and within reasonable staggering distance of Saturday night's party venue. The Friday night team meeting in Haslar was mostly concerned with the logistics for Saturday. We had been next to useless at the starting event, and wanted to be a slick professional operation, for media and supporters. I ended the evening doing a final final video diary session for Sarah, and retiring for the last time to my bunk on Maiden.

I woke several times during Friday night with hot and cold sweats which I put down to either alcohol withdrawal symptoms, or more likely livethat-dream cold turkey. Saturday morning felt very similar to the morning of my wedding day thirteen years before. Everybody's nerves were jangling. Everything had already been organised down to the minute details, but everybody was still looking for something to organise or check. The end result was a totally dysfunctional hive of headless-chicken-like activity. After a while I gave up being part of this mega faff, and lay on my bunk for an hour, staring at the ceiling. My bit of the show was relatively easy. I would ride out on the RIB at 1.30 p.m., to a spot just behind Gilkicker Point, out of sight of Stokes Bay. There we would rig the appropriate sail, have a few warm-up runs, and then at around 2.15 p.m., I would miraculously appear from around Gilkicker point, and blast down to Stokes Bay beach. After thirty minutes of hugs and handshakes, I would change, do a series of TV and radio interviews, and then with everyone gathered in the sailing club, dispense my 'few words of thanks'. The reality was somewhat different.

Saturday, 22 October was also the 'last time' day. I would not have to squeeze my reluctant body into a cold, damp, foul-smelling wetsuit any more. Neither would I have to share a bedroom with ten other travellers, nor spend several hours a day being regularly doused with sea water on the back of a whining jarring RIB. Deep down in my heart I still didn't know whether the relief of completion would override the pain of leaving behind such a vivid existence. Just before leaving Haslar the wind seemed to pick up another notch, and was gusting to over 30 knots on Maiden's anemometer. Various decent-sized yachts were on their way back in obviously having decided that enough was enough. The mouth of Portsmouth harbour was rough and tricky with heavy wind-over-tide conditions, but we found some shelter in the lee of Gilkicker Point to rig a 5.4m sail plugged into Lady Di. I did my warm-up runs fully powered up, but sailing like an absolute novice. I was so churned up inside that gybing seemed impossible. I apparently even made waterstarting look like a radically difficult manoeuvre. This was certainly not the guy who had just sailed round Britain and Ireland. Andy gave me the thumbs up at 2.10 p.m. (he obviously couldn't stand watching me floundering around like a helpless beginner any longer), and I pointed my board towards Stokes Bay. The howling wind and torrential rain seemed to ease slightly as I approached Gilkicker, and within a couple of minutes it was down to F3 and I was going nowhere on such a small sail and board. I had so desperately wanted to put on a show for the kids and cameras, blasting into the beach at speed, and now right on cue at 2.15 p.m. the wind had died. Andy later suggested that maybe the wind gods had watched my wretched warm-up efforts, and decided that this was all I could handle. My view was that this was the final signal that in this world the wind and the weather call all the shots, and transient visitors to their kingdom forget this dictum at their peril.

We quickly decided that there was no time for a change to a bigger sail, but that at least on Katie I could move forwards slowly rather than sink slowly on Lady Di. So my final run to the finish was accomplished at an average speed of about 5 knots, petrified of falling in in front of the crowds, and thus even unwilling to try a few aggressive pumps to bring the board onto the plane. The pain of my pedestrian progress was, however, completely obliterated by a posse of kids led by my daughter Rosie and sons Jack and George who had decided to escort me in by running the last 400 yards along the beach parallel to my course. It was a truly wonderful way to finish, and my four kids got to me well ahead of my wife, as I abandoned my kit and walked onto the beach arms aloft. Hugging and kissing them all after so long apart was a big deep moment. There seemed to be nothing but cameras and familiar faces all around me, and much of the first ten minutes of reunion with family and friends seemed to be a blur of tears, champagne and camera flashes. I remember talking into the Sky TV news camera, and giving various radio reporters their 'back on Stokes Bay beach' soundbites, and then shaking hands with supporters who had followed us diligently but whom I had never met. One elderly gentleman shook my hand for ever and spoke with deep emotion and feeling, as though he had been with me on the board every inch of the way. Through all this interviewing, backslapping and emotion, my two daughters, Rosie and Amy, had stayed firmly latched to either my hand or my shoulders. Three-year-old Amy hadn't a clue what was going on, but she knew who her dad was, and she knew this was his big day. That was enough for me.

After gleefully ripping off my wetsuit alone in the Gents, I wandered up to the bar to get a pint before doing all the media stuff, but Duncan had rescheduled the schedule. I now had to do my thank-you speech. This threw me at first, but after hundreds of hours of fantasy rehearsal on my board, I knew what I wanted to say and how I wanted to say it. I didn't get as emotional as I thought I might, but enjoyed the moment immensely; and afterwards was desperate to get down to some serious mingling and drinking with all the friends and family who I had not seen for months. Duncan stopped me in my tracks as I still had to spend the next hour being interviewed by Classic FM and Mentorn. The big party was looming, as was the probably quite difficult process of becoming a husband and father again. I will look back on the day of 23 October 1999 with great feeling and satisfaction. I can't find a collection of clever words that captures the essence of how I was feeling. My last utterances into the Mentorn camera which were used to end their National Geographic documentary were simple and to the point: 'We did it ... end of story'. They were also very wide of the mark. It had been a towering story for me, but it was far from over.

Main: Emotional family reunion.

Inset: Mum very pleased to see her son home and safe.

Postscript

I must go down to the seas again, to the lonely sea and sky,
And all I ask is a tall ship and a star to steer her by,
And the wheel's kick and the wind's song and the white sails shaking,
And a grey mist on the sea's face and a grey dawn breaking.

I must go down to the seas again for the call of the running tide,
Is a wild call and a clear call that may not be denied,
And all I ask is a windy day with the white clouds flying,
And the flung spray and the blown spume, and the sea-gulls crying.

I must go down to the seas again to the vagrant gypsy life,
To the gull's way where the wind's like a whetted knife;
And all I ask is a merry yarn from a laughing fellow rover,
And a quiet sleep and a sweet dream when the long trick's over.

John Masefield ('Sea Fever')

*T*he most common question asked after my return was inevitably: 'So what next?' The question however had two very different meanings depending upon its source. Those who respected what I'd done, but thought it a bit irresponsible, were asking when would I put this crazy scheme behind me, and resume my sensible father-of-four lifestyle. The rest (who I think were in the majority) were asking what was the next adventure I had in mind. My answer to both was that I intended to take my time finding the right job, which would ideally be something completely different from the corporate drudgery I found myself in before; and that my next major adventure would not be for five to ten years, and then hopefully shared with one or more of my teenage children.

As I'd hoped for before we set off, the venture did open doors to new and very different career opportunities, which was good news because there were no suitable re-entry opportunities available from my old employer. I rewrote my cv, with a paragraph on the front page describing the Round Britain and Ireland Windsurf; and despite having come from a narrow world of biotechnology and animal nutrition, I got interviews for jobs in the Internet, pharmaceutical and leisure sectors. More than half of my interviewers commented that they had wanted to talk to me primarily because of the windsurf venture. They of course needed the solid business background, but the fact that I had broken out of normality and made something very different and quite special happen, presumably helped me stand out from the crowd. I ended up taking a job as Managing Director of Clipper Ventures plc, a business whose main product is a round-the-world yacht race for amateurs and whose chairman is Sir Robin Knox-Johnston. It is a tremendously exciting position, with clear links to the Livethatdream experience. Clipper, with its strong adventure ethos, also took over my Livethatdream domain name and trademark registration, so this book will hopefully not be the last time the reader will come across this brand.

Looking back on what was achieved still amazes me. In fact the more time passes, the more I wonder at how on earth I made it round. I did not go windsurfing again until six months after the finish, and my fitness has declined to its lowest level for five years. If I were turfed over the side to broad reach in a F5 out on the open sea today, I would be surprised if I lasted more than twenty minutes. My other predominant reflection is how lucky we were. The Celtic Sea doldrums seemed a pain at the time, but in reality anything more than a F4 would have made the crossing a logistical nightmare. I had my gripes with the wind gods, but they gave us decent F2/4 conditions for all the major crossings and headland round-ings. It is a colossal tribute to the two Sues and Euan who prepared me, Denise who got me started, and the RIB team who kept me out of trouble en route, that my body remained free of any significant injury. Simon Bornhoft also had a big role in the success of the mission, in boosting my windsurfing ability, my equipment know-how and perhaps most impor-tantly my windsurfing confidence. I also had my gripes about the support team, but like with the wind, it was easy to find fault, yet even easier to take for granted the good things that were quietly happening around me every day. They were a randomly assembled bunch of mostly volunteers, who gave up their normal lives to help me, and live their own adventures. On reflection I also believe I was incredibly lucky with this team. Even John, who irritated others so effortlessly, was still trying hard to do his job right up to the end. So if I was so lucky, how easy would it be for someone to break my record? Theoretically, a better windsurfer than me, with similar fitness and logistical support, setting off in April/May should have a better than evens chance of beating 61 days. Even 35 days is possible with plenty of F4/5 beam-reaching conditions. Theory and practice are, however, incompatible bedfellows, and I will watch with interest.

The other big question was: how has this adventure changed you, Richard Cooper, the archetypal 'mid-lifer' looking for something else? I definitely feel more fulfilled and complete than before, and I cannot deny that the achievement has given me an ever-present warm glow of pride and satisfaction. The sea has dug it's subtle claws deep into my being, and I doubt that this will be my last tempestuous affair with its enchanting but ruthless psyche. Maybe I have become a little more patient and less helter-skelter, in the way my life works, but my wife would be the best arbiter of this claim. If I did have a knawing and disruptive need to prove something to someone, then hopefully this need has been satisfied. I do feel different, but only time will tell whether people around me notice any changes. I feel that my attitude to the world around me has probably changed. I am still looking for thrills and excitement, and achievement, but maybe now beauty, depth and meaning are equally important. I still want to pass that 'fresh air thing' on to my kids, and to experience with them the wonder of our natural environment, but maybe on the basis of 'let it happen' rather than 'do it all'. My hunger to live life to the full is as strong as ever, but this hunger needs to be managed to avoid that feeling of time slipping away between meals of vivid living. My reasons for taking on the challenge were set out at the start of the book, but are equally vague at its end. Maybe the reader is in a better position to decide why I did it. Maybe it was simply the Western equivalent of an aboriginal walkabout.

Looking back at the different elements of the venture, and its five or six main components that I spent so much time on before we started, I would give the highest 'satisfaction score' to my fitness and the quality of the support team and infrastructure. My windsurfing was both better and worse than expected. Our media coverage was well short of my totally unrealistic expectations, but also well ahead of what we should have received with the very limited resources at our disposal. Classic FM were an excellent sponsor and media partner, and also thoroughly genuine, committed people. It was great to be 'someone' in the windsurfing world, and (at least for one edition) to be a hero in the sport that I have loved the most. It also felt good to be on national TV, and radio news; but perhaps the biggest hit was when some friends in Australia were quietly taking in the evening Sky News, and all of a sudden their living room was 'invaded by pictures of Cooper and supporters cavorting around Stokes Bay beach'! My biggest disappointment was our fundraising for the Marine Conservation Society. It was my mistake that we didn't have a fundraising champion on board, and the crew as a whole were not that MCS minded. MCS fundraising was not first and foremost in our minds during stopover time; and I didn't feel comfortable pressurizing friends and family, some of whom were incredibly generous, while others simply forgot to do anything. We expected to raise at least £20k, but in the end were somewhere short of £10k. We, however, apparently did do a very good job on increasing awareness of MCS, and marine conservation issues.

Family life was severely disrupted by my venture, and friends joked that my wife's challenge of looking after our four hyperactive offspring as a one-parent family, was just as difficult as my waterborne adventure. It was not a joke to me. Thanks to Mandy and her phenomenal behind-the-scenes operations, our kids' lives continued as normal, with all necessary school, social and sporting activities implemented like clockwork. Having me back 'under her feet' and trying to resume my role in the family processes was also quite difficult for Mandy at first. The kids were very proud of their dad, especially when I was asked to give a slide show to all their mates at school. They also enjoyed being media stars for a day, and seeing themselves on a variety of national and regional news clips. Normality was difficult for a while. Strange as it may seem, I actually had difficulty sleeping in a normal, warm, large, flat bed between layers of lovely cool cotton! Not so surprisingly I found it difficult to kick the 4,000 calories per day habit, and thus quickly put on weight. After training so hard for so long before the event, and after being away from my family for so long, I virtually gave up serious exercise for six months. It was quite painful seeing my transient super fitness and new musculature disappear in a matter of weeks. Also, within days of my return I had flu, my first bout of any such illness for over a year. I am certain that the clean air and adrenaline kept all such viruses at bay during the trip.

The others on the team all went their separate ways. Tim decided that he would stay well clear of oilfield geology, and took a winter season job with a ski holiday company in the Alps run by Duncan's wife. Andy hooked a great role training the Camel Trophy participants. Sarah went from Livethatdream to making a documentary on men's genitalia, and then on to the Tall Ships Race, also making a documentary. Philippe has bought his own ocean-going yacht, on which he now lives, as a base for his sailing photography and charter business. Terry is still plugging away selling berths and charters aboard Maiden and her sister ship 'Ice Maiden'. Kevin is well into buying his own boat, and breaking into the Caribbean charter market. Peter Head was last heard from in Western Australia teaching windsurfing. Sophie is back at her hospital administrator's job, missing the sea. Denise is back at her sports physio practice, missing Gaz's zany humour. Duncan continues his enviable winter sports photography lifestyle. Steve and Russ's IRS business seems to be going well, and Spider is where he wanted to be, fighting fires in London. John Beecroft has been busy filming a documentary on the making of a Richard Stillgo musical. Predictably I haven't got a clue where Gaz is, and I assume Damian is back in Clifden teaching kids to sail.

A number of individuals, who had read of my exploits, or seen my slide/talk shows, let me know that they had been inspired by my story, and were looking to implement their own dreams. This was perhaps the biggest thrill of all, knowing that my actions had caused other people to bring about changes in their own lives which they in turn felt good about.

I also received a letter and some photos from a lady called Joan. Her husband, Doug, had apparently been a fervent follower of my voyage, and they were on Stokes Bay beach the day I finished. I then remember the emotional elderly gentleman who had pushed through the crowd and shook my hand as though he had been with me every inch of the way. Joan's letter went on to explain that Doug had died suddenly, soon after my homecoming, and that she wanted to know how thrilled he had been that day. The letter made me feel humble, sad and touched. I had taken on the whole journey primarily as a selfish exercise in achievement and adventure. I had never really set out to thrill and inspire other people, and feedback such as this gave me a different, maybe even a deeper satisfaction.

Windsurfing around Britain and Ireland was the toughest, most exhilarating, most thought-provoking, and most satisfying thing I have ever done. At the start I had told people that I wanted to test myself. I wanted to push myself to the limit physically and mentally and see if I could hack it. I think I passed this Cooper-test. I will never forget my nights in Kilrush, lost in my own self-doubt, and my contrasting days on the board going way beyond what I thought was my limit. The highs were so high, and the lows so low, and maybe the most stimulating thing of all was just living this full-on rollercoaster existence. My final words are: thank you to everyone who helped make it happen, and good luck to all those reading this book who have their own dream to live.

Appendix I

Fitness Results

Dear Richard,

Please find enclosed:

1) The results of your VO2 max test and your rowing OBLA test (Onset of Blood
    Lactate Accumulation test) performed on the 15th July 1999. OBLA is a standard
    reference point equivalent to 4.0 mmol of blood lactate.

	THIS TEST	2nd March
Power/Weight ratio @ OBLA:	3.38 watts/kg	2.99 watts/kg
Oxygen consumption @ OBLA:	52.6 ml/kg/min	46.3 ml/kg/min
Heart Rate @ OBLA:	143 beats/min	158 beats/min
RER @ OBLA:	0.99–1.04	0.96–1.03
Body Weight:	81.6 kg	85.7 kg
VO2 max:	62.9 ml/kg/min	55.3 ml/kg/min
Max Heart rate:	169 beats/min	176 beats/min
Body fat results:	11.8%	16.3%

Richard, your recent fitness test has shown a good all-round increase in
your aerobic fitness. This is also coupled with a healthy decrease in body
fat and I'm sure an appropriate increase in muscle mass. You have clearly
put much effort into your fitness training and the all-round improvements
of approx. 13% (VO2 max, VO2 @ OBLA and power/weight ratios @
OBLA & max) are the clear rewards. Your present fitness level is quite
similar to our best Olympic windsurfers and they are on average 20 years
your junior!!

Diet:

When conducting the actual marathon you will roughly need 4,000 calories
per day. Of this figure carbohydrates should amount to 650–700 grams
(2600–2900 calories of carbohydrates per day). As I said it will be excep-
tionally difficult to consume this in complex carbs alone so don't be afraid
of eating simple carbs.

The coming months should be aimed at the following areas:

1) To improve your aerobic base and help improve fat metabolism (aimed at

lowering the RER value).

60 mins to 90 mins at ~ 120–125 beats/min (row pace 2m 02s – 1m 58s) 3 or 4 sessions per week. If cycling the heart rate should be approx. 5 beats lower ~ 115–120 b/min.

2) No need for any more weight training if sailing frequently.

3) 30 mins rowing @ your OBLA heart rate of 142 beats/min (approx. 1 min 47 s pace on a concept rower) or conduct this as an interval session. 1 session per week/fortnight. THIS IS NOT A PRIORITY.

4) Continue with the physio/rehab work that you are conducting under the supervision of Sue & Euan.

Example of Weekly Training Report

From: Richard Cooper
To: Euan McGrath
Cc: Pete Cunningham; Simon Bornhoft
Date: 27 June 1999 22:28
Subject: w/c 21/6 Training/Sailing report

Monday 21/6: 100 mins (4*25) Fat burn session in gym. HR mostly in 130–140 range. Legs tiring towards end.

Tuesday 22/6: 3hrs sailing off Hillhead in F3 with new 9.4m Raptor C3 on 3.05. Comfortable flat water, upwind/downwind stuff.

Wednesday 23/6: 3hrs sailing off Hillhead in F1-2 with 9.4m sail and long board, about half of which was pumping. pm Weights session in Gym.

Thursday 24/6: 30 mins OBLA on rowing machine. Surprised myself with best ever average time/500m@149.3 (Previous best was 151.3). Still v. hard but different from before in that legs tired before arms and back, and breathing easier. Maybe upper body stamina/strength improving.

Friday 25/6: Approx 28 mile am Bike ride in 1hr 22.22, which easily bettered last time for this route of 1hr 25.30. Now use camelback with energy fluid on long bike rides, which maybe helps. Also didn't knacker me for rest of day. pm Gym/Weights session.

Saturday 26/6: Sailing with SB off Hayling in F3 with 9.4m sail and 3.05. Did some long upwind/downwing legs (technique hopefully improving) Approx 4.5hrs on water.

Sunday 27/6: 56 minute (approx 7.5/8 mile) run at relatively gentle pace (HR 135-145).

Made some of my targets but not all:

*Only 10.5 hrs on the water vs target 15
*made target of 3 fat burn sessions and 1 OBLA
*did 2 weights sessions vs target 3
*also did 5*10 pull-ups on old boom hanging off tree in garden, most days, + 4-5 10-minute goes on wobble board, + 2-3 20-minute sit up sessions.

Weight seems to be down to around 83 kg vs 85/86 3-4 months ago. Only problems I have (need to see Physio) are:

> : a stiff right ankle, always after running, and sometimes after sailing
> : Some muscular discomfort in lower left back, always after working at my desk, and/or after standing for long periods, and sometimes after long runs but not after other forms of exercise.

Thanks R.

Appendix II

The Marine Conservation Society

*E*veryone loves the sea, and nobody appreciates it more than windsurfers. But the seas around us are under threat from pollution – by sewage, litter, chemicals and other waste – plus overfishing and damage to habitats. As an island nation, we are surrounded by sea but so often ignore the benefits it brings us, and the life it contains.

British waters are home to a fascinating and rich diversity of marine life. From a lookout point on the shore, you can watch dolphins cavort in the waters off the west coast. A boat may give you views of the second largest fish in the world – the basking shark – which cruises UK waters between May and September, scooping up plankton in its huge cavernous mouth. Orcas and minke whales frequent the seas around the Scottish Highlands and Islands, and seahorses are regularly seen around the Scilly Isles and south-west coast. The geographical position of the UK assures a diversity of life from north to south and west to east, and the often majestic shape of the coastline influences the life that can cling to it. Hundreds of fascinating creatures inhabit the shore, surviving between the tides where conditions can be harsh and changeable. Rockpools are underwater cauldrons of life, where fish and seaweeds, sponges and crabs can be found together. Shallow waters provide breeding and feeding grounds for many fish and shellfish, supporting the wheeling flocks of seabirds and pods of leaping dolphin which bring delight to any viewer.

The sea provides us with many opportunities for sport, enjoyment and work. We depend on the fact that bathing waters are safe, that we can dive and sail without fear of falling into a soup of harmful viruses and litter. We don't want to see boats fouled by oilslicks or with paddles snagged in discarded nets. We have moved on from the days, only a century or so ago, when it seemed that the sea was a vast wilderness which we could not spoil. It is now heavily affected by waste, over-exploitation and coastal development to name just a few. We all suffer from incidents like the *Sea Empress* disaster in 1996, and from continuous polluting discharges of everything from sanitary items to radioactive waste. Small boat users and surfers may be particularly vulnerable to sewage-related disease – water forms an aerosol as it sprays up from the sea surface, concentrating bacteria and viruses in small droplets which are breathed deeply into the lungs. Facts and figures:

- *Every day*, ships throw over **5 million items of waste** into the sea worldwide.

- *Every day*, over **300 million gallons of sewage** are discharged into UK coastal waters.

- *Every day* there are still up to **30,000 miles of drift gill nets** set, killing everything in their path, including more than 1,000 dolphins and 3,000 sharks – every day!

- *Every year*, **three times as much rubbish is dumped into the world's oceans as the weight of fish caught**.

- *Every year*, an estimated **one million seabirds and 100,000 marine mammals and sea turtles** suffer cruel deaths from entanglement in, or ingestion of, plastics.

- *Every year*, over **100 million sharks are killed**, mainly solely for their fins.

- *Every year*, an estimated **20 per cent** of all marine fish landed on fishing vessels are discarded dead or injured back into the sea.

- *Each year*, **three and a quarter million tonnes of oil** enter the oceans of the world.

The Marine Conservation Society (MCS) is the UK charity dedicated to the protection of the marine environment and its wildlife. Many surfers will already be familiar with MCS through meeting members, taking part in beach cleans and surveys, or reading books and reports published by MCS. Most surfers will have a good word for MCS, but not everyone realises that MCS is a charity, completely reliant on membership support and donations to carry out its work.

MCS campaigns for sewage-free seas, beaches free of litter, site protection and sensitive management of our coast and sea – and much more. Over the last few decades, MCS has highlighted many issues of concern, from litter to coral reef destruction, hormone-altering chemicals of overfishing. Achievements range from lobbying the UK water industry to clean up its act, to influencing international and UK government policy on basking shark protection and the disposal of wastes at sea. Into the future, MCS will continue to uncover threats to both marine wildlife and to the wider marine and coastal environment, and bring them to the attention of the public, media, politicians and industries alike.

You can take part in MCS conservation projects and surveys. *Ocean Vigil* and *Basking Shark Watch* are sighting projects for all sea-watchers. *Seasearch* is a habitat and species survey to map the underwater life of our coasts. You can survey and clean your local coastline and contribute information to our national *Adopt-a-Beach* and *Beachwatch* projects, and there are many other ways to help protect our seas and their wildlife.

Join MCS

For just £20 you can join the Marine Conservation Society and support the vital campaign for cleaner seas. In return, we'll keep you in touch with our work and informed of the state of our seas and marine wildlife, plus give you the opportunity to get involved and make a real difference to the future of our seas.

Marine Conservation Society,
9 Gloucester Road
Ross-on-Wye
Herefordshire
HR9 5BU
01989 566017

info@mcsuk.org
http://www.mcsuk.org
http://www.goodbeachguide.co.uk

Richard Harrington MCS
11/5/00

Appendix III

Statistics

Distances and Speeds

Total waypoint to waypoint (straight line) distance = 1,693 nautical miles (1,794 land miles), and sailed distance = 2,060 nm (2,369 land miles)

Did not sail 12 out of 61 days (9 due to Gales, 2 due to RIB problems, and 1 no wind)

Average distance covered per sailing day = 35 nm
Average distance sailed per sailing day = 42 nm
Average board speed = 7 knots
Max sustained board speed = 24 knots (average over 1 hour)
Longest day = 10 hrs on the board
Average time on the board = 6 hrs

Boards and Sails

78% of sailing time on race board (Bertha) and 14% on 3.05 (Katie)
46% of sailing time using 10.0m and 10.7m sails
40% of sailing time using 8.0m and 9.4m sails

Wind speed distribution

Average wind speed per day = 10 knots
28% of time at F2 or less
23% of time at F3
21% of time at F4
8% of time at F5
20% of time at F6 or above (including non-sailing days)

Point of Sailing

43% of time beating or close hauled
41% of time broad reaching or running
16% of time reaching

Tack and gybe angles

Tack angle on Bertha 85–95 degrees, but on Katie 100–115 degrees
Best gybe angle in planing conditions 80 degrees